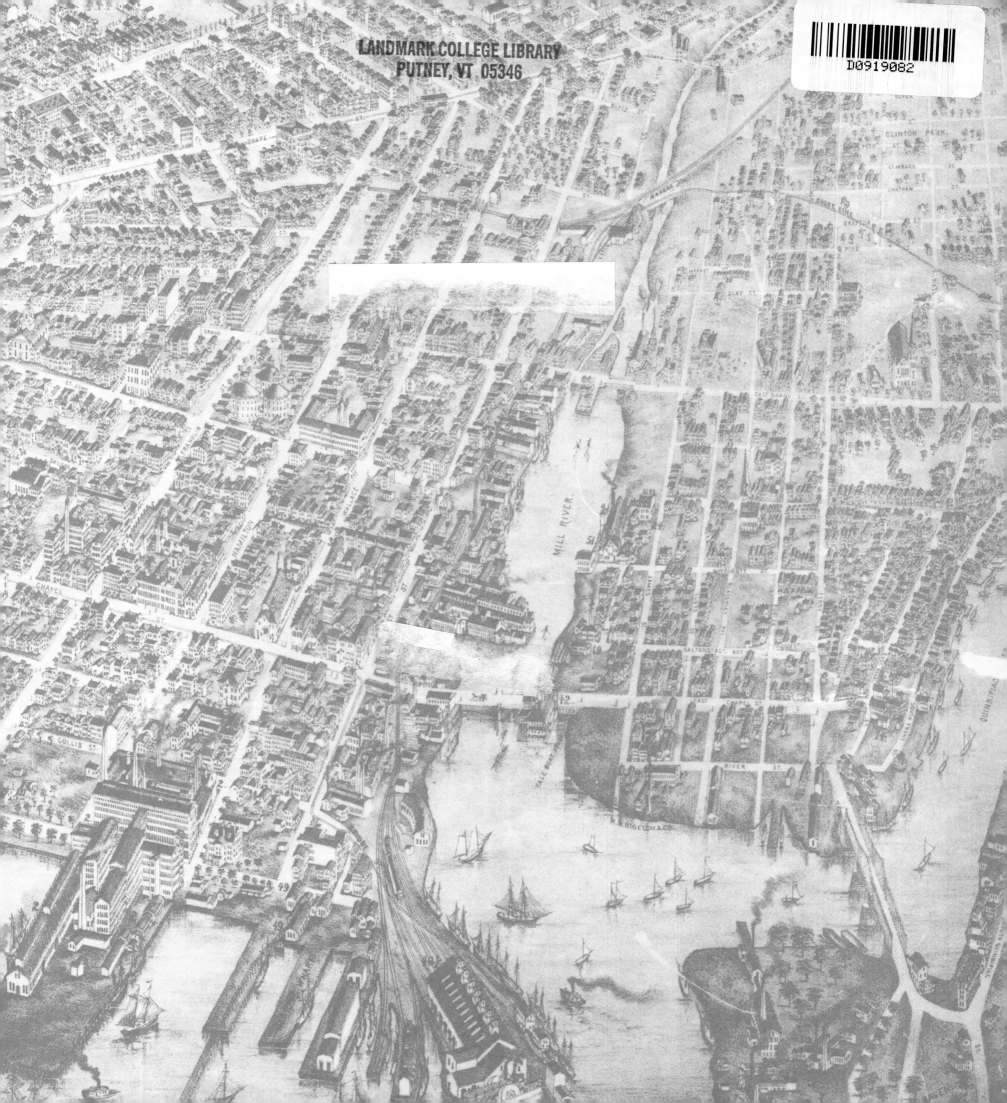

Carriages and Clocks, Corsets and Locks

Carriages and Clocks,

The Rise and Fall of an Industrial City—New Haven, Connecticut

University Press of New England • *Hanover and London*

Corsets and Locks

Preston Maynard and Marjorie B. Noyes, *Editors*

Sylvia M. Garfield and Carolyn C. Cooper, *Associate Editors*

A Project of The New Haven Preservation Trust

Published by University Press of New England,

One Court Street, Lebanon, NH 03766

www.upne.com

© 2004 New Haven Preservation Trust

Printed in Singapore

5   4   3   2   1

LIBRARY OF CONGRESS CATALOGING-IN-PUBLICATION DATA

Carriages and clocks, corsets and locks : the rise and fall of an industrial city, New Haven, Connecticut / Preston Maynard and Marjorie B. Noyes, editors.

p.   cm.

"A Project of The New Haven Preservation Trust."

Includes bibliographical references and index.

ISBN 1-58465-420-1 (cloth : alk. paper)

1. Industrial archaeology—Connecticut—New Haven. 2. New Haven (Conn.)—Antiquities. 3. Historic sites—Connecticut—New Haven. 4. Historic preservation—Connecticut—New Haven. 5. Industries—Connecticut—New Haven—History. 6. Manufacturing industries—Connecticut—New Haven—History. 7. New Haven (Conn.)—History. 8. New Haven (Conn.)—Economic conditions. I. Maynard, Preston. II. Noyes, Marjorie B. III. New Haven Preservation Trust.

T22.5.N49C37 2004

609.746'8—dc22   2004010716

Contents

Contributors

BRUCE CLOUETTE is the director of Historical Services, Public Archaeology Survey Team, Inc., Storrs Connecticut.

ROBERT B. GORDON is on the faculty of Yale University where he teaches and does research in archaeometallurgy and industrial ecology.

CAROLYN C. COOPER is a historian of technology and a research affiliate in Yale's economics department.

DOUGLAS W. RAE is the Richard Ely Professor of Management, School of Management, Yale University and an urban historian.

DIANA BALMORI is principal of Balmori Associates, Landscape and Urban Design, and lecturer at the Yale School of Environmental Studies and Yale School of Architecture.

SANDRA RUX is a managing partner, Leetes Island Enterprises, Guilford, Connecticut, providing consulting services for historical research, and a consultant for National Register of Historic Places nominations.

PRESTON MAYNARD, vice president, the Community Economic Development Fund, is an adviser to the National Trust for Historic Preservation, and former executive director of the New Haven Preservation Trust.

SYLVIA M. GARFIELD, director and chief researcher of the North Haven Historic Buildings Project, is an archivist and local historian.

MARJORIE NOYES has been an editor and/or designer of publications for Yale University and several nonprofit organizations.

Preface

The New Haven Preservation Trust is Connecticut's oldest local preservation organization. Founded in 1962 in response to the excesses of the urban renewal era, the Trust rallied academics, business people, and longtime residents to fight for New Haven's architectural legacy. Large portions of downtown, Oak Street, and other historic neighborhoods were destroyed during this era.

The Trust became a leading advocate for preservation and adaptive reuse. Important landmark buildings like the Federal Courthouse and the New Haven Public Library, both on the New Haven Green, were saved. The Wooster Square neighborhood, once a target for demolition, became an early model for neighborhood preservation. The Trust catalogued thousands of historic buildings through a citywide inventory and produced National Register nominations for more than a dozen different neighborhoods. Public and private sectors invested millions of dollars in historic rehabilitation. Historic preservation today is a value upheld by many of the city's residents.

Former industrial buildings, however, have mostly missed the attention of the preservation or real estate communities. Many manufacturing structures from this era are neglected and underutilized. In many places, the buildings are blights; residents, unaware of the buildings' development potential, want them demolished.

About ten years ago, as executive director of the Trust, I wrote a proposal to pursue an industrial heritage project to evaluate these historic resources and produce education programs describing their importance. Later, Floyd Shumway, the Trust president, assembled a small team of academics and advocates to push forward this effort. It was clear to those he assembled that the Industrial Heritage project would be a major undertaking. We would need to do significant cataloging of the numerous sites under study, extensive research in public and private collections as well as documentation through photographs, maps, and old etchings.

From these meetings a project took shape. We would focus our research and writing on the industries in New Haven's Harborside, leaving out the well-known sites (Winchester Repeating Arms and the Eli Whitney Armory) that have been extensively documented. We would support an extensive research effort that would create a lasting archive. We would write a book that would have a catalog of the sites, and we would ask scholars to write about different aspects of New Haven's industrial history.

Because the book would have a preservation bent, we tried to look at buildings that still exist instead of the ghost sites that have been demolished. In a few cases, however (such as Sargent Hardware and the Candee Rubber Company), we included places that have been demolished because they were important or helped describe a particular industry.

From all the discussions, research, and planning, the Industrial Heritage project took shape. Sylvia Garfield, a local historian, carried out the research effort, creating a tremendous archive of materials about each site. A team of local historians and writers were assembled to investigate different topics. The format and layout were discussed.

None of this major undertaking would have been possible without the support of the Woman's Seamen's Friend Society. This longtime charitable foundation has closely supported efforts to document New Haven's history. Its interest in this project stemmed from the fact that many of the sites were near the harbor or on one of the tidal rivers that ribbon through New Haven. Throughout our labors, the Woman's Seamen's Friend Society has been a patient and generous benefactor.

The staff of the New Haven Colony Historical Society—Peter LaMothe, executive director; James Campbell, librarian and curator of manuscripts; Frances Skelton, reference librarian; Amy Trout, museum curator; and Bonnie Campbell—greatly assisted our efforts. In particular, Frances Skelton made the research for the book her personal mission and James Campbell organized the illustrations from the Colony's archives and manuscripts for reproduction. The Colony's help was invaluable to making this book happen.

We would be remiss if we did not express our gratitude to the many others who have assisted this project. Richard Hegel, local historian and author, supported and encouraged us throughout the project. Henry Lord climbed over rooftops and stood in the middle of city streets to take the remarkable photos of Harborside factories as they look today. Peter DeBretteville of the Yale School of Architecture and Robert Grzywacz helped scope out the content and format of the book. Richard and Marianne Mazan, and Joseph Taylor opened their collections of historic New Haven ephemera. Our volunteer copyeditors, Barbara Folsom, John M. Garfield, and John Maynard, reviewed our text for errors. Bill Sacco helped in numerous ways to reproduce most of the book's illustrations.

I wish especially to acknowledge two individuals who worked tirelessly on the project for more than six years. Sylvia Garfield spent innumerable hours doing research on dozens of sites and checking facts and figures. She created a tremendous archive of materials associated with each site. Marje Noyes managed the editorial and production process; first, by helping to develop the focus and content of the book, then by writing the company profiles and designing and producing a presentation draft for the publishers. Without Marje and Sylvia's contributions, this project would never have happened. We owe them our highest regard and deepest gratitude.

P.M.

Carriages and Clocks, Corsets and Locks

BRUCE CLOUETTE

Introduction:

New Haven, an Industrial City

Cities have a way of acquiring a certain identity. New York is finance; Los Angeles, entertainment; and Chicago, farm commodities. While providing a useful shorthand, such popular images obscure an important point: virtually all modern cities have had large industrial sectors that, historically, were significant engines of growth. New Haven is no exception. Although known today as a center of higher education and medical specialties, New Haven is in large measure the product of the industrial age, when the city had a handful of factories employing a few thousand workers, dozens of factories employing hundreds of workers, and hundreds of factories employing dozens of workers. In the late nineteenth and early twentieth centuries, New Haven's population expanded rapidly, in part because of the large number of European immigrants who flocked to the city seeking work in its many manufacturing enterprises. The density and extent of New Haven's physical development advanced correspondingly, and its religious, social, and cultural life became much more diverse (figure 1).

Part of the reason New Haven has not retained so vivid a memory of its industrial past as some other cities is the sheer variety of products and processes that made up its industrial sector. Unlike Lowell, Massachusetts, where the textile industry had an overwhelming presence, or Waterbury, Connecticut, once the home of several of the world's largest brass mills, New Haven never had just one major industry that gave it its identity. Instead, as one observer wrote in 1895, "The distinguishing characteristic of New Haven business interests is their manifold variety. There is hardly a commodity of extensive use, from a needle to an engine, that is not manufactured in this city. This fact has proved, in itself, of great importance to the welfare of New Haven, as during the recent depression [1893] the variety of her interests rendered the city unusually exempt from the troubles of the times."

The author gratefully acknowledges the contributions to his understanding of industrialization made by Matthew W. Roth during their twelve years of working together on Connecticut history.

FIGURE 1. *The corner of Church and Chapel Streets, New Haven, early in the twentieth century. The public library and Federal Courthouse are in the background and City Hall is on the right.* (New Haven Colony Historical Society Photo Archives)

As another measure, consider the report of T. Attwater Barnes, Special Agent of the U.S. Census Office, who compiled data on 567 manufacturing establishments in New Haven for the Tenth Census of 1880; the establishments proved worth a total of $9.7 million. That year, the leading manufacturers included forty-three carriage- and carriage-parts makers, with a total capitalization of $1,309,599; some fourteen hardware manufacturers, capitalized at $1,004,300; and nine corset factories, worth $500,600. Despite enumerating forty-one specific areas of manufacturing, however, the census still had to put ninety-four factories into the category, "All Other Industries"; together those industries, ranging from ammunition and artificial limbs to wire work and wood turning, accounted for more than a quarter of the city's total industrial output.

One of the first places of English settlement in Connecticut, New Haven dates back to 1638, when five hundred settlers arrived under the leadership of Puritan minister John Davenport. A town government was organized in 1640. As more people arrived, some of the outlying areas were set off as separate towns, so that New Haven became the center of a small colony. The Royal Charter of 1665 merged the New Haven Colony with the rest of Connecticut into a single administrative unit. For more than two hundred years thereafter New Haven shared the status of capital with Hartford, with the twice-annual sessions of the legislature alternating between the two cities. Until the twentieth century, government was so small (the state papers were reportedly carried between the two cities in a single chest) that little direct economic effect, other than increased business for local inns, can be attributed to the city's serving as a colonial, and then state, capital. Nevertheless, the fact that once a year the legislative sessions drew leading citizens from all over Connecticut to New Haven must have raised its visibility at least a little. This contributed in intangible ways to its general prosperity. Similarly, its status as a county seat must have raised its importance in the eyes of the judges and lawyers that attended the periodic sessions of county and state courts.

New Haven's status also benefited from the relocation of the colony's only institution of higher learning from Saybrook, Connecticut, in 1716, a college that was named for British philanthropist Elihu Yale two years later. The fortunes of Yale and New Haven have been linked ever since; to this day Yale remains perhaps the single most important corporate entity in the city. The direct economic impact of a body of students and professors living in the town was probably marginal for most of the eighteenth and nineteenth centuries, but there must have been indirect effects from having virtually every minister of what was long the established church, most of the lawyers, and many of Connecticut's mercantile elite spending their college years in New Haven. Certainly over the years many who came to Yale remained in New Haven, where they pursued careers as professional men, merchants, and industrial entrepreneurs (figure 2).

In addition to serving as an administrative center and the seat of higher education in Connecticut, New Haven was one of Connecticut's leading trading centers in the eighteenth century. The large sheltered harbor was one of the reasons Davenport's followers chose the place, and from the earliest years transatlantic, coastal, and West Indies shipping were business pursuits of many of the colony's residents. As early as 1640, shipwrights were excused from military duty so that progress on vessels under construction would not be impeded; in 1644 a group of merchants built the first public wharf for the harbor. The early years of trade were not nearly so prosperous as the first colonists had hoped. In the second half of the eighteenth century, however, the amount of commerce greatly expanded, primarily due to trade with the West Indies, in which Connecticut timber, livestock, and grain were exchanged for molasses and rum. Trade benefited not only New Haven's merchants but also its coopers, chandlers, teamsters, shipyards, and wagon builders. Money made from commerce also sustained house carpenters, jewelers, tailors, and others who provided goods and services to the merchant class. Most important, the fortunes made from commerce provided the capital, either through banks or direct investment, for New Haven's earliest industrial enterprises.

Recognizing that commerce had made New Haven into a place different from

FIGURE 2. *Yale College.* (New Haven Colony Historical Society Photo Archives)

the average Connecticut town, the legislature in 1784 incorporated the built-up part of New Haven as a city, along with four other coastal and river ports. As such, New Haven was authorized to form a local government that could regulate markets, weights and measures, and other aspects of commerce; provide additional services appropriate to a densely built settlement; and resolve, by means of a local court, contract disputes that previously had to wait for the next session of a county or state court. Commerce was still the driving force of the local economy at this time. Among the attractions that distinguished New Haven was its Long Wharf (figure 3), an earthen and stone pier nearly four thousand feet long, at one time the longest

in the entire country (Boston's longest wharf was half its length). City merchants owned and operated this private enterprise known as the Union Wharf Company. There were forty warehouses and storage lots along its length. The city had 4,049 inhabitants in 1800, a figure that had grown to 8,327 by the time of the 1820 census and 10,678 by 1830. By that time, New Haven was already feeling the effects of its nascent industrial sector.

Like other Connecticut cities that developed a thriving manufacturing sector to add to their commercial and administrative roles, New Haven achieved an early lead in a single industrial specialty, which in its case was carriage building. Making carriages involved a wide range of traditional crafts skills, including joinery, blacksmithing, iron and brass casting, and ornamental painting. Small carriage-making shops typically worked on one or two vehicles at a time and, while they made similar products over and over, there was plenty of room for meeting individual customer needs. While New Haven undoubtedly had such small shops making wagons and carriages in the eighteenth century, the city's nineteenth-century carriage makers operated at a different scale, building dozens and even hundreds of similar carriages at a time and selling them to distant markets. As with other Connecticut products that were tapping into a broad-based consumer market, the carriage industry increasingly relied on mechanized methods of manufacturing.

James Brewster is credited with being among the first to take carriage-making from the small shop to quantity production (figure 4). In business from 1810 to his retirement in 1837, Brewster found he could sell large numbers of carriages in the coastal commercial cities, such as Boston, Charleston, and New Orleans, with which New Haven merchants had long traded. He also exported his carriages to Cuba, Mexico, and South America. In 1827 he formed a partnership with John R. Lawrence and opened a sales office in New York City. The firm went through a series of changes in ownership; under William H. Bradley, the New Haven factory on the corner of Chapel and Hamilton streets was greatly enlarged. Although the Bradley factory was highly mechanized, this apparently was not considered a good marketing point with carriages, as it was in most other industries. One of Bradley & Company's advertisements in 1876 stated: "Their factory is fully equipped with such appliances as can aid in the rapid production of thoroughly good work, but they do not trust to lifeless machinery and thoughtless boys, the labor which only skilled workmen can properly perform."

The claim must be taken with a grain of salt. While final assembly and finish may have involved much hand labor, most parts of the process, and especially the manufacture of subcomponents such as axles, springs, bolts, and lamps, were primarily performed by semiskilled operatives working "lifeless machinery." Other large-scale New Haven carriage makers included Henry Hooker & Company on State Street, started around 1830; B. Manville & Company, Wooster Street, started in 1855; M. Armstrong & Company, Chapel Street, 1859; the Boston Buckboard and Carriage Company, East Street, 1879; Brockett & Tuttle, Goffe Street, 1881; the New Haven Carriage Company, corner of Water and Franklin streets, incorporated in 1891; and the Seabrook & Smith Carriage Company, Park Street, 1895.

In addition to the makers of finished carriages, New Haven had a number of large factories that specialized in particular types of carriage components, relying on the carriage makers to buy their product and incorporate it into a finished vehicle. W. and E. T. Fitch, for example, which moved from Westville to East Street in 1853 to be close to the carriage makers, operated a complex of foundries making cast brass and iron items. The New Haven Wheel Company, started by Zelotes Day in 1845, mechanized the manufacture of wagon wheels to the point where by 1876 its factory was turning out four hundred sets of wheels a week, selling them not only to local carriage builders, but also marketing them throughout the United States and even exporting wheels to Australia, Latin America, and Europe. Other prominent suppliers in New Haven included Dann Brothers & Company, which made seats and other carriage woodwork starting in 1858; the English & Mersick Company, carriage trimmings, 1860; the United States Coach Lamp Company, 1886; M. Seward & Son, carriage hardware, 1891; the James Prendergast Company, coach steps, 1892; and the Safety Axle Company, 1893.

New Haven's carriage industry encouraged a number of significant secondary industries that today would be called "spin-offs." Sargent & Company on Water Street, for example, employed some two thousand people in 1895 making a wide variety of locks, harness items, cabinet hardware, and builders' hardware; its catalog ran to almost one thousand pages, and its plant was one of the largest hardware factories in the country. All of this production derived directly from Sargent's first specialty, the manufacture of carriage hardware.

The towns further north, along the New Haven and Northampton Canal, also felt the effect of New Haven's carriage industry: suppliers of carriage springs, axles, bolts, and trimmings prospered in Hamden, Cheshire, and Southington. Many eventually built businesses that went well beyond their role as suppliers to New Haven carriage makers. The H. D. Smith Company in Plantsville, for example, was relying more on bicycle parts for its profits in the 1890s than the bolts, steps, and other carriage parts with which it had started, and the Clark Brothers in Milldale, an innovator in the production of carriage bolts, made a variety of bolts, rivets, and other fasteners through the 1980s.

New Haven's carriage builders prospered right up to the point when automobiles began to be produced in quantity, then entered a steep decline. Unlike the Flint (Michigan) Wagon Works, which became Buick, or the Abbot-Downing stagecoach factory in Concord, New Hampshire, which shifted over to delivery trucks, the city's carriage makers failed to acquire the expertise in engine design and manufacture that would have allowed them to become automobile makers. One small firm did make a successful transition: C. Cowles & Company, which had begun in 1838 as a supplier of lamps, curtain fasteners, and other carriage hardware, adapted its facilities in the early 1900s to make automobile lamps and later, door locks, ashtrays, and body trim for Detroit. This strategy allowed Cowles to thrive and eventually become the sole survivor of local carriage industry.

As noted earlier, what most distinguished New Haven among Connecticut's industrialized cities and towns was not its dominance in making one particular product but rather its diversity of manufacturing. Not only did the city produce an astonishing number of different products; in several areas, one or more New Haven firms were among the largest manufacturers in the state, if not the nation. Even many products in which other Connecticut cities specialized, notably clocks, firearms, and corsets, were represented in New Haven by firms that were among the most prominent in their fields.

The first Connecticut industry that was taken from the craftsman's shop to factory production was the manufacture of inexpensive clocks aimed at a broad market. Beginning with Eli Terry, who in 1804 received a proposal from two Waterbury merchants to make four thousand identical clock movements, each decade of

FIGURE 5. *Chauncey Jerome.* (New Haven Colony Historical Society, "American Clock Making")

Connecticut clock making was characterized by more mechanization, production in greater quantities, physically larger factory complexes, and more highly capitalized corporations. Although the Bristol-Thomaston-Waterbury area was the center of the industry, New Haven played a major role.

Clock making in New Haven began in 1844 when Chauncey Jerome of Bristol (figure 5) moved his clock case factory to Hamilton Street; two years later, he transferred the production of movements to New Haven as well. Jerome was one of the key innovators in the American clock industry; his clock movements, built with gears stamped from sheet brass, were superior to the wooden movements used by other makers of inexpensive clocks and cheaper to make. Because brass movements could be shipped overseas (the dampness caused wooden movements to deteriorate), Jerome is credited with creating an export market for American clocks. Within a few years, Jerome's New Haven clock factory was the city's largest employer, with 225 workers turning out some 250,000 clocks a year. Jerome, however, was a better inventor than businessman, and in 1855 his company went bankrupt. One of Jerome's local suppliers, the New Haven Clock Company, raised additional money and quickly put the works back into operation, continuing Jerome's models, using the existing machinery, and even hiring back his employees. Over the years the company prospered, and eventually multistory manufacturing buildings were built around the whole perimeter of the block. An early producer of electric movements, the company continued as one of the country's largest clock makers well into the twentieth century. Today much of the complex, mostly dating from the expansion of the 1870s and 1880s, is vacant.

The story of firearms is a little different: New Haven was in on the dawn of industrial-scale firearms production and also participated in its full flower in the form of the Winchester Repeating Arms Company, somehow skipping any intermediate steps. New Haven's Eli Whitney (1765–1825) is justly celebrated for promoting the ideal of interchangeable parts, which was achieved for military muskets by midcentury. Whitney's factory, located just outside the city in the town of Hamden, was an important supplier of rifles to the U.S. government in the early days of the republic and a training ground for local machinists. The company did not grow or innovate much after Whitney's death, however, playing only a minor role in the history of firearms manufacture as the producer of Samuel Colt's first Connecticut revolvers, before Colt's first Hartford factory was ready. Shortly after the Civil War, Eli Whitney Jr. sold off much of the machinery, and in 1888 the factory itself was sold to the company that had become New Haven's leading producer of firearms, Winchester Repeating Arms. Organized in 1858, Winchester operated in New Haven for a few years, then moved to Bridgeport, then returned to New

FIGURE 6. *The Winchester Repeating Arms Company.* (New Haven Colony Historical Society, "New Haven Manufacturing Association Souvenir Book")

Haven permanently in 1870. Winchester was innovative not only in its product, the famous repeating rifle, but also in its management and organization of production. In 1870 the company built a new plant in New Haven and expanded it continually as its business grew. By 1895 Winchester had become the largest manufacturer in New Haven, with some 1,500 employees and some 400,000 square feet of production space (figure 6). Winchester was also a major producer of ammunition, operating its own brass mill on the premises to supply the cartridge division. During the World War I period, the demand for weapons and ammunition was so great that the size of the plant was expanded to more than three million square feet by 1916. Although much demolition has occurred in the years since, the Winchester complex remained an impressive industrial complex throughout the twentieth century.

As might be expected in a city with such a long history of firearms manufacture, Winchester was not New Haven's only gunmaker; at least two other firms tapped into the city's skilled labor pool of machinists and toolmakers and its extensive network of machine builders and other suppliers. John Marlin started making firearms in 1870; instead of relying on government contracts, however, he targeted a civilian market for sporting rifles. The Marlin Fire-Arms Company's large plant on Willow Street was occupied through the 1960s. Even more of a niche was sought out by L. T. Snow, whose Strong Fire Arms Company made signal and salute guns.

Corset production was another industry (though more fully realized in other

Connecticut cities such as Derby and Bridgeport) that became a major source of employment in New Haven. Corset manufacture is a curiously two-faceted enterprise. It is partly a garment trade, characterized by changing fashions and requiring all the cloth-cutting and sewing needed to make any article of clothing, and yet it is also very much a metalworking industry. A nineteenth-century corset appeared to be made of cloth, but the real work was done by spring-steel stays, wire forms, and numerous hooks, eyelets, and other fasteners. New Haven and Connecticut's other corset-producing cities clearly had a unique locational advantage. They were close to New York City, the nation's wholesale clothing and fashion center, and they could draw upon the myriad toolmaking, brass-stamping, metal supplying enterprises that characterized central and southern Connecticut. J. H. Smith and Company began making corsets in New Haven in the 1850s, but soon sold their factory to the firm of I. Strouse and Company. The company was immediately successful; by 1870 the firm was manufacturing 173,000 corsets a year with a workforce that included 105 men, 16 women, and 173 children. By 1895 its Court Street factory covered several acres and employed more than one thousand workers. Of the three principals at that time, Max Adler was a resident of New Haven and oversaw the manufacturing operations, while Abraham Strouse and S. L. Mayer devoted their attention to the New York City end of the business in the company's Broadway salesrooms. In the twentieth century the firm, by then known as Strouse, Adler and Company, grew even more, with employment typically over the 2,000 mark; at one point, some 12,000 corsets were leaving the New Haven plant *each day*.

Of course, not all the city's manufacturing was related to those sectors in which Connecticut played a leading, if not predominant, role. In a city like New Haven, where people had access to capital, good relationships with markets in New York and other commercial centers, exceptional rail connections, and a labor pool that included highly skilled machinists and experienced factory operatives, entrepreneurial drive and imagination could lead to a surprising number of ways to make money by making things. New Haven's Diamond Match Company, begun in 1854 as A. B. Beecher & Sons, owned factories and lumber mills in ten different states by 1895 and had achieved a near monopoly in American match production. That same year, it was estimated that the Andrew B. Hendryx Company, which had a factory on Audubon Street that employed some five hundred workers, made 60 percent of all the wire bird cages sold in the world.

When Alfred Carlton Gilbert came from Oregon to study at the Yale Medical School, he thought he would spend his life as a physician. He did earn his medical degree; however, it was his love of magic tricks that would change his life and the economy of his adopted city. In addition to being an Olympic champion pole

FIGURE 7. *A wire birdcage.* (New Haven Colony Historical Society, "Hendryx Catalog," 1903)

FIGURE 8. *The New Haven Chair Company's caned "Invalid Folding Chair."* (New Haven Colony Historical Society, "New Haven City Directory 1880")

FIGURE 9. *An advertisement in the 1888 New Haven City Directory. What distinguished New Haven among Connecticut's industrialized cities and towns was not its dominance in one particular product but rather its diversity of manufacturing. The Globe Silk Works was one of almost one hundred different manufacturers in the city in the late nineteenth century.* (New Haven Colony Historical Society, "New Haven City Directory 1888")

vaulter, Gilbert was a part-time magician who sold homemade magic kits at his performances. In 1909 he formed the Mysto-Manufacturing Company to produce magic sets; in 1911 (supposedly inspired by the electrification structures of the New Haven Railroad) he invented the Erector construction toy. Over the next half-century, families throughout America bought Erector Sets, microscopes, chemistry sets, magic kits, and American Flyer electric trains made in A. C. Gilbert's New Haven factory.

Gilbert's story was unique only in the details: at one time or another New Haven also had large-scale producers of machine tools, foundry products, furniture (including the caned "Invalid Rolling Chair," a kind of precursor to the modern wheelchair), locks, electrical goods, bank safes and vaults, rubber boots, metal bed springs, toys, bricks, steam boilers, pianos and organs, and patent medicines (figures 7–9).

Some of New Haven's second tier of manufacturers used precision machining and industrial production to make anachronistic items. Edward Harrison, for example, had perfected a self-contained flour-grinding mill in which the stones ran on iron shafts set in machined bearings. While the acme of modern design and production, Harrison's enterprise,

active in the 1870s and 1880s, could not achieve long-term success because the flour industry as a whole was adopting high-capacity steel roller mills in place of the ancient stone-ground method. Harrison's only customers were small rural custom-grinding mills, and only those that could afford to replace their traditional equipment.

The development of a machine and tool-making sector was both a consequence of the establishment of early manufacturing and a factor that facilitated further industrial development. An entrepreneur who wanted to establish a new industry or add a new product to an existing enterprise needed machinists to create unique production machines or, at the very least, adapt standard general equipment such as lathes, screw machines,

millers, presses, and four-slides to make his specific product. The larger companies established their own machine shops once they were up and running; even in these cases, however, local machinists would be called upon to help out. Even a fully equipped factory would need new patterns and dies whenever the slightest change in a product occurred, and dies, cutters, and other tools might have to be replaced just from wear.

As with Hartford and Bridgeport, New Haven in any given period had a number of machine shops that could serve the needs of local manufacturers. An ad for Bush & Company, successors to the William Hillhouse machine works, offered gear cutting and "small machinery and dies . . . *made to order at short notice*" (emphasis added); their location on Whitney Avenue and the specific mention of gun manufacture in the ad suggests that at least some of their work was for their giant neighbor, the Winchester Repeating Arms Company. The Bush shop also made a direct appeal to people undertaking technological innovation by offering "models for patents and experimental machines built in strict privacy if desired." Several New Haven companies both made their own products for market and offered services to other manufacturers. The New Haven Hardware Company on Howard Street, for example, offered a diverse line of builders' hardware, saddlery items, tools, and kitchen knives, but also advertised made-to-order "malleable iron castings of the highest quality."

So far this account has concentrated on the products and enterprises that distinguished New Haven from her sister Connecticut cities and other industrial centers. However, one must also remember that a good deal of New Haven's industrial activity took the form of localized manufacturing commonly found in any city of similar size. New Haven had a large gasworks, for example, in which workers slowly heated coal to drive off flammable gases, which were then collected and stored in huge brick gasholders; prior to the development of natural gas facilities and pipelines, every city made its own gas for streetlights and residential and industrial heat and lighting.

Another industry found in most American cities and larger towns was the manufacture of architectural woodwork. Because of population growth and the attendant boom in residential construction, local builders needed a ready nearby source of the windows, doors, shingles, clapboards, porch turnings, brackets, bargeboard, and other architectural ornamentation that made up even modest Victorian dwellings. The Leonard Pardee Planing and Saw Mill on East Water Street, to take but one example, advertised "lumber in all its branches . . . sash doors, blinds, carved piano legs, all kinds of wood turning, scroll sawing, and architectural carving done to order."

Another localized industry that at one time had several large representatives in New Haven was brewing. Without pasteurization or microfiltering, beer is too unstable to be shipped any distance, so every city had one or more breweries. Most of New Haven's several breweries produced the light German-style lagers that had dominated the American market since the 1870s, such as the large Quinnipiac Brewery still standing on River Street. However, one of the last to remain in production, Hull's Export, made the dark English-style brews that were the traditional drink of the British Isles and early America.

These and other local-market industries reflected the population growth and physical expansion of neighborhoods that transformed New Haven in the industrial age. At midcentury, the population of the city stood at 20,345; in 1860 it had nearly doubled to 39,267. Another 10,000 were added by 1870, and the head count had reached 62,882 by 1880. The population had more than tripled in thirty years. As a consequence, new streets were laid out and old ones more densely built over with multifamily housing; municipal services such as parks, water supply, and sewage disposal had to be continually added and upgraded; and school construction struggled to keep up with the growing population. The social scene had also become more complex: about a quarter of the population in 1880 had been born in Europe. The immigrants brought new cultures to the city as they created ethnically based churches, clubs, and neighborhood businesses.

No account of New Haven's industrialization can be complete without some notice of the role played by railroads. New Haven's harbor was an important resource early in the city's history, and it long continued to be an important avenue for bringing in shipments of coal, iron, and other bulk materials needed by the city's manufacturers. Nevertheless, it was the city's railroad connections, unequaled by any other Connecticut city, that ensured the city's industrialists an exceptional access to materials and markets, and probably accounts for New Haven's sharing in virtually every Connecticut industrial specialty (figure 10).

The city's first connection came in 1839, when it was linked to its co-capital by the Hartford and New Haven Railroad, a corporation that had been chartered six years earlier. Passengers from Hartford rode the coaches to New Haven harbor, where they could board steamboats if their journey continued to New York City. At first, the railroad reserved its steam engines for passenger service between the two cities, hauling freight along the rails with teams of horses. New Haven's second railroad was built by the reconstituted New Haven and Northampton Company, which used the right-of-way occupied by its canal for a rail bed beginning in 1846, slowly building its way into Massachusetts. A more significant connection came in 1849, when the New York and New Haven Railroad completed its line from New

FIGURE 10. *Passengers boarding a train at the Clinton Avenue train station in the late 1870s.* (New Haven Colony Historical Society Photo Archives)

Haven to the Harlem Railroad, which gave it access to New York City. It is a measure of the poor communications of the time that the first train to run the route, on Christmas Day, 1849, had to carry its load of dignitaries back to New Haven when it discovered that the Harlem connection had not been finished; four days later the line actually did open through to New York. Travel eastward began in 1852 with the completion of a line to New London, Connecticut, a line that allowed one to reach Boston by rail if one did not object to the numerous ferry crossings along the way. Other lines followed: to Middletown in 1870 (and eventually on to Boston via the "Air Line"), and to Derby in 1871, a connection that allowed access to the north-south Housatonic and Naugatuck railroads.

In all, six important railroad routes radiated out from New Haven, providing direct connections to Connecticut's major manufacturing cities of Hartford, Bridgeport, Waterbury, and Danbury, as well as to smaller but highly industrialized places such as Meriden, New Britain, Derby, and Norwalk. With three through routes to Boston, the main line to New York City, and two additional routes to the Hudson River north of New York City, New Haven was also well connected to the world beyond Connecticut. In 1871, the New York and Hartford lines were consolidated into the New York, New Haven, and Hartford Railroad Company, commonly referred to as the New York and New Haven. Through acquisition and leases, the company eventually controlled nearly all the railroad lines of southern New England. Despite providing freight service to one of the most highly industrialized parts of the country (and at one point accounting for nearly 10 percent of the nation's total passenger traffic), the railroad rarely enjoyed financial success.

The radial pattern of the railroad construction generated an economic geography for New Haven that differed from Bridgeport and Hartford. Instead of being located in one or two large industrial areas, manufacturing in New Haven tended to be more dispersed, and so, perhaps, less discernible today as a major feature of the city. One should not be too deterministic about the importance of rail access as a locational factor, however; one group of entrepreneurs associated with the Bigelow boilerworks in the Fair Haven section of the city started their own railroad in the 1890s, a street-running electrified line that connected their factories along River Street with the New Haven Railroad's main line at Belle Dock.

In addition to providing good transportation for the city's manufacturing enterprises, the railroad generated a substantial amount of industrial activity of its own. Although the New York and New Haven's earliest locomotives were produced by Rogers and other out-of-state builders, the completion of the company's large roundhouse, machine shop, and forge behind the site of the present passenger station gave it facilities in which it could manufacture its own locomotives and rolling stock. Hundreds of 4-4-0 steam engines were built or substantially rebuilt in the New Haven shop between its opening in 1868 and the late 1880s, when the company again turned to outside vendors. Even in the 1890s and early 1900s, the railroad produced more than fifty home-built locomotives to supplement those built by commercial builders. In the 1920s, the New Haven facilities, which by then included the massive new yard at Cedar Hill, built hundreds of gondolas and hoppers, and in the period from 1926 to 1929, the New Haven shops participated in the rebuilding of more than twelve thousand of the railroad's antiquated wooden boxcars. This was the boxcar fleet that carried southern New England's vast output of war matériel during World War II; not until the very end of the war was the railroad able to obtain a substantial number of modern steel boxcars.

Today New Haven has changed from the industrial city it once was. Entertainment, in the form of theaters and sports venues, has become a proportionally more important part of the economic mix, as have biotechnology enterprises, educational and research institutions, and the provision of general and specialized health care. Nevertheless, New Haven's industrial past remains clearly visible in the physical fabric of the city: railroad tracks running down the middle of streets, brick factory complexes suddenly springing into view, and large tracts of nineteenth-century working-class houses all continue to command our attention. The city today is, in great part, a product of a period of substantial prosperity based upon manufacturing, and we cannot fully appreciate what New Haven has become in the twenty-first century without an understanding of the city's industrial past.

This book attempts to document New Haven's industrial heritage, particularly with regard to the buildings and other physical artifacts that remain today. This introduction is meant as a capsule history that picks out a few of the high points and suggests an overall context for the story. The essays that follow take some of the aspects touched on above and develop them in much greater fullness. Robert B. Gordon recounts the development of the many industries in the Harborside area from the viewpoint of the industrial archaeologist. Carolyn C. Cooper looks at New Haven's carriage and carriage parts industry using C. Cowles & Company, the industry's sole survivor, as a case study. Douglas W. Rae considers the impact of industrialization in New Haven with a model that embraces economics, technological innovation, urban geography, and population movements. Diana Balmori examines the natural and human-made water systems of New Haven and the role that water played in New Haven's history. Finally, Preston Maynard shows the importance of preserving former industrial buildings through intelligent reuse. Historic industrial buildings form an armature upon which historians' accounts of the city can take shape. The buildings' age, size, and unique construction—in short, their very *presence*—appeals to the imagination in way that words and pictures cannot. The essays, photographs, and written histories of specific companies in this book will provide a permanent record of New Haven's industrial past; through the efforts of creative entrepreneurs and enthusiastic community support, that record will also be preserved by the distinctive buildings in which that history occurred.

(Overleaf) *The busy corner of State and Chapel Streets, just north of the Harborside area, in 1901.* (New Haven Colony Historical Society).

ROBERT B. GORDON

Industrial Archaeology of New Haven's Harborside Area

Early European settlers in Connecticut, faced with many tasks and few hands to do them, set about applying mechanical power to ease the labor of man and beast. Because New Haveners lacked water-power sites within their town, they had to go two miles north along the Mill River to find a place to build their grist mill, and to East Haven to set up an ironworks. Through the eighteenth century, craftsmen in town worked in their own shops with hand tools. Eli Whitney's lack of a power source for his cotton-gin shop at Chestnut and Wooster streets so limited his production that he couldn't meet the demand from his southern customers. Whitney placed his 1798 armory at New Haven's grist mill site on the Mill River to get the power he needed to make the ten thousand muskets he had contracted to deliver to the federal government. Because there was no housing nearby, Whitney had to build one of the early republic's first mill villages, later called Whitneyville, to accommodate the armory's artisans at this then remote location.

As the eighteenth century closed, Connecticut entrepreneurs began to gather work previously done by hand in small shops or homes into factories with power-driven machinery. Although the Farmington canal, completed through New Haven in 1826, provided some manufacturers with water to run their machinery (as at the Wilcox machine shop on Whitney Avenue), only steam engines could provide the power needed for a large factory in the city. American machine builders had learned to make reliable engines and safe boilers at affordable prices by the 1830s. Eleven New Haven factories had engines driving their machinery in 1838.[1] In the city, manufacturers had access to transportation facilities and an established community that could provide housing and services for workers. With other shops and factories nearby, entrepreneurs no longer needed to build factory villages or

I thank Sylvia Garfield and Robert Grzywacz for finding much of our primary data on the Harborside area industries, and Carolyn Cooper for background information on New Haven's industrialization. Barbara Narendra generously shared her extensive collection of maps and New Haven documents. Marje Noyes and Preston Maynard kept information for this project flowing freely to those of us who needed their help.

TABLE 1.

Examples of Industries that Moved Into New Haven

Firm	From	Date
Jerome Manufacturing Co.	Bristol	1842
G. F. Warner	Naugatuck	1848
L. Candee & Co.	Hamden	1850
Sargent & Co.	New Britain	1858
Peck Bros. & Co.	New Britain	1862
O. B. North & Co.	New Britain	1867
Henry G. Thompson & Son	Milford	1884

undertake every task needed to complete a product. Instead, neighboring industries could often supply parts and services. A steady stream of entrepreneurs moved manufacturing into the city from outlying districts (table 1), once recovery from the panic of 1837 was under way. By 1887, the year Edward Atwater published a detailed description of New Haven, manufacturers had created a dense cluster of diverse industries in the Harborside area (table 2).[2]

Documents make an incomplete record of industrial history. They may include prices and sales data, and sometimes have drawings and specifications for products or payroll records; rarely, however, do they tell us much about the day-to-day experiences of the people working in industry. Mills and factory buildings, the tools artisans used in them, and examples of the products they made give us a material record of the work people did in the past. The setting of a workplace — its relation to dwellings, shops, schools, churches, and recreational facilities — shows us aspects of the environment in which industrial workers passed their everyday lives. These features, unmediated through the eyes of an observer or participant, are a record of what actually happened in the past, not what someone said happened. Industrial archaeologists read and interpret this physical evidence of the lives and work of artisans and entrepreneurs. They examine the environmental changes caused by industries, the sources of power that ran factories, the transportation systems that delivered raw materials and took products to market, and the places where industries disposed of wastes.[3]

A factory or workplace with all its equipment in place (or, better yet, still in use) is an industrial archaeologist's richest source of material evidence. However, a vacant factory can still tell us about the environment in which artisans worked, and show us architectural choices managers made. It can show us the relation of the workplace to homes, stores, recreational facilities, and civic buildings. Excavations at the sites of razed industrial buildings can yield tools, personal items, and other artifacts of working life; and show us the footprint of past structures and facilities. Some sites lacking physical remains are of interest simply because of their association with important events or people.

The Harborside area remains rich in material evidence of its industrial heritage despite neglect, decay, and the depredations of urban redevelopment. Industrial archaeologists have yet to study this area in more than a cursory manner. Here we can only sample some of the information that more detailed studies could fully develop. We begin with material evidence of the different kinds of work that industrialization brought, and the workplaces entrepreneurs provided for their employees. Then we examine the physical traces of the context of the area's industry,

TABLE 2.

Manufacturing Works in the Harborside Area in 1887

Alling Turnery and Planing Mill	100 E. Water
Atwater Sash & Blind Works, 1847	136 E. Water
Bigelow Co., 1869	River
Bradley Carriage	East at Wooster
B. Manville Carriage Parts	Water
B. Shoninger Organ and Piano, 1865	Chapel and Chestnut
Hale's Carriage Works, 1846	East
H. B. Ives, 1885	St. John
H. G. Thompson & Son, 1884	Chapel
Holcomb Carriage Woodwork	111 River
Hubbel & Morton Carriages, 1839	Brewery
Jerome Manuf. Co., 1842	Hamilton
J. H. Moore Carriage Works, 1881	James and River
L. Candee, 1850	Greene, East, Wallace
Mallory-Wheeler Lock Co.	Greene
New Haven Brewing Co., 1850,	Chapel at East
New Haven Clock Co., 1853	Hamilton
New Haven Horse Nail	Grape Vine Point
New Haven Malt Co.	58 East
New Haven Rolling Mill, 1871	East near Grand
New Haven Steam Saw Mill, 1854	Chapel and East
North Carriage Hardware, 1867	Franklin
Peck Bros. & Co.	Franklin
Pipe Bending Co., 1882	River
Quinnipiac Brewery	Ferry at East Pearl
Reynolds & Co.	East
Sargent Hardware, 1858	Water
Warner Malleable Foundry	East

Note: Dates and locations are for the initiation of the business in those cases where there was a later move to new quarters. All data are from Edward E. Atwater, ed., *History of the City of New Haven* (New York: Munsell, 1887).

its transportation systems, energy sources, community structure, and the resulting environmental change.

Work Places

Work in the industries of the Harborside area (see table 2) called for artisans with many varied skills. Their tasks ranged from running massive machinery at the Bigelow Company and the New Haven Wire Works, through pouring castings at the Fitch foundry, to assembling delicate mechanisms for the New Haven Clock Company, and sewing at the Strouse, Adler factory.

H. B. Bigelow made the move from foreman of a machine shop to proprietor by buying his boss's business at 8 Whitney Avenue, at the head of Church Street, in 1860. He profited from brisk wartime demand for machinery; after the war, he thrived by making Leffel water turbines, small steam engines, and sugar mill equipment. In 1869, to gain room for expansion, he moved his business to a wood-frame factory on River Street in the area then known as Grape Vine Point. After an 1873 fire, Bigelow built a new brick factory on the south side of River Street, and added storehouses on the north side. By 1887 a hundred men made boilers and steam engines in a plant that covered three acres. When an 1889 fire consumed part of the wooden factory, Bigelow rebuilt and enlarged his works using fireproof construction. A high-bay erecting shop with new engines and cranes installed in 1906 completed the plant we see today.[4] Bigelow used it primarily to make boilers.

By the 1880s customers wanted better fuel efficiency for their engines. One way to get this was to use the heat contained in an engine's exhaust steam to preheat the water that would be pumped into its boiler. To make feed-water heaters, H. B. Bigelow joined with several partners in 1882 to start the Pipe Bending Company (later reorganized as the National Pipe Bending Company). The heater piped feedwater through a coil of brass tube placed inside a cast-iron case that received the waste steam. Bending brass tubes into graceful curves required special skills and equipment. The Pipe Bending Company built its factory across Lloyd Street from Bigelow's boilerworks.[5] It broadened its product line over the years, and in 1970 was making 14-foot-diameter coils of stainless steel tubing for chemical works.[6]

In the 1860s, when Bigelow undertook manufacturing, engines ran on steam raised in relatively simple Lancashire or fire-tube boilers constructed of iron plates and straight tubes. In the 1880s, engineers were adopting the more efficient water-tube boilers. Bigelow finally started making water-tube boilers in 1905. By 1911 his firm supplied new water-tube boilers for the New Haven Railroad's rebuilding of its Cos Cob power plant.[7] When railroad magnate J. J. Hill wanted the best of everything for his new mansion in Minneapolis, he had the builders order Bigelow boilers for the heating plant. This equipment can be viewed at the mansion, now operated as a museum by the Minnesota Historical Society.

The prominent name and monograms on a boiler made for the Collins Company (figure 1) show the pride the Bigelow firm took in its products while the gracefully curved hinges indicate the designer's concern for style. The Collins's boiler shows us some of the tasks Bigelow artisans undertook. Pattern makers shaped wood with hand and power tools into patterns for the cast-iron name ring, hinges, monograms, and door frames. Foundrymen using these patterns made sand molds. They melted iron in a cupola furnace, and poured the castings, and then broke them out of their molds. It was a dirty, heavy job. Layout men working in the one-story brick shop on the east side of the office and machine shop that faced River Street (see Figure 3, Profiles of Harborside Industries: Bigelow Boiler Company) made patterns for the boiler shell and door plates. Ironworkers cut the door inserts out of steel plates to these patterns, and riveted them into the cast-iron door frames. They assembled these parts with the tubes and cast-iron headers to complete the boiler, working in the high-bay erecting shop behind the brick

FIGURE 1. *A Bigelow boiler installed at the Collins axe works in Collinsville, Connecticut.*

buildings that face on River Street. In figure 2 two boilermakers are reaming a rivet hole in a nearly completed Bigelow boiler. We can imagine the heavy labor and the noise of the riveters at work in this large, open area.

In the adjoining block, artisans practiced another metalworking skill as they made hand tools. At the Kilborn & Bishop works at 196 Chapel Street they heated steel bars, grasped the hot metal in tongs, and placed it on the die block of a drop hammer. A single blow of the hammerhead shaped the hot metal to the form needed for the tool being made. This shop illustrates the possibilities for adaptive reuse of an industrial building: The Kilborn & Bishop works had earlier housed the Bigelow Company. In 1917 the A. W. Flint Company took over the shop from Kilborn & Bishop. It made wooden ladders of all kinds along with other wood products, such as porch chairs. By 1950 the Flint Company had developed specialized saws, molding, and drilling machines (figure 3). By this time the third generation of the Flint family had entered management of the firm.[8]

Businesses dependent on a single material or technique are at risk when other firms develop new products or methods. Aluminum ladders, increasingly popular with buyers by the 1950s, required entirely different fabrication techniques from wooden ones. Fiberglass could be used where electrical insulation was essential. Rather than adopt these new materials, the Flint Company went out of business.

Across the river from the Bigelow works, artisans also handled large masses of

FIGURE 3. *The managers of the Flint factory arranged molding and drilling machines near the windows where there was good natural light, and used the large open space formerly used for drop forging for assembly of ladders.* (New Haven Colony Historical Society)

metal as they drew billets of iron and, later, steel into wire. In the late nineteenth century a group of iron-fabricating businesses clustered along the Mill and Quinnipiac rivers. E. S. Wheeler & Company, in the business of importing and shipping iron and therefore located near the harbor, invested in the New Haven Rolling Mill Company, founded in 1871, on East Street, and in New Haven Wire, built about the same time on the east side of the Quinnipiac River. The wire company rebuilt its works after fire destroyed its plant in 1882, and soon had a hundred hands at work making a million dollars' worth of iron and steel wire a year, primarily from imported metal and for sale to industrial customers in New England.[9] Hard times in the 1890s led to bankruptcy and several changes in ownership followed by another fire and receivership. In 1908 the American Steel and Wire Company (later a part of the United States Steel Corporation) acquired the works, and added wire rope to the product line.[10] By 1956 some 850 people worked in this industrial complex.

Artisans at the wire factory worked in steel-framed, high-bay mill buildings fitted with overhead cranes for handling steel billets and heavy coils of wire. They drew rods into wire, braided this wire into rope, and, when wanted by customers, attached fittings or spliced eyes on the finished ropes. Closure of the boiler, pipe bending, and wire works in the 1970s eliminated job opportunities for New Haven artisans skilled in the heavy metalworking trades, and diminished the industrial diversity of the city.

Manufacturers often found casting the easiest way to make metal objects having curved or complex shapes (see figure 1). The Yale Ironworks building (figure 4), erected about 1870 and still standing at the corner of Chapel and Wallace Streets, is typical of the local foundries where an entrepreneur with a small staff of artisans poured iron castings and machined them into finished products. Proprietor William B. Parmelee and his men took on just about any product they could make out of cast iron, including steam engines, pumps, machine tools, architectural castings, and drinking fountains. Generalists like Parmelee could help out city factory owners who needed a machine or fixture made quickly or to special order. They were vulnerable, however, to competition from specialist manufacturers, who could offer more sophisticated designs and lower prices on their standard products. Parmelee was out of business by 1880, and replaced by one of these specialists, Miner & Peck, makers of drop presses.[11]

The Yale foundry had a two-story brick section suitable for an office and machine work in front of the high-bay foundry floor where foundrymen made their molds and poured their castings. At the back of the foundry floor they had a core oven (used to dry cores placed in the molds) and two cupola furnaces for melting iron pigs or scrap. When they completed their molding late in the day, the foundrymen would draw molten iron from the cupolas into hand ladles, carry them across the foundry floor, and pour their castings.

The well-proportioned, practical, substantial foundry building could handle almost any job that came along: it later served a machinery dealer, and now houses an upholsterer. The design and comprehensible scale of the building is a reminder of times when entrepreneurial artisans went into business with general skills and small capital to serve the city's manufacturing community. A small corner office

FIGURE 4. *Yale Ironworks building at the corner of Chapel and Wallace Streets.* (New Haven Preservation Trust)

and lots of work space reflects the expanding, diversified economy free of restrictive work rules in which New Haven's small manufacturers once flourished.

New Haven foundrymen added malleable iron castings to their usual trade in gray iron in the mid-nineteenth century. Gray iron was soft and brittle while properly made malleable iron could be as strong and tough as mild steel. A malleable-iron founder cast an object in white iron (an inherently brittle material) and then annealed it to toughen the metal. Designers substituted malleable iron castings for iron or steel forgings in railway equipment, wagons, carriages, and firearms.[12] Connecticut firms built large malleable iron foundries in Naugatuck and Branford. New Haven had several smaller ones, including the works of W. & E. T. Fitch.

When the Fitch Company moved from Westville to its new location on East Street in 1853, it set up its works adjacent to James Brewster's famous 1832 carriage factory, later used by the Rogers Smith Company (makers of plated silverware) and, after 1876, the Boston Buckboard Company. As its business expanded, Fitch added machine shops and other buildings through the 1890s, and in 1907 expanded to the north by razing the old Brewster factory. After 1925, North & Judd and, later, the Connecticut Malleable Castings Company used the Fitch plant. Construction of the Connecticut Turnpike (later Interstate 95) took five and a half buildings out of the complex, leaving the large foundry building in place south of the highway.

A malleable iron founder needed a pattern shop, a molding floor, a cupola furnace for melting his iron, and a set of annealing furnaces. Foundrymen at the Fitch works did their molding in a 150 × 80 ft. open, dirt-floored one-story brick building. At the end of a day of molding each man carried ladles of molten iron from the cupola in the center of the south side of the work space to pour his castings. Later he broke open the molds and removed his castings for annealing in one of the four furnaces in the annex at the back of the shop.

Although widely accepted in the past, most people now find the dirt and heat of foundry work uncongenial. Neighbors are less tolerant of the smoke from foundry cupolas than they used to be. These factors make it virtually impossible for a foundry to operate in New Haven today. Partly because of the difficulty of getting foundry work done, manufacturers have abandoned malleable iron castings in favor of alternative materials such as copper for pipe fittings and pressed or stamped steel for machine parts. Connecticut Malleable Castings closed its works in 1964. Developers razed Naugatuck's Eastern Malleable Iron foundry in 1994, and have torn down most of Branford's Malleable Iron Fittings Company plant. Neither was recorded before destruction. The adaptive reuse of the Connecticut Malleable foundry as retail space for Charette's store preserved the timber-truss roof of the molding floor, and gave viewers an idea of the size of the work area.

Unfortunately, this building is now scheduled to be sacrificed to the demands of highway enlargement.

Sheet metal fabrication required relatively light machinery and could be done in a multistory factory. The Cowles company specialized in this line of work. William Cornwell and Chandler Cowles began making carriage parts in 1838. Reorganizations and several moves to different quarters saw the firm emerge as C. Cowles & Co. in a shop on Orange Street by 1855.[13] It concentrated on making oil-burning carriage lamps. After forty-five years on Orange Street, the company needed more space, and in 1890 built a new, five-story factory at 83 Water Street. It installed freight and passenger elevators to facilitate movement between the floors. Work here followed a pattern common in the second half of the nineteenth century with its reliance on inside contractors: an individual artisan would assemble his own team of workers to make a particular part or product using company-owned equipment within the plant. The Cowles Company adapted to changing markets by making battery-powered lamps for automobiles, and today makes automobile accessories and lamps for outdoor athletic facilities. It adapted to changing labor practices by gradually abandoning inside contractors in favor of hourly wages.

The Cowles plant illustrates successive generations of building style for light manufacturing. In the period of growth and prosperity before World War I, Cowles added a 22 × 60 ft. addition in 1912, and a five-story concrete and brick structure in 1914. New construction techniques allowed the greater floor loading needed to accommodate heavier production machinery. The company made an addition of 50,000 square feet in 1968 to create an air-conditioned work area. Today the elevated portion of the Oak Street Connector sweeps by, almost touching the factory building, and robbing it of its original setting.

The Armstrong factory on Chapel Street is a good example of a building erected specifically for carriage making. Montgomery Armstrong began manufacturing for the Southern market in 1859, which soon offered little future for the carriage trade. He survived the war by making ambulances for the federal government. By 1882, reestablished as a maker of high-grade vehicles, Armstrong was ready to build a new factory on Chapel Street specifically fitted to his needs.

Carriages, made largely of wood and not weighing much, could be made in multistory factories. Armstrong chose six floors, numerous windows to provide good light in the work areas, and an elevator in a tower at the back to move materials between floors. He placed the smithy, doing the heaviest work, in the basement, had office and storage areas on the first floor, assembly of the vehicles on the second, woodworking on the third, and the painting and drying rooms above. He, like his fellow manufacturers, thought the advantages of a factory with a small footprint outweighed the inconvenience of moving materials and parts for assembly between floors. The multistory buildings contributed to the compactness of the neighborhood and kept carriage makers close to their suppliers.

The Armstrong company began making wooden automobile bodies as the carriage trade dwindled. Its factory, designed for handling lightweight products in a cramped neighborhood, was ill-adapted to the demands of the new product. In 1927 the J. P. Smith Company, a maker and seller of wire goods, took over the building for its factory. In 1933 it converted the first floor entirely to sale space. Today several nonmanufacturing businesses use it.

Clock making brought large-scale mass production to New Haven. Although Eli Whitney publicized manufacture of muskets by division of labor and interchangeable parts, it was clock-maker Eli Terry of Plymouth, Connecticut, who in 1809 first achieved this form of industrial production. In 1842 Chauncey Jerome, who learned clock making from Terry, purchased the carriage works used by the failed Isaac Mix & Son firm in order to move clock case making from his Bristol factory to New Haven. When Jerome's clock-movement factory in Bristol burned in 1845, he shifted all his manufacturing to New Haven.

Nearby, in a small two-story building on the north side of Hamilton Street, Jerome's nephew, Hiram Camp, organized the New Haven Clock Company to make clock cases in 1854. The next year, after a period of prosperity, Jerome's want of business skills led his clock company into financial failure. J. E. English, Hiram Camp and others raised twenty thousand dollars to buy Jerome's business. They incorporated it into their New Haven Clock Company. English and Camp weathered the business recession of 1857, and by 1861 their works on Hamilton Street employed three hundred hands making a quarter of a million clocks a year. As its business flourished the company made large additions to its plant in the 1880s. It introduced the dollar watch in 1885, and by 1887 had six hundred hands at work.[14] Men tended milling machines and gear cutters (later replaced by stamping machines for the cheaper grades of clocks and watches) that turned out large numbers of standardized parts. Overhead shafts brought power from the central steam engine to the work areas, where belts drove each machine. A compact factory building minimized the length of this transmission system. Heavy machines were on the lower floors, and lighter ones, often tended by women, above.

Clock making required good light, clean working conditions, and relatively little mechanical power. In Massachusetts the pioneer Waltham Watch Company carried on its business in a factory erected between 1854 and 1914 with narrow buildings and large windows designed so that each watchmaker could work at a bench with natural light.[15] At the New Haven Clock Company, women could sit at benches

doing light machine work under the supervision of a male foreman (figure 5). However, the large floor width meant that others had to work in interior spaces with inferior light. Forty-five years later a picture of assembly work at the New Haven Clock Company showed two rows of women facing each other at a long bench with fluorescent lamps strung overhead.[16] They are working in one of the factory buildings erected before 1879 that provided a large, mill-type room with ordinary windows. It appears that the New Haven Clock Company used standard mill architecture rather than shops designed to facilitate the particular work its artisans did in assembling fine mechanisms. The obsolete design of its factory left the company at an increasing disadvantage relative to other clock- and watchmakers as the twentieth century progressed.

Oliver F. Winchester started a new enterprise for the city when he moved his shirt-making business from Baltimore to New Haven in 1848. Within ten years, Winchester and his partner, John M. Davies, mechanized production with five hundred foot-powered sewing machines. In 1859 they built a five-story T-shaped brick factory on Court Street for their new production system that by then provided jobs for nearly two thousand employees. Winchester retired from the shirt business to give full attention to his arms-making enterprise in 1865. His partner, Davies, moved the business to New York City in 1875 to be closer to his main market.[17]

Isaac Strouse enlarged New Haven's clothing business when he began the manufacture of sewn corsets, which replaced the imported, woven ones women previously used. With Max Adler and others, and trading as Mayer, Strouse & Company, Strouse's firm moved into the former Winchester & Davies shirt factory on Court Street in 1877.[18] Later, as the Strouse, Adler Company, it added the buildings to complete the existing factory complex. Figure 5 in the Profiles of Harborside Industries: Strouse, Adler Company shows the T-shaped Winchester & Davies shirt factory in the foreground with newer Strouse, Adler additions behind. Continued use of older buildings like these is easier where the work in them can still be done with relatively light machinery, such as individually operated sewing machines. The newer, four-story building with large windows shows the heavier construction needed for power machinery, and the greater window area made possible with newer, stronger construction techniques.

Nineteenth-century factories could be an impediment to modernization of production techniques that depended on heavier machine tools. This growing obsolescence became a serious problem at the Sargent hardware factory. Joseph B. Sargent with his brothers George and Edward had a factory built in 1858 on Water Street between Wallace and Hamilton for manufacture of hardware. The Sargents prospered, and by 1871 had two thousand hands at work in a much-enlarged factory. Their firm began production of door- and padlocks in 1884, with further expansion of the plant.[19] Joseph Sargent built his first factory buildings with slow-burn construction: it had brick walls and heavy plank floors placed on wooden beams without joists. Satisfied with his design, Sargent saw no need to spend money on architects, and simply repeated his factory plan each time he expanded his works. By the late nineteenth century, the Sargent Company found that it could not install modern production machinery because its buildings lacked the necessary strength and rigidity.

Not far from the Sargent works, the Henry G. Thompson and Sons factory on Chapel Street illustrates how much factory design had changed by the time Sargent needed to modernize. Here artisans made metal-cutting saw blades. The firm had started in Milford by making book-stitching machinery, flexible-backed saws, and malleable iron tool handles. It moved to a factory at the corner of Elm and State Streets in 1884, and by 1887 had about forty men at work.[20] In 1936 it moved to a new, steel-reinforced concrete building with brick facings at 277 Chapel Street. Here it concentrated on making saw blades. The company marketed its blades under the brand names "Milford" and "Flexible," derived from its earliest businesses.

The Thompson works was typical of the type of business that could thrive in New Haven through the first two-thirds of the twentieth century. It made a high-value product where quality born of technological skill was essential to holding its market share. Thompson relied on the expertise of Arthur Phillips, professor of metallurgy at Yale, to develop methods of reliably hardening the tool steel that went into its saw blades.[21] In the factory, skilled artisans ran strips of tool steel through automatic machines that cut and set saw teeth. They then passed the blades through gas flames and an oil quench to harden the teeth. This equipment had to be supported on a rigid floor so that each machine would hold the adjustments tool setters made for the different types of blades. The wood floors of older factories, as at the clock company, could not provide this rigidity. The Thompson factory is one of New Haven's best examples of the steel-reinforced concrete factory whose strength also permitted large windows to improve light at the workplace. Artisans had cleaner, safer working conditions than in the older brick structures with wood floors.

As firms such as the Thompson works found it increasingly difficult to carry on manufacturing in New Haven, they moved to locations outside of the city, often to new, single-story buildings. The Thompson company moved its works to new quarters in Branford, and new owners adapted the Thompson factory on Chapel Street to dwelling space.

Transportation Infrastructure of Harborside Industry

Factory work depended on the Harborside's transportation systems, fuel sources, and the services provided by the surrounding community and city. Maritime trade gave New Haven its first commercial ties with the outside world, while the rope walk and shipyards along Water Street formed some of its earliest industries. Coasting vessels brought in raw materials and shipped out products made by the city's early manufacturers. The Farmington Canal and then, much more successfully, railroads expanded the city's role as a transportation hub in the first half of the nineteenth century.

New Haven's English settlers had found their harbor getting shallower year by year, and in 1682 began building a pier, later known as Long Wharf, into deeper water for the convenience of their ships.[22] They extended it in 1754 and again in 1772, financing both projects by lotteries, and added 1,500 feet in 1810 to make a total of 3,843 feet. The wharf then reached the wood and stone bulkhead built by merchants on the west side of the main channel in the 1770s to allow vessels to come alongside in all stages of the tide.[23] Long Wharf served the commercial development of New Haven that flourished after town merchants opened trade with the West Indies early in the eighteenth century. Capital generated by mer-

FIGURE 6. *Photograph of Long Wharf as it was in 1864.* (New Haven Colony Historical Society)

chants using the wharf helped finance the early nineteenth-century turnpike roads radiating from New Haven, the Farmington canal, and the city's early manufacturing ventures. Commercial buildings lined the side of the wharf well into the mid-nineteenth century (figure 6).

A group of New Haven proprietors built another component of the city's transportation system from 1796 to 1798: Harbour Bridge (later known as the Tomlinson Bridge), across the mouth of the Quinnipiac River. Timothy Dwight described it as a half-mile long, twenty-seven feet wide, and the only noteworthy bridge in the town. The builders used stone causeways from either shore to cover half the waterway, and placed trestles made with stringer beams supported by piles to span the rest. The bridge proprietors found that boring worms destroyed the piles every five or six years, making maintenance costly. After a storm in 1807 wrecked much of the timber bridge, Isaac Tomlinson and his fellow proprietors extended the stone causeways so as to leave a gap of less than five hundred feet to be bridged.[24]

By 1838, when the U.S. Coast Survey prepared its first chart of the harbor, Long Wharf had no more than six feet of water alongside, sufficient only for small sailing vessels.[25] The Tomlinson Bridge proprietors built a stone wharf out from their causeway to the west side of the harbor channel to reach a depth of ten feet of water alongside. Steamboat operators shifted from Long Wharf to the new pier. Revenue from the dozen or more steamboats then operating out of New Haven gave the bridge proprietors a substantial increment to their income.

From 1835 to 1846 traffic entered the Farmington canal through the Union Basin, formed by building Prism Wharf from Long Wharf to the shore at the intersection of Water and Brewery streets (figure 7). A shipyard, pottery, and the town's tide mill lined the shore of Union Basin along Water Street.[26] The owners of the Canal Line Railroad (built on the canal towpath) extended their tracks onto

FIGURE 7. *Buckingham's 1830 map shows the Union wharf and basin, the terminus of the Northampton canal, Water Street fronting the harbor, and the Tomlinson Bridge with its steamboat wharf.*

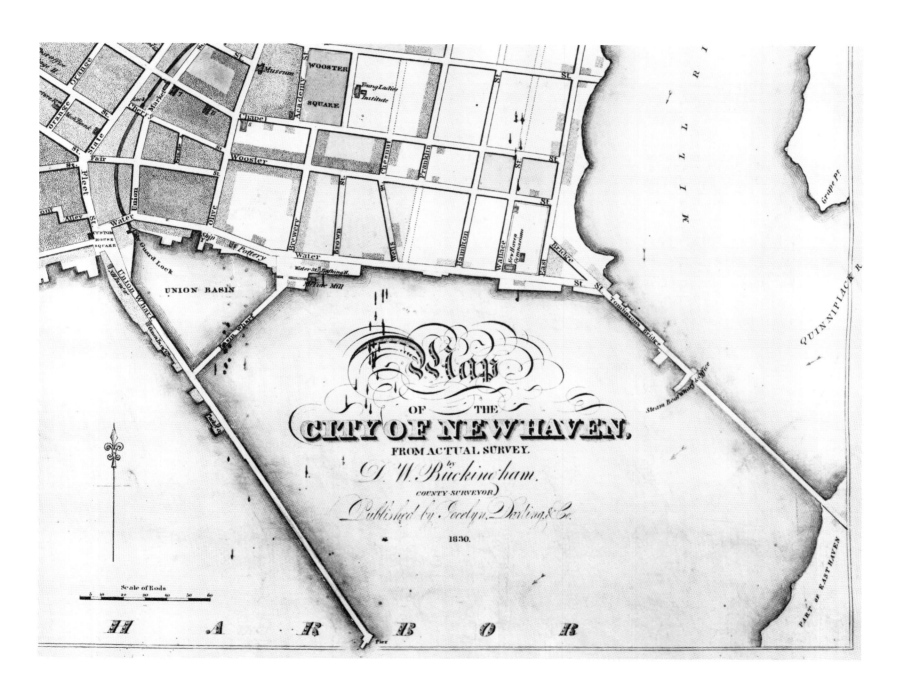

a pier built through Union Basin soon after 1845, and by 1852 had filled the basin for terminal and marshaling yards.

The Hartford & New Haven Railroad purchased the Tomlinson Bridge in 1839 to use as part of its New Haven terminal. Because passengers then completed their journeys to New York by boat, the railroad company constructed a pier where travelers could board the vessels operated by the New Haven Steamboat Company directly from the trains. An 1847 map shows the depot placed next to the boat landing on Tomlinson's bridge (figure 8). In 1841 the steamer *Belle* began service from an adjacent pier, later known as Belle Dock because of the popularity of this boat.[27] Additional piers extended along the shore to the west to Canal Dock (see figure 3 in Balmori, "Industry and Water in New Haven"), including a 1,500-foot long pier the railroad built in 1860 parallel to Long Wharf.[28]

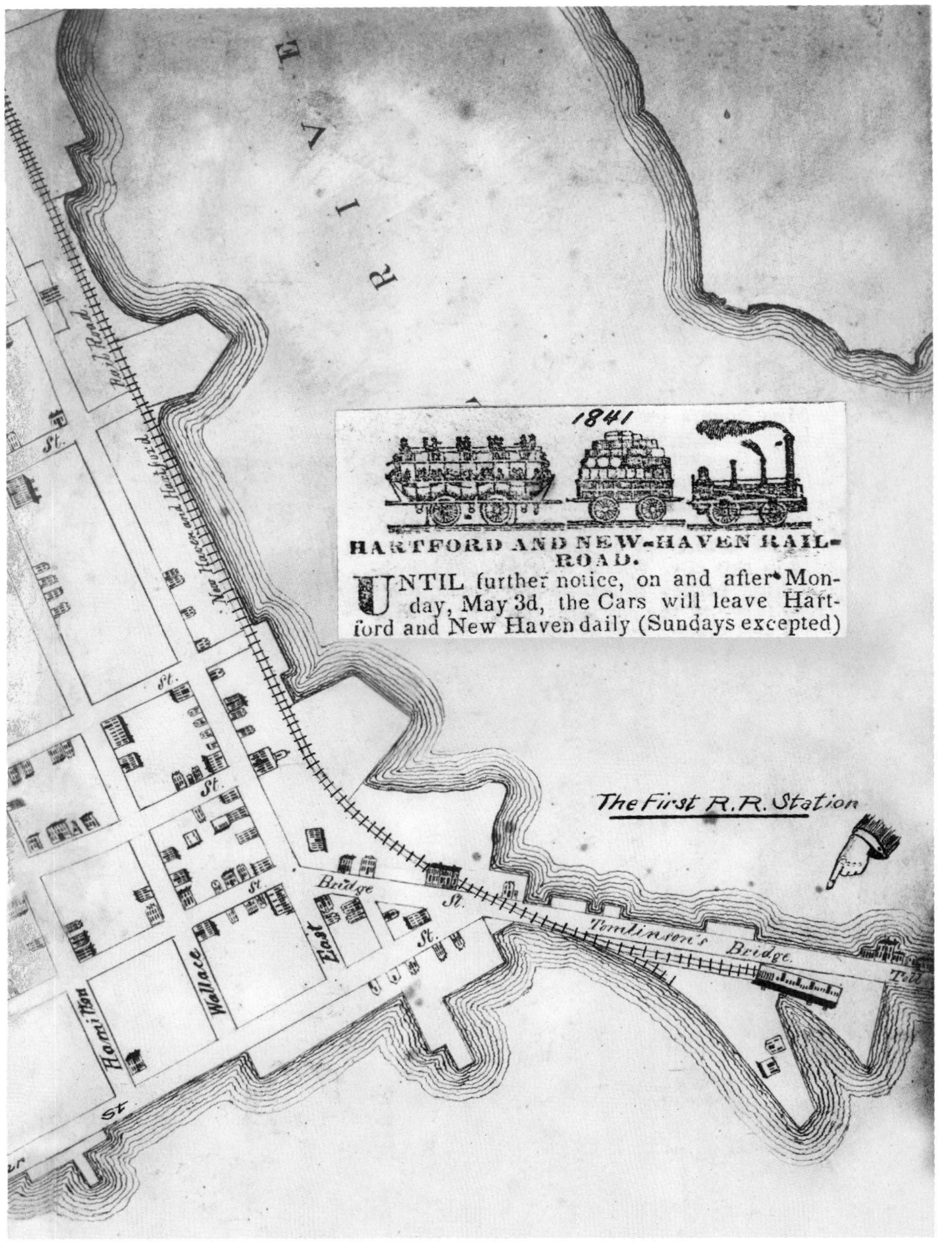

A picture circa 1905 of the National Wire Company plant shows a schooner ready to handle cargo alongside the bulkhead adjacent to the works.[29] Most manufacturers in the Harborside area, however, had to haul their products in wagons along city streets to a railway depot until the Manufacturers' Railway, beginning in 1893, brought rail service directly to many of their doors. As little space existed for a right-of-way from Mill River Junction into the Grape Vine Point manufacturing district, the railroad company laid its tracks in River Street. Horses hauled freight cars along the tracks until 1896, when the company bought an electric locomotive powered by a trolley running on overhead power lines.[30] Wagons and, later, motor vehicles, shared the street with locomotives shunting freight cars onto the sidings that branched off to the industrial buildings along the south side of River Street, creating one of the city's most intensely industrial neighborhoods. An extension over the Tomlinson Bridge allowed the railroad to serve industries on the east side of the harbor. Even though the American Steel & Wire Company (successor to the New Haven Wire Company) had a bulkhead where small vessels could come alongside to work cargo, it relied heavily on rail transportation by 1911. A network of spurs connected all of its buildings to the tracks of the Manufacturers' Railway on Forbes Avenue.[31]

FIGURE 8. *The Hartford & New Haven Railroad's terminus in 1847 was at the Tomlinson Bridge, where steamers from New York docked.* (New Haven Colony Historical Society)

Remnants of earlier transportation systems remain around the Harborside area. By 1900 Long Wharf was already a relic of departed commerce. Today only its outer six hundred feet projects beyond the fill dumped in the harbor over the past hundred and fifty years. The riprap base of the navigational light stands on the site of the eighteenth-century stone bulkhead. Fill covers the masonry structures of Union Basin and its associated industries, and extends out to the site of Steamboat Dock. Future construction projects could offer opportunities for rediscovery of these buried features. Cores, borings, and excavations could reveal the successive episodes of land filling, and allow a reconstruction of the history of environmental change here.

Concrete causeways and a new draw mechanism built in 1922 allowed the Tomlinson Bridge to carry heavy traffic with the railroad and motor vehicles sharing the bridge deck. By the 1970s tugboats often had difficulty getting the larger barges then in use through the draw opening. After collisions repeatedly damaged the draw mechanism, the state decided to build a completely new bridge. Construction was still under way in 2001.

Beginning in the 1950s, the demands of motor vehicle transportation for more space threatened established businesses in the Harborside area. The state highway department threatened to put a new road through the Cowles plant on Water Street. Uncertainty about the department's plans disrupted the firm's business and led to lost orders. Eventually, the highway department placed its road immediately in front of, rather than through, the Cowles factory.[32] Although Cowles survived the onslaught of the road builders, others did not. Construction of the interstate highways through New Haven led to massive destruction of the Harborside's industrial core.

Energy Sources

Virtually every factory in the Harborside manufacturing district had a steam engine to drive its machinery. Coal provided the energy to raise steam, heat buildings, make gas, and, later, generate electricity until the city switched to oil and natural gas. Coal unloading and storage facilities lined the side of the Mill River (figure 9). Carts and, later, motor trucks, made deliveries throughout the city from these yards.

Nineteenth-century factory engines in the Harborside area averaged about a hundred horsepower (table 3). A hundred-horsepower engine consumed two tons of coal in a ten-hour working day.[33] Four half-ton, horse-drawn coal carts had to arrive at the factory gate for each working day just to keep one of these engines

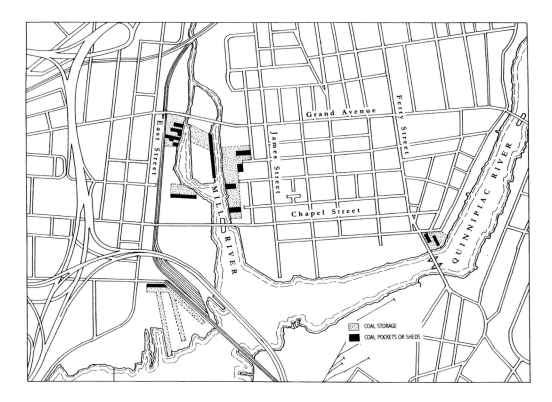

FIGURE 9. *Map showing the Harborside area coal yards.* (Drawn by Eric Vogt)

TABLE 3.
Examples of Factory Steam Power in 1887

Strouse, Adler	75 horsepower
Alling & Sons, planing mill and turnery	150
New Haven Steam Saw Mill	250
Warner's foundry	30
Shoninger organ and piano works	125
Peck's plumber's supplies	100

running. To service engines at the factories listed in table 2, about a hundred and twenty coal wagons a day made their way along the district streets (figure 10). Wagons made additional trips delivering coal to heat workplaces, for the furnaces at foundries, and to stores and residences.

Mineral coal fuel and steam engines allowed manufacturers to locate their works in the city but did not solve the problem of providing adequate illumination for work after dark. Spurred on by the enthusiasm of Benjamin Silliman Jr., a group of New Haven citizens led by Henry Peck obtained a charter for a company that would make gas from bituminous coal. They raised $100,000, and in 1847 organized the New Haven City Gas Company (renamed the New Haven Gas Light Company in 1854). A contractor from New Jersey erected a stone retort house, associated buildings, and a fifty-foot diameter gasometer within a year at the company's site on St. John Street between Franklin and Hamilton. At first it supplied streetlights in the city. Factory owners and residents gradually adopted gaslight after 1860. Some manufacturers found gas a good substitute for coal in specialized furnaces such as those used for heat treating steel.[34] In 1861, the gas company added a new coal-gas plant on East Street. In 1885, it added a plant for making carbureted water gas. It closed its coal-gas works in 1927, as it could then purchase gas from the Connecticut Coke Company. The coke company chose its Harborside location so that it could receive large shipments of coal. The coal was stored in a large yard alongside its bulkhead and served by a traveling crane system.

FIGURE 10. *Coal wagons at the Benedict yard in 1908 delivered fuel to Harborside factories and homes by way of the city streets.* (New Haven Colony Historical Society)

The large coke work's stack served as a landmark for many years. The company supplied coke to users as far away as Troy, New York, by rail, and gas to customers throughout southern Connecticut.

City entrepreneurs organized the New Haven Electric Light Company in 1881, the year before Edison's Pearl Street station went into service in New York City. It set up its dynamos on the ground floor of the C. Cowles & Company factory on the east side of Orange Street (near Crown Street) so as to use Cowles's boilers and engines at night, when the factory was shut down and city customers wanted light. After a reorganization in 1887 the company set up Thomson-Houston alternating current equipment in a plant on Temple Street between Crown and George streets. Wagons hauled coal from the Harborside coal yards through the city streets to fire the company's boilers.[35] Industrial users began to use oil fuel as early as 1890, when C. Cowles & Company adopted oil in place of coal to heat its new plant on Water Street. As the change over to the new fuel was gradual over many years, coal traffic, coal dust, and horse manure continued to be a common feature of everyday life and throughout downtown New Haven as well as in the Harborside area.

Because getting coal to the downtown electric power plant proved difficult and neighbors complained of the noise of the generating equipment, the electric company bought land on Grand Avenue at the Mill River in 1890 for a new generating station. There it had access to cooling water and coal delivery by barge. It built its plant, named after James English, along Grand Avenue in a plain, brick building. Then, in 1899, New Haven Electric Light merged with the Bridgeport Electric Light to form the United Illuminating Company.

Both the gas and electric companies soon needed to expand their works on the Mill River to supply growing demand. Both created space by placing fill in the river. In 1830, East Street ran close along the river's edge, leaving just enough room for the Hartford & New Haven Railroad to run its tracks between the street and the river. Subsequent filling made room for the rail yards, the Fitch factory complex, the New Haven Steam Sawmill, and the expansion of the New Haven Gas Company works along Chapel Street, completed in 1905. By the 1920s the gas company plant included a bulkhead on the Mill River where barges could unload coal for storage in the company's yard, three gasholders along East Street, and an additional fixed tank that, with its red and white checked top, was a city landmark for decades. The electric company built a large addition next to its English power station, which now occupied a substantial island in the river, in 1927, and another in 1947. When the United Illuminating Company completed its new, oil-fired power station on the site of the former Connecticut Coke Company in 1975, it retained the English station for standby power. It looms over the gas company office building and adjacent condenser house, all that was left of the once-large gasworks in 1998 (see Figure 3, Profiles of Harborside Industries: New Haven Electric Company).

As people switched from coal to oil fuel, dealers replaced some of their coal yards with piers and tank farms, as at the terminal at the foot of East Street. Other coal yards now serve new uses. An oyster company stores its clutch (old shells) on the site of the former coal yards on the east side of the Mill River just above Chapel Street. One would not have to dig far below the surface to find traces of the former use of these areas.

Community

People generally lived near their work in nineteenth-century New Haven. Abundant housing helped attract entrepreneurs to neighborhoods where they and their employees could live within walking distance of their workplaces, perhaps even close enough to be able to go home for midday dinner. The area around the Candee Rubber Company was such a combination residential-industrial neighborhood.

Leverett Candee, an entrepreneur in dry goods and other ventures, recognized the value of Charles Goodyear's process for making rubberized clothing. Candee obtained a temporary license from Goodyear, raised capital from New Haven lumber merchants Henry and Lucius Hotchkiss, and organized the L. Candee Company in 1843 with himself as manager. He set up shop in Hamden, struggled through the technical difficulties of making satisfactory rubber clothing, and went through several changes in partners before finally getting the business well under way in 1848. In 1850 Candee expanded the business at a site bounded by Greene, East, and Wallace streets. Nine years later, with additional buildings erected in New Haven, he abandoned his Hamden factory. Candee retired from the rubber clothing business in 1863.

A fire in 1877 destroyed the entire Candee works. The company rented a vacant factory in Middletown, and hired a special train to take its employees there each day for the eight months it took to build an entirely new factory on the New Haven site. The three-story masonry factory buildings occupied the three sides of the block on East, Greene, and Wallace streets, and enclosed a complex of other, smaller build-

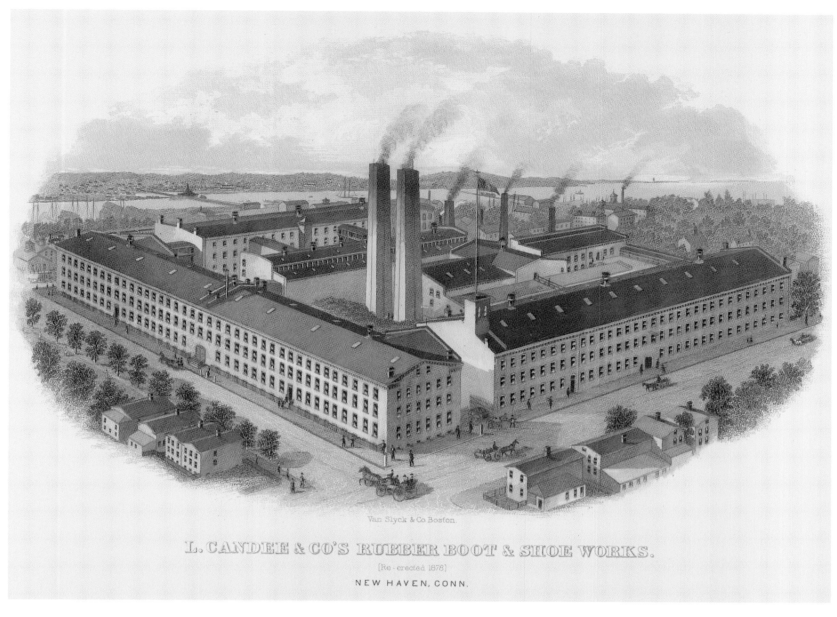

Van Slyck & Co Boston.

L. CANDEE & CO'S RUBBER BOOT & SHOE WORKS.

[Re-erected 1878]

NEW HAVEN, CONN.

FIGURE 11. *The Candee rubber plant as delineated for Atwater's history of New Haven.* (Collection of Richard and Marianne Mazan)

ings within. By 1887 people in New Haven thought it the world's largest works devoted to rubber goods.

In 1868 the Candee works occupied one corner of the block bounded by East, Greene, and Wallace streets with houses adjacent on both sides of Wallace Street. In 1877 the Candee factory, newly built after a destructive fire, occupied all the northern part of the block.[36] Dwellings fronted by sidewalks and rows of trees stood across from the three-story rubber works buildings along Greene and Wallace streets (figure 11). Houses and industrial buildings shared East Street and the rest of the block with the Candee factory. The drawing in figure 11 shows only a trace of smoke from the Candee factory stacks while well-dressed citizens ride in open carriages along the streets. The realities of life here would have been less idyllic, with teams of horses hauling heavy commercial traffic on the streets and no pollution control equipment at the factories. Nevertheless, the block from Greene

FIGURE 12. *Map showing the locations of industrial works, dwellings, and services used by residents in the Harborside area in 1924. In the map, dwellings include single and multiple family houses, boardinghouses, flats, and apartment buildings.* (Drawn by Eric Vogt; *source:* 1924 Sanborn maps)

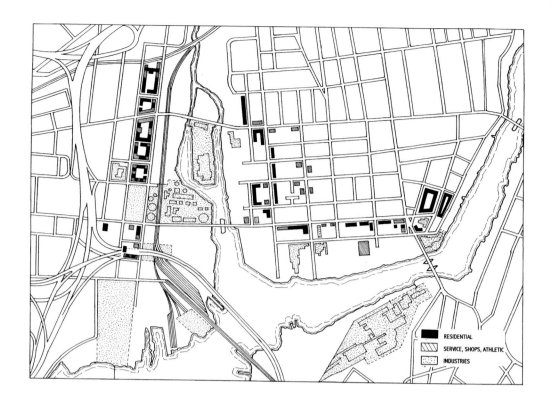

RESIDENTIAL
SERVICE, SHOPS, ATHLETIC
INDUSTRIES

Street north remained a mixture of dwellings and stores at least as late as 1924 (figure 12). Establishments providing services needed by residents—stores, recreational facilities, schools, and churches—mixed in with the dwellings and factories throughout the Harborside industrial area. It was a community peopled throughout both day and night.

The arrival of a new industry could overtax the housing supply. J. B. Sargent put up the first building of his hardware factory on Water Street in an area that had been a summer resort, and therefore lacked existing housing stock. He faced the same problem Eli Whitney and other early manufacturers had solved by building factory villages. Sargent's solution in 1864 was to purchase and convert the adjacent Pavilion Hotel to house a hundred artisans' families. (They must have lived in rather close quarters.) Sargent himself lived on Wooster Street, a five-minute walk from the factory. By 1879 others had built enough neighborhood housing that Sargent could make over the old hotel for factory use.

Environmental Change

New Haven's founders laid out their town on the nearly level ground between East and West Creeks. Through the eighteenth century vessels from overseas could come up West Creek to unload cargo at the foot on College Street. Small vessels could navigate East Creek to Chapel Street until at least 1800. Water Street ran along the northern edge of the harbor.

The *Fulton*, the first steamboat to navigate Long Island Sound, arrived at Long Wharf from New York in March 1815. The advent of steamboat service prompted Mrs. A. Babcock, proprietor of a hotel on Church Street, to move her establishment to Water Street near Tomlinson Bridge, and rename it the Steam-Boat Hotel. In addition to serving passengers arriving from New York by boat she sought customers who wanted to visit the shore in the summer by proclaiming that her establishment was "delightfully situated to receive the refreshing breezes of the sea."[37] The waterfront then served both commercial and recreational needs of the city. Industrial development and land filling would soon change this.

Extensive landfill placed in New Haven harbor over the past hundred and fifty years now covers most of the waterfront's early industrial sites. By showing the exact location of the now-buried West Creek, borings for the New Haven Railroad's 1940s office building fixed the precise locations of the streets and wharves at the head of the harbor.[38] With these locations fixed, maps published from 1830 onward to the present day can be used to show successive stages of filling of the harbor.[39]

By 1826 the builders of the Farmington Canal had altered the landscape by running their canal up East Creek and constructing an enclosed boat basin at the foot of Long Wharf. By 1846 city entrepreneurs had filled in the shallows south of West Creek to create more waterfront land. Railroad companies began building across the shore at the foot of Long Wharf in the 1850s, and continued to fill more of the harbor for yards and terminals through the rest of the century.

The Sargent company created the largest industrial intrusions into the water of New Haven Harbor. J. B. Sargent placed his first factory buildings on Water Street at a time when the area was a fading seaside resort. The flats south of the street were by then bare mud at low tide. Sargent, who owned the shoreline, began dumping debris on the mud to create new land. He began erecting buildings with pile foundations on the made ground in 1869. By 1889 he had the factory enlarged to the complex that would remain in place until 1960, when the company decided to move to new quarters. At that time its foundry at the water's edge was sixteen hundred feet south of Water Street. Fill pushed the shoreline so far south as to leave no hint of the origin of Water Street's name.

The state highway department made the largest intrusion into the harbor in the 1950s by filling in a huge area for the Connecticut Turnpike (now Interstate 95) while creating Sargent and Long Wharf drives. The extensive filling of the tidal wetlands of New Haven harbor is a material reminder of our changing attitudes toward coastal resources. People today would not tolerate the extensive destruction of tidal wetlands that made room for the industries that once brought prosperity to the city, and now accommodate the transportation facilities that New Haven relies upon.

Conclusion

The industrial archaeology of the Harborside area is a record of change of the land to new uses. Successive generations of New Haveners rebuilt the harborside to meet their evolving needs, leaving physical traces of older uses beneath newer ones. People chose railroads over boats for travel and shipment of goods, and then largely abandoned their investment in rail facilities as they adopted motor vehicles. They welcomed imports of mineral coal from Virginia and Pennsylvania, and then gave up coal in preference to imported oil and gas fuel. They found it easier to gain space for new transportation and energy distribution systems by building into the harbor instead of displacing established city streets.

On land, New Haveners built an industrial community in the Harborside area in which they could both live and work. While erecting multistory brick factories, they eliminated the earlier wood-frame shops and mills that had survived the area's frequent fires. Successive generations of entrepreneurs then built factories of stronger, more durable materials that proved a greater obstacle to the late-twentieth-century redevelopers than the earlier, lightly built structures. Now people are beginning to find new uses for these surviving structures. They show us the evolution of Harborside workplaces, and hint at the vibrant community that once thrived here.

NOTES

1. Charles S. Hartley, "The New Haven Clock Company Building," MS. at the New Haven Colony Historical Society, 1982.
2. Edward E. Atwater, ed., *History of the City of New Haven* (New York: Munsell, 1887).
3. For an introduction to industrial archaeology see R. B. Gordon and P. M. Malone, *Texture of Industry* (New York: Oxford University Press, 1994, 1997).
4. Atwater, 595; Matthew Roth, *Connecticut: An Inventory of Historic and Engineering Sites* (Washington, D.C.: Society for Industrial Archeology, 1981), 180.
5. Atwater, 597.
6. *New Haven Register*, 13 September 1970.

7. These boilers are illustrated in a drawing Robert Grzywacz made for the Historic American Engineering Record. The Bigelow boilers were obsolete by the mid-1920s, and other manufacturers moved into the forefront of boilermaking; R. C. Stewart, "Electricity on the High Iron: Cos Cob Powers the New Haven Railroad," *IA: Journal of the Society for Industrial Archeology* 23 (1997): 43–60.

8. Dana MS 1, 123: p. 73; New Haven Chamber of Commerce, January 1952.

9. Atwater, 600.

10. *New Haven Register*, April 1929.

11. An advertisement in the 1880 city directory shows a Miner & Peck press. A cam turned by large reduction gears forced spring-supported dies shut. All the parts are castings, and would have required only modest machining to finish.

12. C. C. Cooper, R. B. Gordon and H. V. Merrick, "Archeological Evidence of Metallurgical Innovation at the Eli Whitney Armory," *IA: Journal of the Society for Industrial Archeology* 8 (1982): 1–12.

13. Atwater, 570. An archaeological study of the Orange Street site was done in connection with the Ninth Square Project.

14. Atwater, 577 and 580; Rollin Osterweis, *Three Centuries of New Haven, 1638–1938* (New Haven: Yale University Press, 1953), 252 and 354.

15. Gordon and Malone, 326.

16. *Guide to the Manuscripts and Archives of the New Haven Colony Historical Society* (1988), 52.

17. The Davies mansion on Prospect Street attests to the prosperity created by these entrepreneurs. Yale University razed Winchester's adjacent mansion to make way for its Divinity School.

18. Osterweis, 255; Atwater, 581–583 and 628.

19. Osterweis, 353.

20. Atwater, 597.

21. President Griswold's decision to close programs in Yale's engineering school that he regarded as overpractical deprived many industries in southern Connecticut of a source of expertise they had come to rely on, and contributed to the increasingly hostile climate for manufacturing that developed in New Haven in the 1960s.

22. Although sea level is rising along the Connecticut shore, enough sediment is carried down the Quinnipiac and Mill rivers and brought in from Long Island Sound to make the harbor shallower.

23. Osterweis, 102, 193, 244, and 277.

24. Timothy Dwight, "A Statistical Account of the City of New Haven," report to the Connecticut Academy of Arts and Sciences (1811); Osterweis, 275.

25. Extract of the U.S. Coast Survey of New Haven Harbor, House Document 202, 25th Congress, 3d Session, Washington, D.C., 1838.

26. These industries are shown on the Buckingham map. [1830] Buckingham, "Map of the City of New Haven by Actual Survey," 1830.

27. G. M. Turner and M. W. Jacobus, *Connecticut Railroads* (Hartford: Connecticut Historical Society, 1986), 21–22; Sidney Withington, "Steamboats Reach New Haven," *Papers of the New Haven Colony Historical Society* 10 (1951): 147–187; see 178.

28. This pier is shown on the 1892 topographic map of New Haven.

29. Dana Scrap Book, 123: 92–93 (MS 1), New Haven Colony Historical Society.

30. Morley J. Kelsey, "The Fair Haven & Westville Railroad," *Journal of the New Haven Colony Historical Society* 29, no. 1 (1982): 21–56.

31. Cassius W. Kelly, "Atlas of New Haven, Connecticut" (Bridgeport, Conn.: Streuli & Puckhafer, 1911), sheet 41.

32. Neil Hogan, *A Certain Distinction, C. Cowles & Co.,* 1838–1988 (New Haven: Cowles, n.d.), 63–64.

33. A typical late-nineteenth-century factory engine required about four pounds of coal per horsepower hour; William Kent, *The Mechanical Engineer's Pocket-book* (New York: Wiley, 1903), 789.

34. Henry H. Townsend, "The Formative Years of New Haven's Public Utilities," in Richard S. Kirby, ed., *Inventors and Engineers of Old New Haven* (New Haven: New Haven Colony Historical Society, 1939), 55–82; see 56; Osterweis, 258 and 280.

35. Townsend, 76–82. With alternating current the company could transmit power to more distant customers than with its original direct-current equipment.

36. Atwater, 591–592; Osterweis, 252. The Candee company merged with the U.S. Rubber Company in 1892. Its works occupied the entire block until it closed in 1929; "Insurance Maps of New Haven" (New York, Sanborn Map Company, 1897, 1923). There are no surviving structures.

37. Withington, 156 and 161.

38. D. P. Krynine, "History of an Old New Haven Landmark," *Connecticut Society of Civil Engineers Annual Report* 64 (1948): 73–98.

39. Buckingham (1830), "New Haven Harbor," Washington, D.C.: U.S. Coast Survey, 1838; "Map of the City of New Haven and Vicinity from Actual Surveys by Hartley and Whiteford" (Philadelphia: Collins and Clark, 1851); and successive editions of the U.S. Geological Survey topographic maps of the New Haven quadrangle since 1892.

CAROLYN C. COOPER

Building an Industrial District: Carriage Manufacture in New Haven

In "horse and buggy days," New Haven was a nationally prominent center of carriage production. During barely more than a century, the industry took root, flowered, and wilted with the arrival of automobiles in the early 1900s, leaving a heritage of wood- and metalworking skills and of factory buildings and worker housing. These social and material heritages became available for adaptive industrial and postindustrial reuse. One company, C. Cowles & Co., adapted to the changing needs of the twentieth century, and thrives today.

The Beginnings of New Haven's Carriage Industry

Before the nineteenth century, travel on the American eastern seaboard was accomplished much more comfortably by water than by land. Inland, people usually rode horseback or walked; goods moved ponderously by wagon on roads that were usually poorly built and poorly maintained. However, stagecoaches did connect Boston, New Haven, and New York during the last quarter of the eighteenth century. Private "pleasure carriages," mostly imported from England or France, were rare and expensive. In mid-eighteenth century, we are told, "there were not more than four or five coaches in New York city,"[1] and "but four chaises and chairs" in New Haven.[2] Very few wealthy carriage owners would risk them on the rough roads outside towns. By 1796, however, 458 carriages were on Hartford's Grand List, 109 on New Haven's.[3] In order to build better roads, the post-Revolutionary movement to incorporate turnpike companies in Connecticut resulted in turnpikes begun between 1797 and 1802 from New Haven to Litchfield, Derby, Hartford, Cheshire, and Milford.[4] At about that time, too, New Haven's earliest known carriage maker,

John Cook, began in 1794 to build two-wheeled carriages in a small shop in a back lot on Chapel Street where Orange Street was later laid out.[5]

By 1809 there were several carriage-building establishments in town when James Brewster, after his apprenticeship to a carriage-maker in Northampton, Massachusetts, headed for New York City by a stagecoach that broke down in New Haven. Brewster promptly accepted employment by John Cook, and after a year at wages of five dollars a week had saved enough to get married and set up his own business in New Haven, at the corner of Elm and High streets (now in the heart of Yale University). Brewster expanded the range of two- and four-wheel carriage styles offered, took pride in paying wages in money instead of store credit or "truck," and prospered. His was one of the nine carriage manufactories that in 1811 were together producing ninety to a hundred carriages a year in New Haven.[6]

As his business grew, Brewster moved a short distance from Elm and High streets to the corner of York and Broadway, still later to John Cook's "old stand" on Chapel Street. By 1830 Brewster vehicles were being exported to Mexico, South America, and Cuba, as well as closer destinations.[7] Brewster's sons James B. and Henry grew up making carriages; he set them up with branch manufactories in Bridgeport and New York City. Later the sons ran two separate Brewster carriage-making establishments in New York City. In 1832 Brewster Sr. moved his operation from downtown New Haven to the banks of Mill River and built a grand new factory on East Street. He was an early pioneer of industrial location in the "New Township" east of New Haven's original nine squares.

This area had been farmland, and then had gradually become a suburb, with rather substantial houses along extensions of Chapel Street and Water Street, and even a hotel or two overlooking the harbor. In 1794 Eli Whitney had set up his cotton gin workshop in the New Township on a lot where Chestnut Street later intersected Wooster Street.[8] Nearly forty years later and farther east, Brewster bought acreage where Wooster Street ended at East Street, and laid out adjacent streets to encourage other manufacturers of carriages and carriage parts, and their workers, to settle in what became known as "Brewsterville."

That year, 1832, Louis McLane, the U.S. secretary of the treasury, gathered statistics on American manufactures. In the category "coach and wagon," New Haven outstripped the other reporting Connecticut towns in all respects reported (see table 1). In New Haven that year 217 men working ten-hour days produced 800 coaches worth $221,00 from $43,500 worth of domestic and foreign materials, using $41,000 worth of capital invested in land, buildings, and equipment.[9] In Bridgeport, the nearest competitor, thirty-five men worked eleven-hour days to produce $45,000 worth of coaches and wagons that year from domestic and

TABLE 1.
Coach and Wagon Manufactures in Connecticut, 1832*

Town	Value of materials	Capital invested	Value of product	Employees	Workday
Meriden	$350 domestic	$700	$4,000	4 men	12 hours
Hartford	—	$13,400	$42,000	90 men	12 hours
Torrington	—	$500	$2,500	5 men	12 hours
Norwich	—	—	$19,000	29 men	12 hours
Bridgeport	$1,000 foreign; $28,000 domestic	$4,000	$45,000	35 men	11 hours
Middletown	—	$3,000	$1,200	3 men	12 hours
Berlin	—	$1,500	$6,500	14 men	—
New Haven	$12,000 foreign; $31,500 domestic	$41,000	$221,000	217 men	10 hours

*Louis McLane, comp., *Documents Relative to the Manufactures in the United States . . .* Washington D.C. 1833 (The McLane Report) Vol. 2, doc. 9, #1. pp. 990–991. The value of domestic materials reported for New Haven coaches on p. 990 is $31,500, but on p. 1033 it is $21,500; foreign materials worth $12,000 are reported at both places, so the total is either $43,500 or $33,500.

TABLE 2.
Carriage Manufacture in Bridgeport, Hartford, and New Haven, 1845* & 1860**

City	Year	Factories	Capital invested	Annual value	Employees
Bridgeport	1845	4	$101,000	$153,253	169
Hartford	1845	5	$15,000	$21,980	29
New Haven	1845	24	$287,600	$553,400	460
Bridgeport	1860	13	$223,600	$604,550	415
Hartford	1860	21	$89,850	$205,080	217
New Haven	1860	41	$1,174,000	$2,462,057	1,829

*Daniel P. Tyler, comp., *Statistics of the Condition and Products of Certain Branches of Industry in Connecticut, for the Year Ending October 1, 1845* (Hartford, Conn.: John L. Boswell, 1846), 6, 39, and 92. Tyler prepared this report from the returns of the tax assessors of all but one of the 144 towns then in Connecticut. The figures may not be strictly comparable, as they are for Bridgeport's "car, coach, and wagon" factories, Hartford's "coach, wagon, &c." factories, and New Haven's "coach, wagon and sleigh" factories.
**J. Leander Bishop, *A History of American Manufactures from 1608 to 1860* (Philadelphia: Edward Young, 1864), 2:736, 757, and 764. Bishop cited the 1860 federal census returns for these cities.

foreign materials worth $29,800, using $4,000 capital invested.

Growth of New Haven Carriage Manufacture to 1860

New Haven and Bridgeport continued to be the most active carriage production centers in Connecticut. Both towns' capital invested, output value, and employment in carriage industries grew rapidly in the three decades after the McLane report, especially Bridgeport's, but New Haven's remained much larger (see table 2). Hartford's carriage industry seems to have declined sharply between 1832 and 1845, but grew by 1860 to about the size New Haven's had been in 1832, in employment and value of output. New Haven's carriage industry was roughly three times larger than Bridgeport's in 1845 in terms of employment and output value; by 1860 it was four times larger than Bridgeport's.

New Haven carriage manufacturers generally emulated the Brewsters in building relatively expensive, high-quality carriages, even while the national industry mechanized, generally lowered prices, and expanded, following population westward. The number of New Haven carriage manufacturers, which had risen from nine in 1811 to twenty-four in 1845, climbed to forty-one by 1860.[10] Prominent among New Haven firms in 1860 were Lawrence, Bradley & Pardee, at Chapel and Hamilton streets (figure 1) and G. & D. Cook & Company at State and Grove streets. Both firms had Brewster connections.[11] The Cooks' catalog for that year shows 145 different styles of carriage, ranging in price from a stripped-down "skeleton wagon" for $80 to $95, through a "farmers buggy" for $140 to $175, to heavier and more ornate barouches, rockaways, bretts, and coaches, from $200 up to $1200 apiece (see figure 2).[12]

A coach made at about that time by Lawrence, Bradley, & Pardee is now exhibited at the Pardee-Morris House in East Haven (see figure 3). Like many other New

Haven carriages, it was shipped to a customer in the South.[13] Indeed, while some New Haven carriages went to New York City, most were shipped further, first by water and later by railroad, south and west. New Haveners also bought carriages: the assessed total value of carriages on the Grand List for 1859 was $82,078, ranking just below the value of New Haven horses and mules ($98,270) and far above that of its citizens' timepieces ($50,026) or their musical instruments ($50,668).[14]

By the eve of the Civil War, New Haven was an astonishingly important producer of carriages on the national scene, especially considering its modest size (population 39,267). An editor of the *New York Coach-Maker's Magazine* reported in 1858, "As a coach-making city, New Haven stands forth among the most extensive in the country, and perhaps, in the world."[15] It was outranked in output of vehicles only by the states of New York, Pennsylvania, and Connecticut itself.[16] At least 10.5 percent of the persons listed in the New Haven directory of 1860–61 were employed in the carriage industry.[17] The G. & D. Cook & Co. manufactory alone was employing three hundred men. According to clock manufacturer Chauncey Jerome, who lived in its "immediate vicinity," the Cook Co. was turning out ten carriages a day; that is, "a finished carriage every hour."[18] Within Connecticut, New Haven carriages contributed disproportionately to the state's earnings from the industry. Of the 154 carriage-making establishments in Connecticut counted in the 1860 census, more than one-third (56) were in New Haven County. Constituting slightly less than nine percent of the county's 642 manufacturing establishments, these 56 companies produced carriages valued at $2,745,056, which was nearly two-thirds the value ($4,171,804) earned by the whole state in carriage production.[19]

The 56 New Haven County carriage establishments in 1860 were also larger on average than the others in the state, for they had more than two-thirds of the state's total investment in carriage-making ($1,220,400 out of $1,776,450), and employed

2,096 men and 80 women, or nearly two-thirds of the state total of 3,313 men and 98 women so employed. The size of the average carriage manufactory in New Haven County was about 39 employees, compared to the state average of about 22 workers per carriage factory. New Haven County carriage employees were paid $395 annually on average, which was below the state average of $435 for carriage workers. At $561, the amount of capital investment per carriage worker was seven percent higher in New Haven County than in the state as a whole—$521.[20]

Wartime Shock, Gilded Age Recovery but Decline in Rank, Twentieth-Century Demise

New Haven carriage manufacturers survived the business panic of 1857, but were subsequently hit hard by the Civil War, during which they lost their southern customers. Nevertheless, many recovered and prospered again after the war. They were fewer in number, however, down to 35 and 33 in the city directories of 1870 and 1880, though rebounding up to 40 in 1890 and 1900.[21] New Haven carriage manufacture was less prominent on the national scene than it had been before the war, for the carriage industry had spread westward. In 1880 the city ranked fifth in the value of carriages and wagons produced, after Cincinnati, New York City, Philadelphia, and Chicago.[22] Censuses showed New Haven County carriage manufacturing was employing fewer workers than before the war: such employment was down from 2176 in 1860, to 648 in 1870, and 588 in 1880.

The trend was statewide, too: by 1900 the number of wage earners in the carriage and wagon industry of all Connecticut was 2,192, which had increased from 1,457 in 1890,[23] but was down more than a third from the total of 3,411 men and women in 1860. In 1900 the value of carriages and wagons produced in Connecticut was nearly $4.5 million—somewhat more than in 1860—but now the state ranked only tenth behind first-ranking Ohio, whose carriages and wagons earned nearly $16.5 million that year.[24]

New Haven carriage-maker William H. Bradley summed up the situation in the last quarter of the century: "New Haven has lost the Western trade for cheap carriages and cannot compete with the Western builders for the Southern trade. New Haven will always be a market for fine, nice carriages; coming down to a cheaper grade, the West will beat us."[25] New Haven carriages maintained their reputation for high quality and style, receiving favorable mention at the 1876 Centennial Exhibition in Philadelphia and the 1893 Columbian Exhibition in Chicago.[26] After the advent of the automobile, carriage-making in New Haven continued at least two

FIGURE 1. (Opposite top left) *As successor in New Haven to the prestigious Brewster Company, the firm of Lawrence, Bradley & Pardee built high-end carriages with a maximum of handwork. Its factory-and-repository complex was one of the largest in New Haven. The only extant New Haven carriage in New Haven today was built in this factory around 1860.* (Lawrence, Bradley & Pardee, *Illustrated Catalogue of Carriages, Sleighs, Harness, Saddles, &c.* [New Haven, 1862], frontispiece)

FIGURE 2. (Opposite bottom left) *Carriage styles manufactured by G. & D. Cook & Co.* (G. & D. Cook & Co., *Illustrated Catalogue of Carriages and Special Business Advertiser* [New York: Baker & Godwin, 1860], 75, 101, and 147)

FIGURE 3. (Opposite bottom right) *Although very similar to the Cooks' "Hamilton Coach" shown in fig. 2, a coach built by Lawrence, Bradley & Pardee circa 1860 was shipped to a customer in Kentucky and returned in the 1930s to New Haven. It is now owned by the New Haven Colony Historical Society and on view at the Pardee-Morris House. In design it closely resembles the "Scroll-Back Quarter Caleche Coach" shown in the firm's catalog.* (Lawrence, Bradley & Pardee, *Illustrated Catalogue of Carriages, Sleighs, Harness, Saddles, &c.* [New Haven, 1862], 109)

decades into the twentieth century. In 1918 *A Modern History of New Haven and Eastern New Haven County* reported that "despite the supposed decline in the use of the horse in the large centers of the east, New Haven has today thirty concerns [making] . . . carriages for the country."[27]

Ultimately, however, the automobile, a technological offspring of the bicycle rather than the carriage, killed the carriage industry nationally as well as locally. For instance, the New Haven Carriage Company, beginning confidently in 1887 in a new building that stretched south on Franklin Street from Collis Street most of the way to Water Street, became "one of the last of the large local carriage concerns," and built its last carriage in 1907. It adapted to the new age as "Builders of Automobile Bodies of Wood and Metal," offering "Automobile, Carriage and Wagon Wheels" and "Repairs of All Kinds," but went out of business in 1924.[28]

SPECIALIZATION OF PRODUCTION

During its rise in the nineteenth century, the carriage industry not only grew, but also differentiated into specialties. Separate wheelworks and axle works, for instance, supplied more than one carriage-maker. A visitor to New Haven in 1858 noted not only that "1700 men find employment at the various branches directly connected with coach and carriage manufacture," but also that there were "almost half as many more [employed] in the manufacture of stocks, such as springs, axles, malleable castings, lamps, laces, finishing hardware, etc. etc." Among the specific "stock manufacturers" he noted were the wheel-maker G. F. Kimball (figure 4),

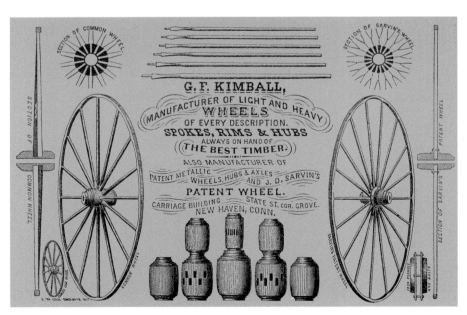

FIGURE 4. *American wheels made of elm wood hubs and hickory spokes and rims were particularly lightweight but strong, and were prized in foreign as well as domestic markets.* (G. & D. Cook & Co., *Illustrated Catalogue of Carriages and Special Business Advertiser* [New York: Baker & Godwin, 1860], 128)

the Dann Brothers' manufactory of "running parts," the coach lace manufactory of Laban Pardee, the wood-carving establishment of James H. Campbell, the lamp-making business of A. J. Cutler, and the "trimming and finishing hardware manufactory . . . of Messrs. C. Cowles & Co."[29]

In describing New Haven industry, J. Leander Bishop's *History of American Manufactures from* 1608 *to* 1860 also emphasized the manufacture of "parts of carriages, as wheels, axles, springs, etc."[30] In addition to carriage manufacturers, dealers, and repairers, in the 1860s the business section of the city directory listed headings that recognized the separate manufacture of carriage bodies, carriage woodwork, carriage irons, coach lace, coach lamps, coach trimmings, carriage and saddlery hardware, and wheels.

Clearly, carriage manufacturers were at this time already able to buy many of their parts ready-made by other firms. In fact, J. Leander Bishop singled out a relative newcomer to New Haven carriage-making, the steam-powered and mechanized factory of George T. Newhall, for *not* doing so: "Mr. Newhall not only makes more of that class of vehicles known as "Buggies," in a year, than any other manufacturer in the United States, but makes more of the constituent parts of a carriage. Nearly everything belonging to a carriage is made on his own premises."[31]

After an apprenticeship at the Hooker and Osborne factory on Park Street and two partnerships, Newhall had established his factory circa 1851 at an old barites mill[32] northwest of the built-up area of town, on the New Haven and Northampton Railroad. He quickly expanded his operation to two hundred workers, and like Brewster two decades earlier, bought adjacent land, opened up streets, and built houses.[33] Thus situated on his own eponymous Newhall Street in Newhallville, he was apparently more self-sufficient than the older carriage establishments in the center of town or those that were, following Brewster's example, increasingly concentrating in the New Township and becoming interdependent.

Hand Craft and Machine Power

Town histories that mention Newhall consistently credit him with introducing steam power to the local carriage industry in 1855, thus implying it had not been used much (if at all) before then, and that thereafter it was used. However, Brewster's successor firm Collis and Lawrence had been using an eight-horsepower steam engine for ten years in 1838, for "sawing, turning and grinding."[34] Nevertheless, contrary to popular impressions nowadays, factories did not necessarily require use of powered machinery. New Haven, situated below the tidewater line on its rivers and streams, only gradually replaced muscle power, where needed, with steam engines, of which all Connecticut had only forty-seven by 1838.[35] One had been in use to fan forge fires at the pioneering axe factory at East and Greene streets in the New Township, which failed financially sometime after a visit by President Andrew Jackson in 1833.[36] More were no doubt beginning to be used at other metalworking establishments in New Haven that supplied springs, axles, and carriage hardware to the carriage factories.[37] By 1860, steam-powered machines were also used at woodworking shops that made wheels,[38] but not necessarily at the carriage factories themselves. Even after George Newhall showed the way in 1855, there was no stampede among New Haven carriage-makers to mechanize their operations.

However, division of labor within a carriage factory was an effective way of increasing efficiency and therefore output, even without the use of powered machinery.[39] A visitor in 1855 to the G. & D. Cook Company factory at State and Grove streets did not mention machinery, but praised its size of operating space and organization of production:

> The manufactory which they now occupy, from a small brick building 50 by 28 [feet] has grown since 1850 to be a mammoth model establishment, worthy of a visit by those who are about to erect large and commodious factories for the business. . . . Each process has its appropriate room, and each workman the duty for which he is best fitted, accompanied with a due share of responsibility. A written description of the carriage to be made and the workman's duties respecting it, is suspended in each room. . . . No carriage leaves their shop without an inspector's stamp of approbation.[40]

A proprietor, probably George or David Cook, attributed their early success to having reduced

> every department to as perfect a system of operation as possible. . . . We made only one style of top and one of no-top carriage, thereby enabling us to make them very perfect and very cheap. We found sale for about three jobs per week the first year; but since the completion of our shops we finish from twenty to twenty-five per week and find ready sale for all we make. . . . We [now] employ 110 hands and have not less than $50,000 capital. Connected with us is New Haven Spring Co., who make all our springs.[41]

The New Haven Spring Co. (figure 5) was using steam engines in heating, hammering, and rolling iron into springs for Cook carriages, but it is likely that the carriage factory itself was not using steampower.[42] A few years later, however, Chauncey Jerome commented in 1860 not only on the Cooks' systematization of work, but also on "much of the work being done by machinery."[43] Another writer in 1860 even more fulsomely praised not only the Cooks' system by which three hundred workmen were now producing ten carriages per day, but also the Cooks'

> beautiful and powerful steam-engine, every revolution of whose ponderous wheel gives life and activity to over fifty beautifully working machines, adapted to almost any conceivable part of their work, performing an amount of work equal to the whole number of their men, and with far greater accuracy than can possibly be

done by hand labor . . . we no longer wonder that their elegant pleasure-wagons are completed at the rate of one per hour.[44]

FIGURE 5. *Workers at the New Haven Spring Co. combined handwork with machine work to forge, temper, and grind iron and steel into axles and springs for carriages. The predominant type of carriage spring was the elliptical design that New Havener Jonathan Mix had patented in 1807.* (G. & D. Cook & Co., *Illustrated Catalogue of Carriages and Special Business Advertiser* [New York: Baker & Godwin, 1860], 46)

By 1876, when several New Haven carriage companies and suppliers displayed their products at the Centennial Exhibition in Philadelphia, mechanization had advanced in the carriage industry nationally. Nevertheless, William H. Bradley & Co., the successor to Lawrence, Bradley & Pardee, considered mechanization a dubious practice. A visitor to the large factory building, which occupied frontage of 220 feet on Chapel Street and 280 feet on Hamilton Street in the New Township, said it was

fully equipped with such appliances as can aid in the rapid production of thoroughly good work, but they do not trust to lifeless machinery and thoughtless boys, the labor which only skilled workmen can properly perform. The utmost care is exercised in every department of manufacture, under the immediate supervision of members of the firm.[45]

In 1886 the Bradley factory along Chapel Street, now under operation by the A. T. Demarest Co. with one hundred "hands," was reported by the Sanborn insurance map to be still using "hand power," while William H. Bradley & Co. had shrunk into the Hamilton Street wing. The next year the William H. Bradley & Co. was absent from the city directory, while William H. Bradley himself was listed as superintendent of the A. T. Demarest Co.[46] In 1901 the A. T. Demarest Co. occupied the buildings on both streets, and continued to use "hand power."[47]

Other carriage manufacturers continued at least into the late 1880s to build carriages with hand power instead of steam power. At least eight of Bradley's nearby contemporaries, employing twenty to one hundred workers each, were doing so in 1886. Across Hamilton Street from the Bradley/Demarest complex, the Durham & Wooster Carriage Builders employed fifty persons to work by hand. In the other direction, the Henry Hale & Co. Carriage Manufactory at 60 and 62 Franklin Street had forty-five workers employing hand power. Farther north at 108 Franklin Street, P. Cullom & Co. Carriage Works and Livery Stable employed twenty workers using hand power. The fifty employees of Kean and Lines Coach Builders at the cor-

ner of Chapel and Wallace streets, worked by hand, as did the twenty employees of J. H. Booth, coach lace manufacturer and carriage trimmer, around the corner at 15 Wooster Street. Across Wooster Street in that block, J. F. Goodrich & Co. employed eighty workers to build carriages by hand, as did Crittenden & Co.'s one hundred workers in the same block. At the corner of Wallace and Wooster Streets, B. Manville & Co. Carriages' factory was manned and powered by seventy-five persons.[48]

How did all these hand-working carriage-makers actually make carriages? Images of the interiors of factories making other wood-and-metal products in the last decades of the nineteenth century usually show machinery, run by offstage steam engines through belting and line shafting. Pictures of the interiors of carriage factories themselves, however, as distinct from factories for various carriage parts, are scarce. The few pictures that are available convey the impression that machines were not much used in carriage factories, at least not in eastern producers of high-style carriages. Views of operations as late as 1879 in Brewster & Co.'s carriage manufactory on Broadway between Forty-seventh and Forty-eighth streets in New York City show plenty of handwork, but no machine work except for bending wood and grinding ingredients for paint.[49] Instead of ranks of machines powered from overhead line shafts, men are shown busy with hand tools. First, pieces of wood—"ash, elm, oak, and whitewood . . . according to the service the part is to undergo"[50]—were manhandled into and out of a steam box and then bent into required shapes by "a powerful bending machine" (figure 6). Then men wielding hand tools—rulers, saws, planes, drills, screwdrivers, and hammers—shaped and connected the wooden pieces into a carriage body (figure 7). Meanwhile, men in the blacksmith shop worked with hammers, tongs and files at forges and anvils to shape iron for the running gear. At some point workers fastened together wheels, axles, and springs that were apparently obtained from elsewhere. Once they had bolted the body and undercarriage together, workers tested the carriage "in the white" for tightness and strength (figure 8) before taking it apart again for painting and varnishing the body. Varnishing was a particularly meticulous process of repeated layers for weatherproofing and glossiness.

Presumably the workers rejoined the body and its undercarriage for display in the company's adjacent "repository," or carefully packed them into separate crates for shipping to a more distant destination. At some point before its departure from the manufactory, they would "finish" the carriage by adding malleable cast-iron steps

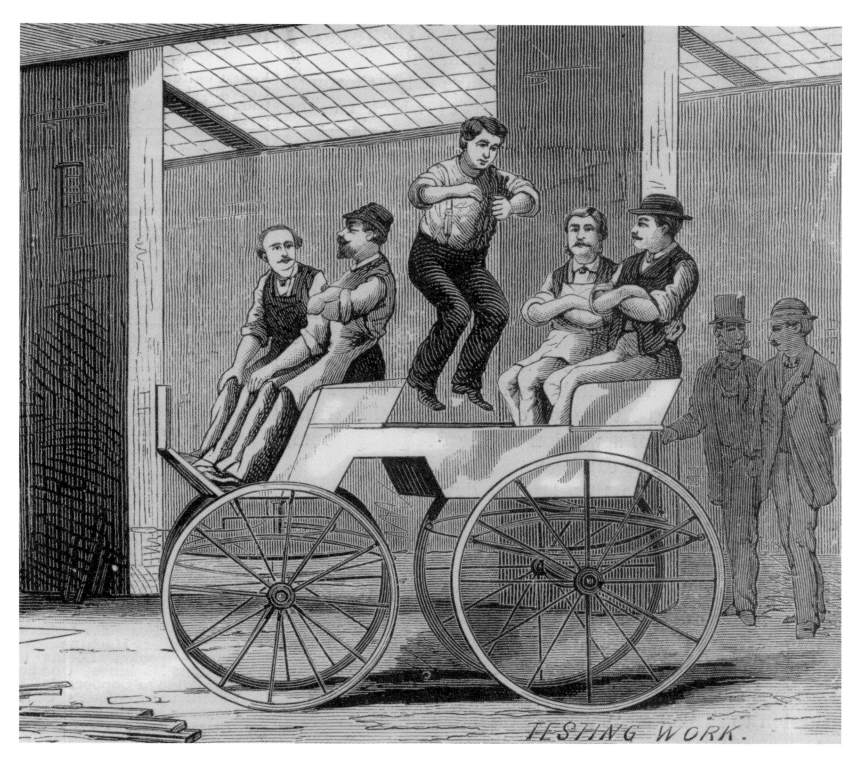

TESTING WORK.

FIGURE 8. *Before painting, the body of a carriage was fastened to its running gear and tested for its ability to withstand some serious bouncing by surrogate passengers. After testing the carriage body, workers would remove it from the running gear for painstaking painting and varnishing.* (*Scientific American*, n.s., 40, no. 6 [8 February 1879], 79)

and brackets, coach lamps, upholstery, coach lace, carpets, possibly glass windows, and (depending on the style) possibly a folding top. These items would have arrived from parts manufacturers.

It is possible that New Haven manufacturers of carriages, following the Brewster example at the high-style end of the spectrum, took longer than the national average to mechanize their operations. A detailed Labor Department study of the effects of mechanization on the manufacture of buggies (at the low end of the style spectrum) between 1865 and 1895 found that it took only one-fifth of the time and less than one-fifth of the labor cost to make a buggy "by machine" (more than half the operations done with power equipment) as "by hand" (all operations done by hand.).[51] The biggest savings in time and labor came in woodworking: "the time it took to cut out material for the gear, body and seat shrank from about 20 hours to about 20 minutes." While the number of distinct operations in making one buggy rose somewhat (from 64 to 72), the number of workers needed to do them rose much more sharply (from 6 to 117).[52] The results of this study must reflect to a large extent the growth of separate production of carriage parts in specialized parts factories.

In the 1860–61 *New Haven Directory*, fifty carriage manufacturers outnumbered thirty-four suppliers of carriage parts, but in the 1880 directory New Haven's thirty-eight parts manufacturers only somewhat outweighed its thirty-four carriage manufacturers. In 1887 the balance was tipped even farther: thirty-seven manufacturers of carriages were served by fifty-three manufacturers of carriage parts, even without counting the five wheel manufacturers, two axle manufacturers and two whip socket manufacturers.[53] This progression strongly suggests that New Haven's manufacturers of carriage parts acquired customers elsewhere as well. Differentiation of carriage-making into separate specialties was a nationwide trend in the carriage industry, so much so that in 1900 the author of the census monograph on carriage-making grumbled: "A considerable number of so-called manufacturers of carriages and wagons are in reality merely assemblers who slip on the wheels, attach the top to the carriage part, adjust and tighten the bolts and nuts, and touch over any part of the polished parts accidentally marred in transport from the several factories to the assembler's repository, or so-called factory."[54]

Formation and Function of New Haven's Carriage Industrial District

Not all New Haven carriage manufacturers followed Brewster to the New Township. Nodes of carriage-building remained in other outskirts of the central "nine squares": besides Newhallville there was a northern node out Ashmun Street near Winchester's gun factory, and to the south, another node between Congress Avenue and West Water Street. The New Haven Wheel Company's plant grew immensely and remained through depressions and fires for decades, just where Zelotes Day began it in 1845 at Grove and York streets, the northernmost corner of New Haven's original nine squares.[55] (Its site is now occupied by Yale University's Hall of Graduate Studies.) And carriage manufactories persisted on Park Street, just beyond the original York Street boundary.[56] But the flourishing center of New Haven's carriage industry gravitated eastward, helping, together with other industries and housing, to fill in streets between State Street and the railroad Brewster had helped build alongside Mill River.

By 1860, sixteen of the fifty carriage manufacturers listed in the New Haven business directory and thirteen of the thirty-four listed carriage-parts suppliers were located on State Street or eastward.[57] By 1880, sixteen of the thirty-two carriage manufacturers listed in that year's directory and nineteen of the thirty-eight listed carriage-parts suppliers had addresses on State Street or eastward.[58] By this rough measure, we can see that the fraction of the city's carriage industry—both carriage and carriage-parts manufacturers—that was located in this area of the city increased from about one third to one half in those two decades.

Despite a great growth in carriage ownership since the eighteenth century and the beginnings of a street railway with horse-drawn cars, in those days most New Haveners walked to work. Zoning regulations did not yet separate residences from industrial workplaces, so walking to work was easier than it is now. In the New Township, industries and their workers moved into what had been a suburban residential area of large lots and substantial houses. Detailed insurance maps of the area, which began only in 1880, show denser residential occupation nearer to downtown, while on the streets from Olive eastward, two-to-three-story dwellings with deep backyards had checkered the space and were already coexisting with carriage factories and "heavier" metalworking industries. The housing stock included a scattered mix of largish separate houses, duplexes, and row houses. This coexistence of industry and domesticity persisted for decades.

For instance, in 1886 M. Armstrong & Co.'s carriage manufactory looked across Chapel Street at seven houses between Hamilton and Wallace. The long lots behind those houses backed on the long lots of more houses on Wooster Street and of the Wooster Public School. On its own side of Chapel Street, M. Armstrong & Co. was flanked by Durham & Wooster's carriage manufactory and the foundry temporarily occupied by F. C. & A. E. Rowland's boiler shop.[59] Together with W. Johnston's carriage woodwork manufactory around the corner at 71 Hamilton Street, these four industrial plants took up about five-eighths of the block bounded by Wallace, Chapel, Hamilton, and Greene streets. Except for a store at 68 Wallace and two saloons at 38 Greene and 80 Wallace, residences filled the rest of the block. Two tenements already existed; another was being built. Fifteen years later the quantitative mix of housing and industry in that block was virtually the same, except for an additional store on the corner of Greene and Wallace. Among M. Armstrong's industrial neighbors, however, the boiler shop had been replaced by the Miner Peck Manufacturing Co. and its machine shop, while W. Johnson's twelve makers of carriage woodwork had departed from where Connecticut Cutlery Co. had arrived, and Durham & Wooster's carriage factory building now housed the Kickapoo Indian Medicine Co. instead.[60]

Meanwhile, the complex of buildings at the site of Brewster's original factory on East Street had undergone many changes during its shifts in proprietorship and product since the 1830s. Following occupation of the old carriage manufactory building by the Rogers Smith Co., makers of silverplated ware, the Boston Buckboard Company moved into it in 1879, restoring it to carriage production, and added height to two of its wings so that it resembled a giant letter E. The Boston Buckboard Co. went out of business in the mid-1890s. The W. & E. T. Fitch Company, an iron- and steelworking firm, had already moved in 1853 from Westville to steam-powered adjacent buildings south of the Brewster complex, commenced making saddlery hardware and currycombs, and in 1868 built a malleable iron foundry. Fitch's plant expansions eventually overtook the former Brewster building a decade after the Boston Buckboard Company ceased operation. Fitch demolished the main two wings during further construction before it, too, closed in 1919. After miscellaneous interim uses, the foundry that Fitch expanded sometime between 1886 and 1901 to fill the obtuse angle of Bridge and East Streets has survived, and most recently has found adaptive reuse, serving in part as a source of art supplies.[61]

Fitch's neighborhood was less residential than M. Armstrong's. Looking westward in 1886, Fitch's immediate neighborhood of carriage factories on East Street (J. F. Goodrich & Co.) Wooster Street (Cruttenden and Co.) and Chapel Street (Kean and Lines) was undoubtedly of benefit to them all, as was its contiguity to the Boston Buckboard Co. next door. Toward the harbor, between Fitch and the massive presence of the Sargent's hardware factory on the next block diagonally across Collis Street, a few residences, a restaurant, a store, and a saloon probably added a friendly respite from an otherwise predominantly industrial ambience. In addition, a sizeable and presumably well-patronized saloon at 138 East Street was directly across from Fitch's buildings. Behind the factory, however, the rail yards fronting the Mill River prevented convenient neighborhood commerce in that direction.

Measuring availability of late-nineteenth-century worker housing in the no-longer-so-new New Township is not possible without much more elaborate study; however, at least a trend can be perceived by counting the boardinghouses listed as such in the city directories. The 1860–61 city directory lists sixty-two boarding houses, twenty-eight of which were located from State Street eastward to East Street. The 1887 directory lists fewer boardinghouses in New Haven (41), but proportionally more of them (27) were in the State-to-East streets area.[62] Private families who took in a boarder or two (including not-yet-married relatives, as was quite common) would not be reflected in the listing of boardinghouses. But the change of proportion from less than half to nearly two thirds of the city's total number of boardinghouses suggests that the area was becoming a place of younger and less-established residents than before, perhaps a place of entry for industrial workers arriving from elsewhere, even overseas. They needed to walk no more than a few blocks from the harbor and railroad if they wanted to work in a carriage factory or a factory producing parts of a carriage.

In this era of Civil War stress, postwar recovery and Gilded Age prosperity, the New Township carriage manufactories, together with neighboring suppliers of carriage parts and accessories, and nearby carriage workers' houses, eventually constituted what can be considered an "industrial district." As such, it was smaller but similar in many respects to that of Birmingham in England, where many separate and specialized craft "trades" interacted in producing firearms and other consumer goods made up of parts. Propinquity among carriage manufactories, suppliers, and workers had mutual advantages. It meant that they could easily exchange information on styles and market conditions, refer customers to one another, subcontract when needed, maintain a convenient labor pool, and save on space in the plant and time for deliveries.

Wood of specific sorts for different parts of the carriage seats, body, and wheels was readily available from the New Haven Steam Sawmill at the foot of Chapel Street and from lumberyards along East Water Street. In fact, nearly all of New Haven's sawing, planing, and turning mills were in the carriage-making industrial district.[63] Among specific carriage-parts producers, the Dann Brothers carriage woodworkers and wheel manufacturer Henry Stowe moved eastward from more central New Haven locations to the carriage industrial district between the 1860s and the 1880s, providing a closer source of woodwork and wheels to the increasing numbers of carriage manufacturers there.[64] Foundries like Fitch's for carriage hardware manufacture gravitated into the area as well.[65] They might recruit and exchange workers trained there at Sargent's giant hardware factory. However, axle manufacturer Leverett F. Goodyear, located at the Bridge Street junction of East Water Street in 1860, had retreated somewhat northwestward to 881 State Street by 1887; Ives & Miller, the other axle manufacturer listed in 1887, was even more distant, out the Canal Line Railroad in Mount Carmel.

The transportation nexus of railroad and harbor, on which the carriage district fronted, facilitated obtaining raw and semiprocessed materials and shipping out the finished products. On 26 July 1875, English & Mersick (a carriage hardware manufacturing firm that remained downtown) reported to the carriage trade publication *The Hub*:

> Carriages transported during the 6 months ending June 30, 1875 were 3459; Carriages transported during the 6 months ending June 30, 1874 were 3383, showing an increase the present year of 76 . . . corroborating the opinion heretofore expressed to you that such was the case. . . . This market, we believe, is now more favorably known throughout the country than ever before.[66]

C. Cowles & Co.: Versatile Specialization

Among other "first-class stock manufacturers" in the carriage industry of New Haven was C. Cowles & Co, located between 1855 and 1890 at a site on Orange Street in New Haven's "ninth square."[67] From 1890 to the present the company has been situated at the corner of Water and Chestnut streets in the New Township. From early on C. Cowles & Co. advertised and traded well beyond New Haven boundaries. Not only did the firm win a prize at the 1876 Exhibition in Philadelphia, it also joined four other New Haven carriage-related companies in exhibiting at the 1880 Exposition in Melbourne, Australia.[68] An observer in 1882 noted that Cowles did business "throughout the United States and also largely in Australia, Canada, the British provinces, South America, Mexico, the West Indies and Europe" and employed "two to three traveling salesmen" as well as "150 operatives."[69]

Cowles produced a wide range of utilitarian and decorative parts for carriages, ranging from "the simplest iron trimming to the most expensive nickel and gold-plated goods used on the highest finished coach."[70] From its beginning in rented space on York Street in 1838 the initial partnership of William Cornwell and Chandler Cowles made a specialty of carriage lamps; later the company produced "a larger variety than any house in this country, averaging over a thousand pairs a month" by 1887.[71] Figure 9 shows two models of Cowles lamps from 1880. In addition, in the 1840s Cornwell and Cowles began offering a wider range of "harness, saddlery and carriage hardware." The company's 1855 catalog for its products offered such arcane items as:

> self-adjusting pad trees, rein hook levers, pole crabs and yokes, curtain frames, dashes, brass or silver bands and sand bands, stump joints, hang and joint riv-

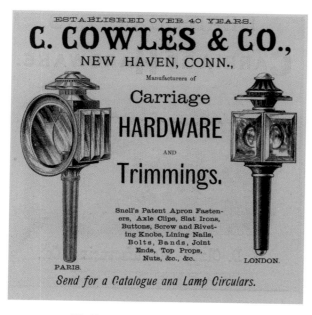

FIGURE 9. *The Paris and London lamps were only two of many styles that C. Cowles & Co. offered its customers in the Gilded Age, each available in different sizes and finishes.* (*Carriage Monthly Advertiser* 16 [1880–81], xxxvii)

ets, carriage knobs, top props, brass or silver shaft sockets, door locks, blind catches, brass or silver inside handles, silver or brass lining nails, ivory head screws . . . etc.[72]

Cowles also sold, in addition to its own products, "patent leather, rubber cloth, oil carpet, coach lace, tufts, tassels, seaming cord, coach door slide bolts, buggy seats, carriage springs, carriage axles, hubs, spokes, any kind of dash and seat rails made to order."[73] Elsewhere Cowles advertised "Nuts, Turned Collars, Washers . . . Carved and Plain Carriage Parts,"[74] and "Kimball's Improved Carriage Top Prop," with "Capped Nuts and Rivets of all patterns, furnished to order, at the lowest prices."[75] As dealer of others' products in addition to its own, Cowles purveyed a great range both of supplies, from textiles to metals, and of custom jobbing for carriage-makers.

At the 1876 Centennial Exhibit in Philadelphia C. Cowles & Co. received praise for its

> good display of carriage and baby carriage mountings, and hardware combined, comprising door handles, crabs with and without hooks, curtain rollers, lamps, etc. In addition to the mountings in silver and gold, there is a fine line of ivory goods, such as card boxes, inside handles for locks, pull-to handles, glass holder slides, buttons, etc. These mountings and ivory goods occupy the center of the case; at the right of these, carriage hardware is placed, consisting of clip bolts, stay ends, etc., at the left, stamped stove plates, representing figures, flowers, etc. are arranged.[76]

COWLES' MANUFACTURING PROCESSES

In short, C. Cowles & Co. dealt in a dizzying array of objects. Even if we recognize that Cowles did not make *all* of the items that it advertised for sale, it is clear that at the Orange Street premises the "hands" worked with a wide variety of material, including at a minimum iron, brass, silver, ivory, glass, rubber, and wood. Their facilities and equipment had to give them capability variously to forge, melt, cast, mold, bend, stamp, cut, and enamel such materials, as well as heat-treat them for different effects. For instance, in 1857, "having secured George Conover . . . to superintend their foundry," Cowles advertised the "Brass foundry. Rear of Orange St. . . . superior work cannot be obtained in this city or elsewhere. Cash paid for old metals."[77] Once in possession of such facilities, the company could and apparently did also take on "jobbing in sheet metals" and in brass castings.

A visitor to the "store and mammoth work-shops" of Messrs. C. Cowles & Co. in 1858 found many processes "novel and interesting":

> The cutting of steel dies, used in the manufacture of curtain frames, ornaments, &c., is an ingenious process, involving the use of more than a thousand tools, among which are a great variety of files, or rather, tools of every conceivable shape with files upon the points or sides. The "spinning" (or rather shaping in a lathe) of lamp-caps, sockets, &c., from silver shell; also, the cutting, grinding and engraving of glass, used in the manufacture of coach lamps, is done here in a very perfect and artistic manner. The refuse chips of silver, which fall from the lamp and curtain-frame factories, are used in the manufacture of ornaments and silver-headed nails, as are the tin scraps into buttons and black-headed nails, by a long row of *chattering* machines, worked by *silent* women.[78]

The company was proud not only of the quality of its materials, but also of its production system. Elsewhere on the tour, the reporter noted, "Plating, dash-making, bending, turning and casting—each is done systematically in its own department."[79] In 1882, the Cowles lamp catalog likened its production system to that of the National Armory:

> Our lamps are made on the same principle as a Springfield musket, the parts being interchangeable. Every piece is cut and formed by dies and this in connection with the fact of our making often five hundred pairs of a kind at one time, enables us to make a better article at a less price than can be done by the old fashioned process. These improvements are patented and we propose to protect them.[80]

COWLES RELOCATES

FIGURE 10. *C. Cowles & Co. occupied this complex of buildings on Orange Street from 1855 to 1890.* (Courtesy of C. Cowles & Co.; Neil Hogan, *A Certain Distinction: C. Cowles & Co., 1838–1988* [New Haven: C. Cowles & Co., 1988], 14)

In 1887 the physical establishment of C. Cowles Co. at 47–49 Orange Street was described as covering "three sides of a hollow oblong square, 200 by 90 feet in area. The buildings are of brick, five stories in height"[81] (see figure 10). At that time a 70-horsepower steam engine ran mechanical equipment that cost $45,000.[82] (This capital investment alone, it may be noted, outstripped the $41,000 capital investment that was reported fifty-five years earlier for the whole of the New Haven

FIGURE 11. *The Cowles & Co. building since 1890, at the corner of Chestnut and Water streets. In moods exuberant to solemn, workers pose in, on, and outside the building for this photograph.*
(Courtesy of C. Cowles & Co.; Neil Hogan, *A Certain Distinction: C. Cowles & Co., 1838–1988* [New Haven: C. Cowles & Co., 1988], cover)

carriage industry; see table 1.) Cowles had long used steam power. A visitor in 1858 had reported that

a large and powerful engine drives the machinery, and a well situated in the cellar furnishes water for the whole establishment. . . . Cool, retired and pleasant, this establishment stands buried in the luxuriant foliage of shading elms, and the busy hum of life pervades the whole.[83]

The surrounding neighborhood by 1886 consisted almost completely of retail stores, especially furniture and carpet stores, banks, restaurants, wholesale and retail drug stores, oil and paint stores, printing presses, and office buildings. Although a wholesale outlet for iron and steel was conveniently next door at 53 Orange Street, Cowles and its associated brass foundry had become an industrial island in a sea of commerce.[84] The "busy hum of life" now surrounding them was not their tune.

Cowles's catalogs expanded from 11 pages in 1855 to 69 pages in 1872, to 117 pages in 1874, and 144 pages in 1890.[85] Cowles had outgrown the Orange Street complex it had occupied for forty-five years, and relocated by the end of 1890 to its present site at the corner of Water and Chestnut streets, purchased from Halsted, Harmount & Co., lumber merchants[86] (see figure 11). This New Township location was a very different neighborhood from downtown in "the ninth square." In 1886 the block bounded south, east, north, and west by Water, Chestnut, Wooster, and Brown streets was entirely residential except for a large and mostly vacant lot fronting on Water Street (which Cowles was to occupy) containing a mattress factory no bigger than a large house and some stacks of lumber.[87] Almost all of the twenty-seven dwellings around the block were two-and-a-half stories high, freestanding on deep lots. One back lot on Chestnut Street contained a small two-story joinery shop for two men; on another stood a small one-story work shop. Otherwise that block was very suburban. To the east across Chestnut Street, however, was a block containing only nineteen dwellings, one saloon, and two substantial industrial complexes: the Henry Killam Co. carriage factory and the American Corset Co. factory. At its southern end on Water Street, a large estate surrounding a mansion set back from Water Street seemed vulnerable to industrial incursion: on the next block farther eastward, a factory was being built on Franklin Street for the New Haven Carriage

Co., as mentioned above, filling in that vacant lot and leaving the mansion's lot a conspicuously large open space.

By 1901 the Cowles Co. was operating in several large buildings covering most of the lot formerly occupied by the small mattress factory and the stacks of lumber. The westward remainder of that lot contained the D. C. Beardsley sash, door, and blind factory. The rest of the block was little changed since 1886 and still primarily residential when the building and workers in figure 11 were photographed. In the next block eastward, the corset factory had been replaced by John T. Doyle Co. (manufacturing "Drugs and Grocer Specialities"), but the Henry Killam Co. was still producing carriages. The saloon had become two narrow stores, but the dwelling houses were still dwelling houses, including the large mansion set back from Water Street in splendid isolation and still defying industrial incursion.[88]

"NEW LAMPS FOR OLD": C. COWLES & CO. OUTLIVES
THE CARRIAGE INDUSTRY

C. Cowles & Co. has remained on Water Street for more than a century. The firm adapted better than the rest of the New Haven carriage industry to the opportunities and exigencies of manufacturing for the automobile industry. Symbolically, battery-operated electric bulbs replaced the candles or oil in Cowles-produced carriage lamps. The 1900 catalog said "We take your old lamps or furnish you new ones of our own manufacture, put electric lights into them and furnish two sets of Batteries neatly put in a tin case. The Batteries will burn one hundred hours."[89] The company has continued adapting to changing conditions, including a very close proximity of its upper stories to an interstate highway exit ramp. Today C. Cowles Co. still makes parts for the automobile industry; its processes now, however, include plastic injection molding and plastic extrusion as well as metal stamping and machining and electric wiring. Its product range has also expanded beyond its historical roots in vehicle-parts production. Its five divisions produce controlled-beam lighting systems of many sizes bigger than an automobile,[90] electronic water-level controls for industrial and home-heating boilers, automobile components for sale to manufacturers and decorative and protective trim for sale to retailers of automotive accessories.[91] Its versatility continues.

By 1937, in the depth of the Great Depression preceding World War II, New Haven's carriage industry was only a memory. Its passing was mourned and mapped by Arnold G. Dana in his book *New Haven's Problems*. His map "Remains of Old Factory Center" (figure 12), emphasizes demolition and decay.[92] C. Cowles & Co.

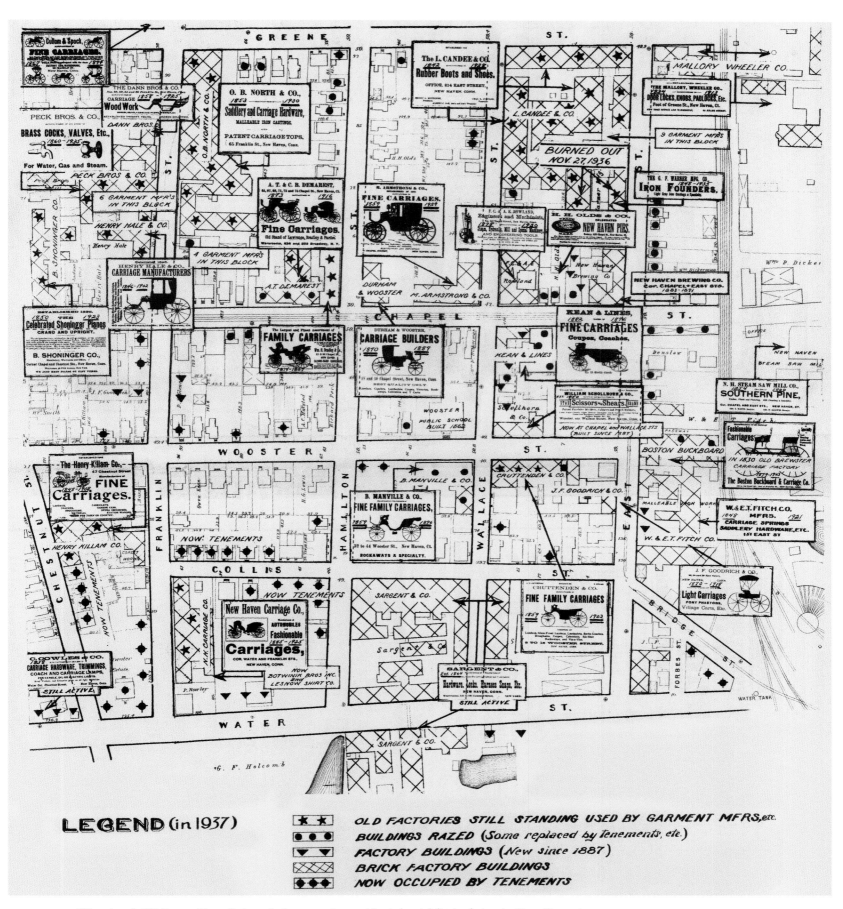

FIGURE 12. *"Remains of Old Factory Center," shows the former carriage-making industrial district during the Great Depression.*

(Courtesy of James and Richard English; Arnold B. Dana, *New Haven's Problems* [1937], map between pages 12 and 13)

and Sargent's were the only two survivors of the New Township industrial district that Dana identified on his 1937 map, and Cowles is the only survivor today. Because of the carriage industry's structure as a network of symbiotic specialist firms, however, the skills learned for building carriages were not lost, but available for application in other metalworking and woodworking industries once the economy began to recover. Those skills helped outproduce the Axis powers and win the war. They helped bring a prosperity that is now again unsure at the beginning of another century.

Understanding the system of specialized flexibility and interaction that caused the New Haven carriage industry to succeed so amazingly in the nineteenth century might help Americans regain prosperity on a sounder basis in the new global economy than would the standardized mass-production model that we have followed in producing automobiles and Barbie dolls.[93] Some buildings besides those of the C. Cowles Co. have also survived even the rigors of 1960s redevelopment in the "Old Factory District." Rehabilitating and reusing the structures from that older era will pose problems, but will help us learn its secrets. If we allow them to, the material and social heritages of our industrial past will enrich our future.

NOTES

1. James K. Dawes, "Carriages and Wagons," in *U.S. Census of Manufactures* (1900), 10:320.
2. Timothy Dwight, *A Statistical Account of the City of New-Haven* (New Haven: Connecticut Academy of Arts and Sciences, 1811), 31.
3. Elizabeth Mankin Kornhauser, *The Face of the Young Republic* (New Haven: Yale University Press, 1991), table 2.2, p. 72.
4. Edward E. Atwater, ed., *History of the City of New Haven* (New York: Munsell, 1887), 353–354.
5. Atwater, 557.
6. Dwight, 31.
7. Paul H. Downing and Harrison Kinney, "Builders for the Carriage Trade," *American Heritage* 7, no. 6 (October 1956), 91 and 95.
8. Whitney's cotton gin manufactory was located on a lot at the northeast corner of Wooster and Chestnut, now occupied by one of many pizza restaurants on Wooster Street in New Haven's "Little Italy." An undated but obviously very early map of the New Township recently found at the New Haven Colony Historical Society shows lot ownership, including Whitney's. When he decided in 1798 to manufacture firearms, Whitney went up the Mill River to its abandoned first grist mill site to obtain waterpower, and built his factory at Mill Rock.
9. Louis McLane, comp., *Documents Relative to the Manufactures in the United States Collected and Transmitted to the House of Representatives in Compliance with a Resolution of January 19, 1832 by the Secretary of the Treasury*. House Executive Document no. 308. 22d Cong., 1st sess. Washington, D.C. 1833. (The McLane Report), vol. 2, doc. 9, #31, p. 1033. (Reprint, New York: Burt Franklin, 1969.)

10. Dwight, 32; Tyler, 39; Bishop, 757. The local count for New Haven was fifty carriage manufacturing establishments, in *Benham's New Haven Directory* (1860–1861), 387.

11. Carriage firms changed names as partners came and went. The path by which Brewster & Lawrence in New York City in 1827 became Lawrence, Bradley & Pardee in New Haven, and subsequently William H. Bradley & Co., is traced in *Asher & Adams' Pictorial Album of American Industry* (New York: Asher & Adams, 1876), 142, and by Atwater, 557. Concerning G. & D. Cook & Co., Edwin T. Freedley, ed., *Leading Pursuits and Leading Men: A Treatise on the Principal Trades and Manufactures of the United States* (Philadelphia: Edward Young, 1856) says, : "The firm is composed of George Cook, David Cook, and Mr. James Brewster, who has been favorably known as a prominent manufacturer of carriages for forty years" (110). In another shift of partners in January 1863, Henry Hooker, Edwin Marble, James Brewster, and Leverett Candee bought out the Cooks' firm to form Hooker, Candee and Co., which upon the death of Candee two years later became Henry Hooker & Co. (Atwater, 564). Richard Hegel, *Carriages from New Haven* (Hamden, Conn.: Archon, 1974), fig. 11, p. 54 shows a large expansion of the plant by 1887.

12. *G. & D. Cook & Co.'s Illustrated Catalogue of Carriages and Special Business Advertiser* (New York: Baker & Godwin, 1860,) New Haven Colony Historical Society library, 8, 9, 11, 75, 101, and 147.

13. The carriage returned to New Haven in the 1930s. A plaque giving the names of its makers and their customer in Kentucky disappeared during its "restoration" in the 1980s. In design it closely matches a model shown in the Lawrence, Bradley & Pardee catalog of 1862, at the New Haven Colony Historical Society library.

14. *Benham's New Haven City Directory* (1860–61), 334. Dwelling houses in New Haven were assessed at $9,906,993 in 1859, ten times the value of manufactories ($972,780). Household furniture and libraries were assessed at $309,558.

15. "Notes of Travel" by the "Junior Editor," *New York Coach-Maker's Magazine* 1, no. 3 (August 1858), 45.

16. Hegel, 18, on 1859 output.

17. The population of New Haven increased more than two and a half times from 14,390 in 1840 to 39,267 in 1960, according to U.S. censuses those years, which counted men, women, and children residents and transients. Of these, *Benham's New Haven Directory* (1860–61), 25–319, listed approximately 11,200 individuals, mainly men, a few widows or otherwise independent women, and no children. These entries would tend to be heads of households. A thirty-page sample consisting of every tenth page contains names of 125 men in carriage-related occupations, conservatively defined. For instance, of the forty persons listed on page 35 from "Ball" through "Barker," two were "carriage makers"; one, a "carriage painter"; one, a "carriage manufacturer"; and one, a "coach trimmer." From the average of 4.17 such carriage-related names per sample page (excluding pages consisting of ads instead of names), I estimate about 1,180 such names or 10.5 percent of the total, are in the directory. A similar calculation for the names in *Patten's New Haven Directory* (1844–45) yields 5 percent carriage-related names, confirming a vigorous growth of the industry between 1844 and 1860.

18. Hegel, 18; Chauncey Jerome, *History of the American Clock Business For the Past Sixty Years and Life of Chauncey Jerome* (New Haven: F. C. Dayton Jr., 1860), 136.

19. *Eighth Census of the United States,* 1860, Manufactures, 44, table 1, "State of Connecticut Manufactures, by Counties, 1860"; 49, table 3, "State of Connecticut Manufactures," totals.

20. *Eighth Census,* tables 1 and 3.

21. Hegel, 79. These numbers differed somewhat from those of carriage and wagon manufacturers found in New Haven by census takers in 1880, 1890, and 1900: 26, 37, and 24, respectively,

reported by Hegel, 80. As Hegel also notes, the number of establishments is not a very satisfactory measure of an industry's size; the size and output of individual establishments can grow as their numbers decline.

22. Hegel, 79, 80.

23. Dawes, table, 295.

24. Dawes, 301.

25. *Carriage Monthly* (October 1877), 133, quoted in Neil Hogan, 24.

26. Hegel, 63, 67.

27. Quoted by Hegel, 68.

28. Hegel, 69. A Sanborn insurance map of 1886 shows "carriage factory being built" where the 1887 city directory lists and advertises the New Haven Carriage Co. at 5 to 19 Franklin St. on the corner of Collis. Sanborn Map Company, *Insurance Maps of New Haven* (New York: The Company, 1886), sheet 7; *New Haven City Directory* (Price, Lee, & Co., 1887), xxvi and 335. Its role as automobile body builder, etc., is advertised in the 1911 *New Haven City Directory*, ix.

29. *New York Coachmaker's Magazine* 1, no. 3 (August 1858), 45–46.

30. J. Leander Bishop, *A History of American Manufactures from 1608 to 1860* (Philadelphia: Young, 1866), 3:431–432.

31. Bishop, 430.

32. Barite (barium sulfate) was an ingredient in paint. The mill presumably ground it into powder.

33. Hegel, 38.

34. Levi Woodbury, *Letter from the Secretary of the Treasury, Transmitting in Obedience to a Resolution of the House of the 29th of June Last, Information in Relation to Steam-Engines, &c.*, House Document 21, 25th Cong., 3d sess. Washington, D.C., 1838, p. 65. Collis & Lawrence was the only carriage factory among the eleven "mills or manufactories" listed for New Haven as using a steam engine. The manufactory was located at 257 Chapel Street when listed in *Patten's New Haven Directory* for 1844–1845. The Woodbury report erroneously printed its name as "Collins & Lawrence."

35. Woodbury Report, 379, quoted in Carroll W. Pursell Jr., *Early Stationary Steam Engines in America* (Washington, D.C.: Smithsonian Institution Press, 1969), 74. This report found 1,616 stationary steam engines in the United States. Louisiana had 274 steam engines in this 1838 tally; Pennsylvania, 383; Massachusetts, 165; New York, 87; Ohio, 83; and all other states fewer than 60 each. Connecticut, with plenty of water power upstream from New Haven and other coastal towns, had only 47 steam engines at mills or manufactories, averaging seven horsepower each, of which 11 were listed for New Haven.

36. Atwater, 535.

37. In 1838, four of the eleven "mill or manufactory" steam engines listed in the Woodbury Report were for metalworking establishments: two foundries, one machine factory, and a lock factory (65–66).

38. The advertisement for "G.F. Kimball, Wheel Manufacturer," in G. & D. Cook & Co.'s *Illustrated Catalogue of Carriages and Special Business Advertiser*, 18, shows nine specialized machines, driven by belts from a steam engine, for separate operations in making a wheel. The Woodbury Report in 1838 listed four woodworking establishments—two sash and blind factories, one turning mill and one planing mill—in its list of steam engine–equipped mills and manufactories, but no wheel manufactory (65–66).

39. Kenneth L. Sokoloff, "Was the Transition from the Artisanal Shop to the Nonmechanized Factory Associated with Gains in Efficiency? Evidence from the U.S. Manufacturing Censuses of 1820 and 1850," *Explorations in Economic History* 21 (1984): 351–382.

40. Edwin T. Freedley, ed., *Leading Pursuits and Leading Men: A Treatise on the Principal Trades and Manufactures of the United States* (Philadelphia: Edward Young, 1856), 111.

41. Ibid.

42. The office of the New Haven Spring Co. at 147 State Street in 1860 was close to G. & D. Cook & Co., but its factory was elsewhere, on Howard. By 1880 G. & D. Cook had been out of existence since 1863, and the New Haven Spring Co. had moved east to 70 Franklin Ave. By 1887 it too seems to have expired, for it is not listed among other carriage-spring manufactories that year, and does not appear on the 1886 insurance map for that block of Franklin Street. New Haven directories, 1860–61, 1880, and 1887, Sanborn Maps 1886, sheet 8.

43. Jerome, 136.

44. *G. & D. Cook & Co.'s Illustrated Catalogue*, 226.

45. *Asher & Adams'*, 142. James Brewster's partners Solomon Collis and John R. Lawrence were, as Collis & Lawrence from 1837, operating at this site (then 257 Chapel Street) as early as the mid-1840s, according to *Patten's New Haven Directory* for 1844–45. The firm became Bradley & Lawrence in 1850 and Bradley, Lawrence & Pardee in 1857, in which year the factory doubled in size to that described in *Asher & Adams'* in 1876. Pardee retired in 1872, leaving William H. Bradley to head William H. Bradley & Co. at the same location.

46. Sanborn Maps, 1886, sheet 8; *New Haven Directory* (1887), 69. The insurance maps not only show the shape, size, height, and material of which buildings were made, but also the source of illumination and heat, the number of "hands" employed, and the type of power—water, steam, or "hand."

47. Sanborn Map Company, *Insurance Maps of New Haven* (New York: The Company, 1901), sheet 16.

48. Sanborn Maps, 1886, sheets 7, 8, and 9.

49. Hamilton S. Wicks, "The Manufacture of Pleasure Carriages," *Scientific American*, n.s., 40, no. 6 (8 February 1879), 79–80.

50. Wicks, 80.

51. Edward Duggan, "Work and the Mechanization of Carriage-Making," *Carriage Journal* (Autumn 1985): 71–73. The carriage-making study described in this article was part of a much larger study of manufacturing mechanization conducted by Carroll D. Wright, U.S. commissioner of labor, and published in the *Thirteenth Annual Report of the Commissioner of Labor*, 1898.

52. Duggan, 72–73. The steeper increase in workers per buggy than operations per buggy probably reflects additional attention to "flow" production, in which slower operations that cannot be subdivided into shorter operations are performed by more workers simultaneously in order to "catch up" with the shorter operations. This subdivision and duplication of operations is of course possible only in a sizeable factory. See, for instance, Carolyn C. Cooper, "The Production Line at Portsmouth Block Mill," *Industrial Archaeology Review* 6, no. 1 (Winter 1981–82): 28–44.

53. *Benham's New Haven Directory* (1860–61), 387, 388, 389, 382, and 406; Price and Lee, *New Haven City Directory* (1880), 301 and 302; Price and Lee, *New Haven City Directory* (1887), 492, 493, and 499; wheel manufacturers and whip socket manufacturers in 1887 are listed on 559, axle manufacturers on 482. These numbers agree poorly, however with the census records. Hegel (80) says the 1880 census showed 26 carriage and wagon manufacturers in New Haven, and 17 manufacturers of carriage and wagon materials; the somewhat comparable figures for the 1890 census were 37 coach and wagon manufacturers (including custom and repair work), and 21 manufacturers of coach and wagon materials; in 1900, some 24 coach and wagon manufacturers, 6 coach and wagon materials manufacturers. The discrepancy perhaps reflects a difference in definition of "materials."

54. Dawes, 320.

55. *Asher & Adams'*, 130. Its illustration and the 1879 New Haven birds-eye map show a massive structure with wings along York and Grove streets. Zelotes Day was listed in the 1844–45 city directory as grocer on Broadway, whose house was at 126 York Street. Atwater (557) says Zelote

Day's carriage factory "burned about thirty-five years ago," that is, about 1852. Nevertheless, the 1860–61 directory listed him as carriage manufacturer, still residing at 126 York Street, where carriage manufacturer Augustus P. Day and bank clerk Wilbur F. Day, presumably relatives, boarded. The New Haven Wheel Company's address in 1860–61 was at 148 and 150 York, and (after street renumbering) at 334–360 York in the 1887 directory. Zelotes and Augustus Day were no longer listed, but Wilbur F. Day, now president of the National New Haven Bank, (still) lived at 310 York Street.

56. A short list of fifteen carriage manufacturers persisting (including through different partnerships) from 1860 to 1880, compiled from the city directories of those years, shows Charles Blackman's manufactory at 27 and 188 Park street in those respective years, and John Osborn's at 13 and 132 Park. (This pattern of addresses suggests Park Street was renumbered between those years, while the firms stayed at the same locations.) Henry Hooker, however, who was a carriage dealer at 33 Park in 1860, was a carriage manufacturer at State and Grove in 1880, as successor to the G. & D. Cook Co.

57. *Benham's New Haven Directory* (1860–61), 387–388, 406, for listings of carriage manufacturers, carriage repairers, and manufacturers of carriage irons, carriage bodies, carriage woodwork, carriage seats, carriage and saddlery hardware, carriage shafts and poles, coach lace, coach lamps, coach trimmings, and wheels. Firms listed under more than one heading were counted only once.

58. Price, Lee & Co., *New Haven Directory* (1880), 294ff. contain listings for carriage manufacturers, and manufacturers of carriage hardware, carriage back lights, carriage makers supplies, carriage poles, carriage springs, carriage steps, carriage woodwork, carriage and coach trimmings, coach lace, and coach lamps. Firms listed under more than one heading were counted only once. Wheel manufacturers were not included, so the numbers are not strictly comparable with those of 1860.

59. Rowland's occupation of the otherwise vacant foundry at the corner of Wallace and Chapel Streets, which was owned by the Yale Iron Works, was apparently temporary during expansion of Rowland's works across Hamilton Street at 413–417 Chapel Street. I thank Sylvia Garfield for this information from her research in New Haven land records.

60. Sanborn insurance maps for New Haven, 1886 and 1901, sheets 8 and 16, respectively.

61. This adaptive reuse enterprise, named "Charrette," unfortunately lies in the path of the scheduled expansion of the I-95 bridge across the Quinnipiac River.

62. *Benham's New Haven Directory* (1860–61), 383–384; Price, Lee & Co., *New Haven City Directory* (1887), 486.

63. All ten lumber dealers listed on p. 397 in the business directory section of *Benham's New Haven Directory* (1860) were located east of State Street, eight on the harbor front along East Water Street, at the feet of Olive and Warren Streets or at Custom House Square or Heaton's Wharf. Two were inland on Grand Ave, nos. 163 and 170. The business directory in the 1887 Price & Lee *New Haven Directory* lists on p. 525 fifteen lumber yards, nine of them on Water Street between Chestnut and Union streets, and only two west of State Street (both on Church Street, near Chapel and Crown.) Of the five sawing, turning, and planing mills listed on p. 403 in the 1860 Business Directory, four were in New Township, including the New Haven Steam Saw Mill at the foot (eastern end) of Chapel Street; one was on Park Street. In the 1887 business directory, p. 547, only one of the eight sawing, turning, or planing mills listed was located west of State Street (Hotchkiss sawmill in Westville).

64. The Dann Brothers, formerly located on State Street at the corner of Wall, moved to 80–82 Franklin Street by 1880 and were offering both carriage woodwork and wheels in 1887; Henry Stow, who was associated with Zelotes Day in the 1840s and became part of the New Haven

Wheel Co., on York Street, was producing wheels at the New Haven Steam Saw Mill in the 1860s and eventually set up on his own on Wooster Street before 1887. *Asher & Adams'*, 130; Atwater, 568; *New Haven Directory* (1860–61, 1880, and 1887 eds.) entries for "Carriage Wood-work" and "Wheel Mfrs."

65. The 1860–61 city directory (388) shows seven manufacturers of carriage and saddlery hard-ware, only one of which was in the New Township (Plants Manuf. Co., 56 Grand). In the 1887 directory (493), five of the eight carriage hardware manufacturers were in the New Township.

66. *The Hub*, 17, no. 6 (1 September 1875), 182.

67. During the Cowles Co. occupation of the site, it was designated first as 29 Orange Street, later as 47–49, still later as 67–69 Orange Street. Orange Street was among others repeatedly renum-bered as New Haven grew and filled in spaces with buildings.

68. *Carriage Monthly* (October 1880), 136–137, cited in Neil Hogan, *A Certain Distinction: C. Cowles & Co., 1838–1988* (New Haven: S. Z. Field Printing Co., n.d. [c. 1989]), 24.

69. New Haven Chamber of Commerce, *Commerce, Manufactures and Resources of the City of New Haven and Environs* (New Haven: O. A. Dorman, 1882), 54–55, cited in Hogan, 24.

70. Atwater, 570.

71. Hogan, 11, 79; Atwater, 570. The enterprise was first known by the names of its founders, Cornwell and Cowles. Between 1844 and 1850 Cornwell and Cowles had a third partner, Lewis B. Judson, which changed the name to Judson, Cornwell and Cowles during that period. Chan-dler left the partnership in 1853; in 1855 Chandler Cowles, his half-brother Ruel P. Cowles, and John N. Babcock formed a corporation named C. Cowles & Co. Hogan, 11–13.

72. Hogan, 18. The 1855 catalog is among four preserved at the Beinecke Rare Book and Manu-script Library, Yale University.

73. Hogan, 18.

74. *New York Coach-Makers Magazine* 1 (1858), advertisement following 40 and 80.

75. Advertisement in G. & D. Cook & Co.'s catalog for 1860, 96.

76. *Carriage Monthly* (July 1876), 71; quoted by Hogan, 23.

77. Advertisement in *New Haven Palladium* (4 July 1857); quoted by Hogan, 18.

78. *New York Coach-Maker's Magazine* 1, no. 3 (August 1858), 45–46. To demonstrate for the visitor the malleability of Cowles's hot-swedged carriage nuts, the proprietor had "one of the human machines" set a cold one on its edge and hammer it "into an elongated slug."

79. *New York Coach-Maker's Magazine*, 46.

80. Quoted by Hogan, 25

81. Atwater, 570.

82. Atwater, 570. In 1880–81, Cowles had supplied steam power at night to dynamos generating electicity for arc lights in downtown New Haven commercial establishments; Hogan, 28.

83. *New York Coach-Maker's Magazine*, 46.

84. Sanborn Maps, 1886, sheet 3.

85. Of these four catalogs, the last three are illustrated with pictures of the products. Yale Univer-sity, Beinecke Rare Book and Manuscript Library.

86. New Haven land records 420:52. My thanks to Sylvia Garfield for identifying the seller, Halsted, Harmount & Co., lumber dealers.

87. Sanborn Maps 1886, sheet 7. William B. Trewhella's mattress factory was at 81 Water Street. *New Haven Directory* (1887), 527.

88. Sanborn Maps, 1901, sheet 10. Arnold G. Dana, *New Haven's Problems: Whither the City? All Cit-ies?* (New Haven: Tuttle, Morehouse & Taylor, July 1937), identifies this Water Street mansion as "the Atwater Estate," in a map "Remains of Old Factory Center," between pages 12 and 13.

89. Quoted by Hogan, 45.

90. In 1985 Cowles bought the ABS Lighting Company of Bloomfield, Connecticut, producers of "specialty lighting for airfields, ball fields, tennis courts, parking lots and highways"; Hogan, 70.
91. Website, www.ccowles.com.
92. Dana, map, between 12 and 13.
93. For a view of American industrialization that emphasizes the importance of production methods other than "mass production," see Philip Scranton, *Endless Novelty: Specialty Production and American Industrialization, 1865–1925* (Princeton: Princeton University Press, 1997).

DOUGLAS W. RAE

Technology, Population Growth, and Centered Industrialism: New Haven, 1850–2000

An old and familiar customer ambles in to purchase two small rolls of tape, yet leaves with two larger rolls and a dispenser bought for six dollars: "Seven dollars worth, I give it to you for six." Joseph Perfetto is still a businessman after seventy-four years on the job. Yet his "New England Typewriter & Stationery," at 120 Crown Street in downtown New Haven is under water. As we talk, rain drips into a large coffee can on the table between us, the tail end of a storm from the night before. It has made its way layer by layer through the remnants of four stories above the shop. Perfetto has covered much of his stock with plastic sheeting to keep it dry. During the worst of yesterday's storm, whole buckets filled with rainwater in an hour's time. Much as he hates the idea of retirement, Joe Perfetto is looking for someone to buy his stock and his printing equipment. Entertaining a visitor who shows no interest in office supplies, he tells a story:

My father came from Italy. Benevento. Little town called Cuzon. The whole town my father came from, *everybody's* Perfetto. My brother went there looking for Perfettos: Which one? The mayor, the priest, the whole town! Here in the city, my father worked for Cowles & Company. He was their top locksmith. He spent over fifty years there. All the locks, all the repairs. In fact, I think he invented most of their locks. He worked for the company, never got anything for it, just steady work for fifty years. I lived with him and my family on Vernon Street, that's a block above the hospital. Lived there till I got married.

I started in 1924, working for somebody else—talked me out of going to high school, paid for one year of business college for me. Probably would have gone to Commercial [High]. We had all three—Commercial and Boardman Trade and Hillhouse—all over by Broadway and Whalley Avenue then. So in 1924 I started

This essay is substantially excerpted or otherwise derived from my previously published book *City: Urbanism and its End* (New Haven: Yale University Press, 2003).

out working for Barnes Typewriter at the age of fourteen. Barnes would take off for Florida, leave the place in the charge of his daughter, and she was never there, always out with George Weiss or some guy. So I ran the place more or less. Took my first typewriter apart the first day there and put it together. Mechanically inclined, I suppose. Worked for him five, six years until the Depression started in. One morning I was home, supposedly on vacation, which most of the time I never got—got paid for it but worked anyway. I got a letter saying that he was gonna reduce my pay from $27 a week to $20 a week, on account of the Depression. Everybody was cutting, the telephone company, Winchester. They weren't paying anything, $13 a week. So I asked how come he had to cut mine. He said "We're not making any money, everybody's doing it, we have to do it." I said, "Mr. Barnes, I'm making about $400 a month for you, all your work, all your guarantee work, any deliveries not included, just what I tell you to charge customers for my work. Think about all that work for the Register. You're only givin' me $100 a month, taking in $400, think about it." [Barnes responds] "You don't know what you're talking about." "Yes I do, every time I give you a slip, I keep a duplicate." [Barnes retorts] "You're not supposed to do that. Anyway I treat you like a son, I'm like a father to you." I says I'll go to work for Blakeslee with a pick and shovel but I still gotta have that $27. He wouldn't do it so I said I'm gonna have to quit. I emptied out my tool bag, all the spare parts, and put 'em in the drawer, left 'em there. I said, "How about a letter of recommendation?" He said, "You won't need it, you'll be back next week." I said, no, I'd like to have a letter. He wrote one about how I was honest and trustworthy, nothing about how good I worked. Not that I was the errand boy, the shoeshine boy or what: I was just honest and trustworthy.

So I went out, that was on a Saturday. I went down to a friend of mine used to help out at Dorer's Music Shop; he was quite famous there. I told him, and he said, "What are you worried about?" He took me over to Commerce Street, to a printshop there, and we had some name cards made up. Monday morning I went out, passed out some of those cards, telling people I was working for myself now, and if they could use me I'd appreciate it. Would you believe I made $113 the first week working for myself! I didn't have anything but a tool bag, not a ribbon to sell, not anything. So I made the $113 that first week, and I've been at it ever since. I've had my ups and downs. At one time I had six or seven people working here. Last two or three years I'm losing money, but I just hate to give it up. I live in Hamden, been there almost 50 years. . . . Right at the beginning of Hamden, Davis Street. Last house on the block in those days. Out the front door, you got the [East Rock] park; out the back door, you go hunting. That was 1950, June or

July. I could work on the house, take time off, I had five, six people in here, order taker, bookkeeper, printer, errand-boy. Originally, I had everybody [for customers]. City hall, hospital, Seamless Rubber, Register. I was *the* typewriter man.

Joe Perfetto (figure 1) has lived nearly nine decades of New Haven's history, and has absorbed perhaps another three decades of family lore, making him a messenger from the era of centered industrialism to those of us living in its wake. More important, his story poses the critical question: Why did these people make the choices they made? Why did they crowd into New Haven when they did? Why did they disperse to the suburbs when they did? The Perfettos of course chose jobs, terms of employment (or freelance entrepreneurship) and home addresses for themselves, year by year. But they did not chose in a vacuum: to understand what they did requires understanding the powerful forces operating on New Haven, its region, and the world at large. The result of these forces is a sort of geography of opportunity. They used that geography as they understood it, and the result brought them to New Haven, and gave them structured choices once they arrived—choices that shifted with the passage of time. As it happens, the Perfettos' decisions form something of an archetype for our population history: a long journey of migration, a founding generation of shop-floor industrial work, a shorter flight to the suburbs, usually with an accompanying leap beyond factory walls. The occupational shifts and the spatial ones are of course linked: (1) the immigration journey toward a central-city factory job is a move *up-and-in* from a preindustrial homeland, and (2) the suburbanizing journey away from a central-city factory job is a move *up-and-out*. Joe's parents made the first; he and his wife made the second. Likewise, the overall story of New Haven's population follows this two-phase movement: (1) a dramatic run of *centering development* with increasing core city densities and increasing capital investments in city housing, commerce, and manufacturing, and (2) a second period of *decentering development* leading to a dispersion of population around the central city and a relative dispersal of capital investment toward those same perimeter locations. This essay is organized around those two phases of our history, treating the material forces that distinguish them and the human forces they call into play.

Centering Development, 1850–1920

In 1850, the American economic system was still overwhelmingly based on very small firms. Owners controlled their firms directly, acting as their own managers. Having a business usually meant sole proprietorship with little or no capital invested by others. Where shared investment did occur, the equity was held by a partnership; each owner was a joint manager of the firm. Manufacturing was done in small shops, each with very little capital and relatively few employees by modern standards. Each firm carried out only a fraction of the full production cycle from raw materials to sold goods, so that a product was passed along a string of firms—as raw material, as intermediate products, as finished goods on the plant dock, as wholesale goods in a warehouse, finally as retail product on display in a store. Market contract upon market contract organized the progression.[1] This was an era of precorporate capitalism, and New Haven was a representative case with hundreds of small industrial firms, each supporting only a few workers, each supervised directly by an owner right on the shop floor each morning.

Let's use the year 1845 (three years before New Haven got its first railroad service to New York), as we have unusually fine data on the city's economy in that year.[2] Table 1 lists some representative examples of "industries" in the New Haven economy. These are mostly small firms, with modest capital (the average is $8,154) and smallish workforces (most are under ten workers, and the mean is just fourteen).[3] There are, to be sure, a few larger firms in the mix. Chauncey Jerome's clock factory—with ninety workers—was producing the lowest-priced clocks in the world at this time, due in part to his having discovered a way to stamp rather than to cast the gears.[4]

As is characteristic of nineteenth-century capitalism, radical change was immi-

TABLE 1

Industry by product	Firms	Total capital	Total employment	Mean employment
Cotton Gins	1	?	1	1.0
Musical Instruments	2	$2,000.00	3	1.5
Brass Foundries	2	$1,000.00	4	2.0
Steam Engines & Boilers	2	$2,000.00	6	3.0
Soap & Candles	4	$12,200.00	16	4.0
Cordage	2	$4,700.00	8	4.0
Tin & Sheet Iron	8	$24,400.00	35	4.4
Tanneries	6	$29,600.00	27	4.5
Hats & Caps	3	$3,500.00	15	5.0
Files	2	$3,500.00	10	5.0
Chairs & Cabinets	9	$26,050.00	71	7.9
Worsted Fabric	4	$8,000.00	37	9.3
Sashes & Blinds	3	$14,800.00	32	10.7
Castings (metal)	4	$64,900.00	71	17.8
Carriage Springs, etc	4	$38,500.00	74	18.5
Coaches, Wagons, & Sleighs	24	$287,600.00	460	19.2
Paper	1	$50,000.00	30	30.0
Latches, Locks, & Handles	3	$74,500.00	115	38.3
Clocks	1	$40,000.00	90	90.0
Indian Rubber Suspenders	1	$14,000.00	100	100.0
Total of Sample	86	$701,250.00	1205	14.0

TABLE 2

Town	Anthracite tonnage	Anthracite cost or value
Branford	60	$360.00
Derby	2,636	$13,640.00
Meriden	920	$5,980.00
Middlebury	30	$240.00
Naugatuck	314	$2,349.00
New Haven	3,552	$17,310.00
North Haven	100	$670.00
Oxford	36	$216.00
Wallingford	67	$469.00
Waterbury	834	$7,146.00

nent: change acting upon change, constant shifting of competitive relations. Economist Joseph Schumpeter conceived capitalism itself as a method of change to which he gave the enduring title *creative destruction* and he was surely right about New Haven in the decades following 1850. Even the 1848 *Communist Manifesto*'s more febrile expression— "all that's solid melts into air"—was not altogether overstated in New Haven's case. Larger and larger firms, seeking markets in more and more distant places, absorbing greater and greater capital investments, requiring larger and larger workforces were being formed, partly due to massive changes in technology. Connecticut's 1837 Corporations Act, anticipating a world to come, would also have something to do with the revolution brewing in this period. These were the changes that would set in motion a seventy-year storm of centering development in New Haven and a host of similar cities in the United States and Europe.

A first hint of things to come is hidden in the 1845 economic data for New Haven and other towns in the surrounding county. Table 2 records the burning of anthracite coal for New Haven and nine other nearby places, with tonnage and its value or cost for each. Notice, of course, that there is considerable variation in the total tonnage burned: New Haven and Derby leap off the page. But the interesting datum concerns *price* per ton (estimated as value/tonnage). Waterbury anthracite is the costliest, at $8.57 per ton. Middlebury, Naugatuck, Wallingford, North Haven, Oxford, and Meriden also confront higher than average prices. They are too far away from cheap fixed-path transportation as was provided already by coastal shipping, and would soon be provided by the coming of rail (see figure 2). New Haven's cost was $4.88 per ton, and Derby's was only a little higher at $5.17. This fragment of information foretells a growing force in the economic and social history of New Haven over the next seventy years: a premium would be attached to central-city locations for manufacturing; with it an implicit penalty would be

FIGURE 2. *Cedar Hill freight yard, New Haven, early twentieth century.* (New Haven Colony Historical Society)

imposed on peripheral locations. Half a century later, in 1892, a promotional writer would assert that

> among the conditions which have for many years aided in promoting the growth of the city is the cheapness of fuel for domestic use and the supply of our manufacturing industries. No towns in New England have been able to obtain their fuel at rates as low as have been afforded our consumers. . . . The right place to manufacture successfully is evidently at a point where raw materials accumulate naturally, is contiguous to and easy of access from the original sources of supply, and where, at the same time, there is cheap power, cheap fuel, and advanced and ample facilities for marketing the products. New Haven has always furnished these conditions in preeminent degree. Situated at a focal point of six lines of railroads, connecting the city with the markets of the East and West, the lumber regions of the North, and the coal fields of the South, and bordered by the water of the Sound, with a harbor and channel that accommodate ships of the largest size, material necessarily accumulates here, and cheap power is amply provided and assured for all time.[5]

While the forecast of cheap power "for all time" turns out to have been badly mistaken, the basic story told here is correct and powerfully so. Capital would flow into the core city, and build itself into Strouse-Adler, Cowles, Sargent, Fitch, Candee Rubber, Cowles, Bigelow, National Pipe Bending, Winchester, and all the others. Housing would follow, being built close by these sites so as to attract workers dependent on shoe leather commuting to the plant gate. Retailing would be organized around the housing, with the material stuff of life provided on more than a thousand street corners across a growing industrial city. Church, school, and all the rest of civil society's built imprint would follow exactly the same logic of centering development.

This complex of centering technologies has three essential features. First, it depends on the development of *low-cost, high-reliability fixed-path transport*. This transport is designed to carry high volumes of materials, goods, or people to a relatively small number of predetermined destinations. Low cost is achieved by high volume and rigid targeting; one did not move one thousand tons of coal, or a trainload of immigrants, nimbly and flexibly from door to door, village to village. The terminal points of fixed-path transportation were, or soon became, central place locations. Heavy shipping was well developed in New Haven by 1800; rail would come full-blown in 1848 with the first operations of the New York & New Haven (later New York, New Haven & Hartford).

Second, the complex depends on *an energy technology attaching a penalty to consumption at long distances from the point of generation*. The burning of coal to make steam is a classic case. Coal in great quantity is economically delivered only close to rail and shipping heads, hence New Haven's price advantage. Unlike alternating current electricity (which travels well across long distances), steam is a localizing energy technology: its distribution (by mechanical belts and pulleys) is economical only over very short distances[6]. The mechanical force must therefore be consumed close to the point of its generation as steam. And it must be generated close to fixed-path transport if it is to be competitive with other locations. Use of steam creates a high premium for central-place industrial development. The siting of Sargent & Company at New Haven's confluence of rail and shipping is exactly what this technology rewards—and in the long run requires—of manufacturers (figure 3).

A third and last feature is the *absence of high quality variable-path transportation*. In 1850, horses and shoe leather were dominant methods of going to destinations not scheduled by rail and ship—to the store, church, home, school, and work. These were very nimble yet very slow methods of getting around, practical only over short distances, thus limiting to the development of peripheral locations for house, school, church, and the like.

Where these features came together, as they did in midcentury New Haven,

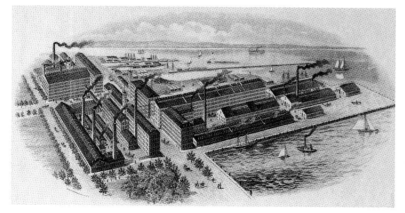

FIGURE 3. *Sargent and Company plant.* (Sargent Manufacturing Company)

one should expect a powerful compression of capital investments, people, and activity around the heavy transport core of a central city. Where that city combines shipping and rail in a small area, one should expect to see the flowering of intensive manufacturing and all that goes with it. As Robert Gordon suggests elsewhere in this book, steam had begun to emerge in New Haven by the late 1830s, and the stage was set.

For many centuries leading up to 1850, waterwheels and animal muscle had been dominant energy technologies worldwide. These were both decentering forces. Animals—horses, oxen—were most efficiently stationed across the land in proximity to forage. Water power was to be found where rivers fell rapidly, not at their languid meetings with the sea, as in the case of New Haven's Quinnipiac and Mill rivers. An idea of falling water technology's impact on New Haven can be gathered from cotton-milling data from the 1845 census of manufacturing. New Haven County had five mills combining to produce 500,000 yards of cotton cloth (not a yard of it in New Haven itself). Windham County—inland, sparsely populated, and upstream from the coastal plain—had fifty-nine mills producing 17,500,471 yards of cotton cloth.[7] The small Windham County town of Canterbury burned no fossil fuel in 1845, yet produced 798,944 yards of cotton cloth by the ingenious exploitation of fast-running water.[8] Nature's gift in these upland towns was the steep gradient of river beds, offering to transfer mechanical energy at great rates for the asking. The very force advantaging upstream locations in the era of water power would decisively disadvantage them in the era of steam, fast rivers being poor arteries of fixed-path transport. Such was already apparent in 1845, when upstream Winchester (the town, not the company) was compelled to pay $9.00 a ton for anthracite (New Haven, $4.88). Once steam power began to dominate manufacturing, as it did in the decades after 1850, the comparative advantage of upriver mill towns would decline steadily, vanishing almost altogether in the early twentieth century.

Similarly, the relative importance of animal muscle would decline steadily over the last half of the nineteenth century. The absolute total of animal horsepower in the U.S. national economy grew in every decade between 1850 and 1920, starting at an estimated 5,960,000 horsepower in 1850 and ending up at 22,430,000 horsepower by 1920.[9] In Connecticut, no comparable data are available, but it is quite probable that the total began falling after about 1900 as the competitive force of western agriculture made itself felt. But nationally its *relative* importance declined in every decade of the same period. Animals accounted for roughly 70 percent of the national horsepower pool in 1850, rivaled distantly by steam and water. By 1880 their share was down to 45 percent, to 29 percent in 1900, and to less than 5

TABLE 3

Year	Total horsepower × 1,000
1920	453,450
1910	138,810
1900	63,952
1890	44,086
1880	26,314
1870	16,931
1860	13,763
1850	8,495

TABLE 4

Year	New Haven population
1850	20,345
1860	39,367
1870	50,840
1880	62,882
1890	86,045
1900	108,027
1910	133,605
1920	162,567

percent by 1920 (scarcely 0.01 percent today). The really important trend is in the *total* horsepower of the U.S. economy. Between 1850 and 1920, total horsepower expanded more than fiftyfold. By the 1920s horsepower equivalent to the national total in 1850 was being added to the economy every 90 days (see table 3). And a very high fraction of the total added between 1850 and 1920 was devoted to centering technologies: rail, heavy shipping, and steam-powered factories producing goods for export beyond the city and even beyond its region.

As these changes in fundamental technology unfolded, the scale of manufacturing production in core locations like New Haven grew by an order of magnitude. While Chauncey Jerome's clock works in 1845 employed 90 people, its successor firm would employ 2,000 by the 1920s, and would be shipping 3.5 million timepieces per year. New Haven Clock had assumed corporate form, with professional management, and had penetrated world markets through the brute force of mass production in capital-intensive factories run on cheap fuel. National Pipe Bending, a smaller firm, would list customers in places as distant as Kansas, Alabama, Idaho, Arkansas, Florida, Mexico, Sweden, Peru, and Bolivia for its "Feed Water Heaters." Candee Rubber would employ 1,500 people making boots for nationwide markets by 1890. American Steel and Wire would start modestly in 1908 with 29 workers, but expand to more than 900 by 1945, by which time it would be a subsidiary of U.S. Steel Corporation. Winchester Arms, arriving in 1858, would eventually become New Haven's largest industrial enterprise, employing about 20,000 workers by the era of World War I.

The city's population was driven hard by these explosions of economic energy (table 4). As the concentration of manufacturing grew more intense, capital migrated toward the city in search of profit made possible by centering technology's growing dominance. The New Haven "grand list" (a rough summary measure of taxable property inside city limits) would expand from scarcely $10 million in 1850 to nearly $47 million in 1880, and more than $242 million in 1920.[10] A large fraction of this would surely have been in manufacturing plant and equipment, and in the housing stock required by its workforce. The year 1880 denotes the beginning of a forty-year run in which most of New Haven's total growth since 1637 is concentrated. In that one longish generation (1880–1920), New Haven added 100,000 (net of deaths and departures) to its population—roughly 60 percent of its total growth over three and a half centuries. The city we see today (most of all, its housing stock) is to an inordinate degree the product of this brief period. Put another way, 60 percent of New Haven's total growth occurred in just over 10 percent of its history as a city.

These newcomers were drawn primarily from Europe, beginning with the Irish

TABLE 5

Year	Total foreign-born	Irish	Italian	Russian
1880	15,668	9,360	102	0
1890	22,994	10,574	1,876	1,160
1900	30,804	10,491	5,262	3,193
1910	42,848	9,004	13,159	7,980
1920	45,834	7,219	15,084	8,080

just after 1850 (table 5). The biggest movements are concentrated in the forty-year window between 1880 and 1920, and are most dramatic among Italians and "Russians" (for the most part Jews escaping persecution from all across Russia and Eastern Europe). What had been a fairly homogeneous and provincial New Haven population would become heterogeneous and cosmopolitan. Neighborhoods would take shape around jobs, but also around churches and temples. In the case of Roman Catholicism, the early-arriving Irish had come to dominate the priesthood, and it would eventually seem wise to develop "nationality parishes" for the Italians and other groups. For example, Saint Michael's—originally a Protestant church—off Wooster Square would become an early hub for Italian immigrants. A feel for neighborhood texture can be approximated by looking at the residents of Fair Street, between Prindle and Union, in the year 1913. This is a working-class street (as can be seen from the occupations listed), close upon the harborside manufacturing district, with an overwhelming number of first-generation Italian families.

RESIDENT/HEAD OF HOUSEHOLD	ADDRESS ON FAIR ST.	OCCUPATION
Raffaele Freccia	1	proprietor, Furturro Freccia & Co., 634 Chapel St.
Dominico Prete	6	mason
Guiseppe Carrano	7	laborer
Mrs. Jenny Nanton	7	widow of James H. Nanton
Gaetano Dattolo	8	fruit vender
Michele Dattolo	8	—
Tommaso Cretella	8	laborer
Sabato Del Franco	9	—
Antonio Carrano	12	Sargent & Co.
Andrea Costantinopoli	12	—
Aontoni Cretella	12	laborer
Bonaventure Savino	12	laborer
Luigi Laudano	12	Sargent & Co.
Giovanni Sica	13	laborer
Mrs. Giovanni Colavolpe	13	—
Antonio Cicalese	15	laborer
Cosimo Gargano	15	laborer
F. Roveta	15	lives at 37 Fair St.
Giacomo Perretti	15	laborer
Pasquale Testa	15	Sargent & Co.
Aneillo Amatruda	16	barber at 224 Wooster
Antonio Proto	16	laborer
Filippo Corso	16	laborer
Francesco Scappace	16	laborer
Giovanni Durso	16	laborer
Maria D'Amico	16	widow of Alfonso, boards
Raffaele D'Amico	16	laborer

G. Rosalio Variety Store	16.5	lives at 12 Warren St.
G. Ferrailo Horse Dealer	20	horse dealer
Guiseppe Scappace	20	laborer
Vincenzo Scappace	20	laborer
Pasquale Surrentino	22	laborer
Fair Street School	25	
Antonio Consiglio	26	Sargent & Co.
Antonio Dattolo Fruit Dealer	26	fruit dealer, at home address
Cosmo Williams	26	fruit dealer, 32 Fair St.
Ernesto Barbato	26	salesman, W. H. Galvin, produce, 253 Water
Gioacchino Cretella	26	laborer
Guiseppe Cavallaro	26	peddler
J. Cavallaro	26	wholesale fruit dealer
Pasquale Volpe	26	barber
Vincenzo Paulillo	26	laborer
Gennearo Consiglio	29	Candee & Co.
Massimo Del Pizzo	29	laborer
Joe Williams Fruit Dealer	30	fruit dealer, at home address
Angelo Langella	31	peddler
Guiseppe Nisto	31	shoemaker, 77.5 Lamberton, Guiseppe Nisto, Shoemaker
Cosmo Williams Fruit	32	lives at 26 Fair St.
Pasquale Mangini	32	Sargent & Co.
Vincenzo Lettieri	32	laborer
Tripoli Athletic Club	34	
Luigi Amatruda	35	laborer
Michele Amatruda	35	shoemaker
William Olson	35	—
Iragi Rosario	36	—
Pasquali Corso Fruit Dealer	36	fruit dealer
Vincenzo Pauso	36	laborer
Domenico Raiano	37	Sargent & Co.
Ferdinando Roveta	37	confectioner at 15 Fair St.
Filippo Mangier	37	painter
Francesco Pacilio	37	driver
Geraldo Cappiello	37	laborer
Mrs. Raffaela Perrelli	37	—
Tomasso Corso Fruit Dealer	37	
Gargano Firovante Grocer	39	grocer, at home address
Francesco Di Mello	40	laborer
Rosario Setaro	40 (grocery)	grocer, at home address
Filippe Gambuto	42	laborer
Philip Sansone	42 (fruit dealer)	fruit dealer, at home address
C. Costello	43 (lodging house)	—
Israel Hershman	45	paperstock dealer
Guiseppe Della Sala	46	Sargent & Co.
Antonio Guglielmino	48 (fruit dealer)	fruit dealer, at home address
Leopoldo Colavolpe	50	laborer
Salvatore DiPalma Meat Market	50	meat market, at home address

Antonio Apuzzo	50	laborer
Alfonso DeMaio saloon	52	saloon keeper, at home address
Mairino Bros saloon	52	

What is there to learn in these names and occupations (culled from the 1913 *New Haven Directory*)?[11] First, of course, this is an Italian block: among roughly five dozen heads of household, only Cosmo Williams, widow Jenny Nanton, and Israel Hershman don't seem to fit that generalization (Williams lives on the block and runs his fruit business there, Nanton just lives there, Hershman deals in paper stock on the block yet lives some distance away on High Street.) Second, in this era before zoning homogenized land use in American cities, this is a mixed-use neighborhood. There are plenty of residential units, most of them tenement flats, but these are mixed in with retail stores selling fruit, meat, even horses. There is a saloon, and there is the Tripoli Athletic Club right next to the Fair Street School. This mixing no doubt had its downside, but it had an organic wholeness sadly missing from today's residence-only streets. Third, as noted, this is very obviously a working-class street: twenty-seven heads of household are laborers, many of them doubtless working construction in a strong housing market. Seven are members of the Sargent workforce; one is a member of the workforce at Candee Rubber. Three are peddlers, one a saloon-keeper, two are barbers, two are shoemakers, one is a confectioner, and one is a mason.

Among these workers, there is another very important pattern. Even though this is a neighborhood built in close proximity to manufacturing facilities of massive scale, only a small fraction of those surveyed actually appear on a manufacturing company payroll. Some of the laborers may well have been doing short-term work for Bigelow, Candee, Sargent, Winchester, or one of the other big companies, but most were probably working for smaller firms in construction. This is the last (and in many respects most important lesson) to learn from the Fair Street block: while manufacturing accounts for the rapid population growth, much of its impact is indirect. Manufacturing wages create increased demand for foodstuffs, liquor, clothing, movies, and countless other products. Centralized manufacturing therefore supports many economic niches made possible by the circulation of payrolls on streets like this, and such streets are richly represented in the working-class neighborhoods of New Haven.

All this develoment was part of a vast centering historical process, drawing people and capital and energy from hinterlands to core cities across the capitalist world. In many cases, it entailed rural populations from the south of Italy (or the Russian steppe) coming to urban places like New Haven—or Providence, Boston, and the like. It also, however, entailed a local concentration in central places. Referring to the 1890s and after, Mary Mitchell quotes one informant on the Connecticut scene:

> The cities have attracted men of all vocations to them, causing a decline in rural populations. Formerly there were many small manufactories in the country and many country mechanics: wagons, shoes, clothes, harness, and all the various articles used in the country were largely made in the country. As the country blacksmith, wagon-maker, shoemaker and tailor have gone to the cities and now do their work there, the country lawyer and store-keeper have followed. As the rural population has decreased from these causes, and the farmer, who saw his farm decreasing in value, his capital shrinking, his crops no longer paying fairly because of Western competition, has turned his thoughts also to other fields of enterprise.[12]

Decentering Development, 1920–2000

The reader will recall that centered development depends on the combination of three key features: (1) strong fixed-path transportation (rail, shipping) focused on central place terminals; (2) the dominance of coal-to-steam energy technology (and the extreme difficulty of transmitting steam energy at a distance); and (3) continued weakness of variable path transportation (shoes, horses). Remove any one of the three, and the whole contraption comes apart. Such was happening even in the last twenty years of centered development. It is true that strong fixed-path transportation continued as a dominant fact of life for another generation after 1920, but neither of the other two considerations stayed in place much beyond 1900. A hint of the first change is offered by the 1892 appearance in *North American Review* of a curious essay by Thomas Alva Edison entitled "The Dangers of Electric Lighting." In this shameless polemic, the great inventor argues against the safety of alternating-current electricity (AC) and for government intervention against this menacing technology:

> As for the alternating current, it is difficult for me to name a safe pressure. Its effect on muscular action is so great that even at exceedingly low voltage the hand which grasps a conductor cannot free itself, and it is quite possible that in this way the sensitive nervous system of a human being could be shocked for a sufficient length of time to produce death. . . . My personal desire would be to prohibit

entirely the use of alternating currents. They are as unnecessary as they are dangerous.[13]

Edison is not a disinterested expert here, but an advocate for his direct current (DC) system of energy distribution, which is visibly faltering in its competition with George Westinghouse's alternating-current system of distribution.[14] What Edison appears really to have hated most about alternating current was its unique capacity to distribute energy through very long transmission lines with very great efficiency (that is, very little marginal loss of power as distance increased). This was a competitive disaster for Edison, and it was a revolutionary breach of the technological basis for centering development in New Haven and hundreds of other cities like it. It meant that energy from steam (or any other source) no longer needed to pass through belts and pulleys on its way to work: it could fly through copper wires, and could be brought into the shop floor through the working of very small, highly efficient electric motors, and through incandescent bulbs. This ease of transmission greatly reduced the premium formerly enjoyed by central places for manufacturing activities; it now became quite unnecessary to bring coal anywhere near the manufacturing enterprise itself and *vice versa*.

In exactly the same historical period, right on the cusp of the twentieth century, a second and even more fundamental revolution occurred: the advent of automotive transport. Here was a method of moving people and goods that combined relatively high speeds with variable-path design. We are so accustomed to the impact of automotive freedom that this combination of speed and flexibility seems a commonplace. But seen from, say, 1880, it is a revolution as profound in its impact on daily life as the political revolutions of 1776, 1789, or 1917. The change came with remarkable swiftness. In 1893 Karl Benz demonstrated his first four-wheel auto,[15] and Henry Ford demonstrated his prototype for a cheap gasoline-fueled internal combustion engine. In 1899, William McKinley would become the first U.S. president to ride in an automobile when he boarded a Stanley Steamer. The Olds Company would initiate "mass" production of cars by rolling out four hundred copies of the same vehicle in 1901. By 1913, with the maturation of Ford's rolling assembly process making the Model T accessible to middle-income buyers, the basis for a new regime of national governance would be launched. In 1909, Ford charged $950 for each of the 12,292 Model T's sold; by 1916, the company had dropped its price to $390 and sold a remarkable 577,036 copies of the same design that year.[16] By 1921, with the federal Highway Act, the most powerful political alliance of the twentieth century would begin to take shape among the driving public, automobile manufacturers, the UAW, the oil industry, the road-building industries (cement, asphalt, construction contracting), and an uncounted hoard of real estate developers. For decade after decade, the apparent resolve of American society and government was the reorganization of life around the car and its ugly cousin, the tractor-trailer truck.

Between these two changes—electricity and cars—the advantages enjoyed by central-city manufacturing, central-city housing, and central-city retailing would be swept away. Roads would be built in dense filigree across the region, forming a radial geometry around the central city. Electric lines would swiftly follow each road, offering access to power for light and heat, eventually even for the garage-door motor. Phone lines would share the same wooden poles, providing instant voice communication to even the remotest suburban or still-rural locations (New Haven hosted the first telephone exchange anywhere.) In truth, a new system of regional technology was forming, and would serve to reverse the centering effect of rail–steam–shoe leather urbanism (figure 4).

This decentering regime contrasts in each particular with its predecessor, and in one additional respect: in a centering system, fixed-path transport is the *only* form of low-cost, high-volume service to be found. In a decentering regime, relatively flexible bulk transportation is provided by the trucking industry. While this does not greatly facilitate the movement of very heavy materials (say, coal or metallic ores), it does provide very great flexibility in the movement of finished goods. A plant can be located near almost any interstate highway off-ramp and be assured of access to continental markets. This access greatly decreases the comparative advantage of rail and shipping terminals in core cities. Second, the energy-transfer technology provided by AC electricity wholly nullifies the concentrating power of steam power distributed along belts and pulleys. The direct use of such steam mechanisms declines, and is supplanted by the use of electric motors. The effect is once more to undercut the pulling power of central places. Third, the introduction of automotive transport produces high-speed flexible-path movement previously unimagined. This new freedom serves to detach workplace from homeplace, allowing housing to shift from core toward periphery. (And, as we know historically, this is a choice millions embrace—with a little help from the federal tax code and the banking industry.)

Finally, a decentering regime has as one of its features the fossil remains of centered industrialism; the buildings and infrastructure created in the previous era around the core city. With the decaying buildings stays the chemical residuum of manufacturing technology—PCBs, petroleum distillates, acids—that now greatly decrease

FIGURE 4. *Generating plant for early electric utility, New Haven downtown.* (New Haven Colony Historical Society)

the economic value of core city property. These "brownfield" sites become objects of environmental regulation, increasing the cost of redevelopment. They are in virtually every economic sense inferior to "greenfield" sites outside the core city. They remain of great historical importance, and may, as Preston Maynard suggests, be open to adaptive reuse. But their days as competitive industrial buildings have passed.

Decentering lives up to its name, pushing people and resources from center to periphery in region after region throughout the advanced industrial world. Twentieth-century New Haven is most assuredly a specimen of the process. Let's use New Haven County as shorthand for the region (it is perhaps slightly too broad, including a second urban core in Waterbury, but this is not a sufficiently large or dynamic part of the county to compromise the analysis). Begin with population change. New Haven itself is shrinking as the decades roll past (table 6). Over the seventy-year span (1920–1990), New Haven loses 32,093 people, which is to say 20 percent of its initial size. The county, in contrast gains about 380,000 people in the same period, growing by 90 percent from its initial base. Thus, the core city in 1920 held 38 percent of the population and only 16 percent in 1990—a consequential decline by any test. Town-by-town details are shown in Table 6. Some six once tiny communities grew tenfold or more, North Haven being perhaps the most important. On the one hand, North Haven is a suburban development story; an industrial expansion story, on the other. With Pratt-Whitney and other heavy industries building plants along Route 5 we have a peripheral version of the old manufacturing story. With U.S. Surgical at exit 9 off I-95, we encounter a classic car-fed industrial site, replete with structured parking "on campus." The most important changes, however, are in places with less spectacular rates yet even more consequential impacts. Here two groups are important. First are the high-income bedroom communities such as Guilford, Madison, Cheshire, and Woodbridge. These have become enclave communities for relatively affluent business and professional people, commonly enjoying important structural advantages in taxation, education, and real estate appreciation over time. A second important and distinctive group of towns are the inner suburbs of Hamden, West Haven, and East Haven. These are heterogeneous communities, not radically unlike New Haven itself. And they have grown to considerable size: 132,559 in total, just larger than New Haven in 1990.

TABLE 6

Town	Population 1920	Population 1990	% gain 1920–90
Wolcott	719	13,700	1805.4
Southbury	1,093	15,818	1347.2
Prospect	550	7,775	1313.6
North Branford	1,110	12,996	1070.8
North Haven	1,968	22,247	1030.4
Bethany	411	4,608	1021.2
Cheshire	2,855	25,684	799.6
Oxford	998	8,685	770.2
Madison	1,857	15,485	733.9
East Haven	3,520	26,144	642.7
Guilford	2,803	19,848	608.1
Woodbridge	1,170	7,924	577.3
Hamden	8,611	52,434	508.9
Middlebury	1,067	6,145	475.9
Milford	10,193	49,938	389.9
Branford	6,627	27,603	316.5
Wallingford	12,010	40,822	239.9
Beacon Falls	1,593	5,083	219.1
Seymour	6,781	14,228	109.8
Naugatuck	15,051	30,625	103.5
Meriden	34,764	59,479	71.1
Waterbury	99,902	108,961	9.1
Derby	11,238	12,199	8.6
Ansonia	17,643	18,403	4.3
New Haven	162,567	130,474	−19.7
Orange	16,614	12,830	−22.8
West Haven	Incorporated 1921	54,021	
Totals	423,715	804,159	89.8

TABLE 7

Town	Equalized Grand List (EGL), 1996	EGL per capita, 1996
North Haven	$2,700,674,565	$121,395
Orange	$1,556,009,570	$121,279
Woodbridge	$923,518,428	$116,547
Southbury	$1,749,296,802	$110,589
Madison	$1,707,236,735	$110,251
Middlebury	$661,650,585	$107,673
Guilford	$1,824,070,896	$91,902
Branford	$2,454,707,187	$88,929
Milford	$4,385,055,780	$87,810
Bethany	$400,214,016	$86,852
Cheshire	$1,964,029,796	$76,469
Oxford	$648,934,515	$74,719
Wallingford	$3,048,791,070	$74,685
North Branford	$886,236,228	$68,193
Prospect	$504,908,500	$64,940
Seymour	$875,534,208	$61,536
Hamden	$3,169,740,168	$60,452
Wolcott	$814,903,400	$59,482
Beacon Falls	$297,995,958	$58,626
Derby	$667,907,449	$54,751
East Haven	$1,324,350,464	$50,656
Ansonia	$878,816,862	$47,754
Meriden	$2,554,563,571	$42,949
Naugatuck	$1,306,983,125	$42,677
West Haven	$2,283,683,754	$42,274
Waterbury	$4,106,522,168	$37,688
New Haven	$4,572,200,382	$35,043

The outward flow of private capital—largely in the form of new housing and commercial construction—has been even more pronounced than the outward flow of people. New Haven's grand list grew steadily throughout the period, at least in nominal terms (that is, neglecting inflation). As might be guessed, however, the county's total grand list grew far faster. In 1920, New Haven accounted for 42 percent of the total grand list for all towns in the county. By 1990, it accounted for about 9 percent of that total. In table 7, the grand lists of each town have been adjusted to market (equalized) taking out the impact of varied assessment practices and varied frequencies of revaluation.[17] The key indicator here is equalized grand list (EGL) per capita. New Haven stands at the very bottom of a regional hierarchy by this measure with $35,043 per capita—a figure trebled by six towns, doubled by eight more, and exceeded by all. This is to some degree an artifact of laws placing Yale University's real property largely off the grand list, and of the fact that New Haven has a remarkable density of untaxed HUD public housing facilities. But these are relatively modest factors in the big picture. The essential truth is that capital has been flowing toward the perimeter towns for most of the twentieth century.

This, like the earlier centering story, has local texture framed within national structure. New Haven is joined in its "decentering" by scores and scores of other perfectly respectable manufacturing centers of the steam era. Here are some of the cities which have lost larger proportions of their peak populations than did New Haven: Birmingham, Hartford, Wilmington, Washington, D.C., Augusta, Chicago, East St. Louis, Gary, Covington, Louisville, Newport (Ky.), New Orleans, Bath (Maine), Baltimore, Boston, Chelsea, Fall River, Holyoke, Lawrence, Somerville (Mass.), Bay City (Mich.), Detroit, Flint, Saginaw, Minneapolis, St. Louis, St. Joseph, Bayonne, Camden, Hoboken, Jersey City, Trenton, Albany, Binghamton, Buffalo, Elmira, Poughkeepsie, Rochester, Schenectady, Troy, Syracuse, Utica, Akron, Canton, Cincinnati, Cleveland, Dayton, Altoona, Erie, Johnstown, Philadelphia, Pittsburgh, Reading, Scranton, Wilkes-Barre, Williamsport, Newport (R.I.), Providence, and Wheeling. Here is another way to see how *un*exceptional is the phenomenon of decentering. Begin with the 240 cities that ever (1790–1990) ranked among the hundred largest in the United States (and that have not since been annexed to another municipality, as, for instance, Brooklyn). How many of these are now smaller than they were at their population peak? Answer: 159 or 66 percent.[18] If we exclude cities the key sunshine states of California, Texas, Florida, North Carolina, Arizona, and Nevada, the percentage of population-losing cities climbs to 79 percent (154 of 195 having lost population.) New Haven is assuredly not alone.

Conclusion

Joe Perfetto—resident since July 1950 of Davis Street in suburban Hamden, proprietor of New England Stationery in downtown Crown Street—faces a predicament that sums up our story. His family heritage was rooted in centered industrial New Haven, defined for the clan by his father's fifty-year career locksmithing on the shop floor at C. Cowles & Co. on Water Street. Perfetto himself was responding to decentering technology (and contributing to its impact) when he moved his household from the city to Hamden decades ago. His move signaled his success— up and out from the old industrial core of New Haven. But his business remained anchored in its place of origin, and gradually declined as its customer base disappeared from the central business district, much as Perfetto himself had done. Not only had the office supply business drifted away toward suburban locations; the organization of office retailing had shifted radically toward corporate form, placing national management behind "big box" retailing in places like Staples or Office Max. These were stores so lacking in symbols of locality that a customer standing in front of one had no indication of whether he was in Connecticut, California, or Arkansas. We must not let them efface the very local, place-specific heritage of industrial New Haven.

If we reach all the way back to 1800, before centering technology began to draw people and resources so forcefully toward New Haven's core, New Haven was home to 5,157 of the county's 33,920 souls. In 1990, deep into the age of decentering technology, New Haven is home to 130,474 of the county's 804,159 people. In 1800, 15.2 percent; in 1990, 16.2 percent, little net change in the balance at day's end. Similarly, the energy economy of 1800 was decentered by the dominance of water power and work animals; the energy economy is of 1998 is decentered by the influence of electric utility costs that are among the highest in the nation (and that are also among the highest in a state that stands among the most expensive nationally).[19] But the region's growth has been enormous, and the accretion of total wealth remarkable. New Haven's core manufacturing district—Bigelow, Sargent, Cowles, Winchester, National Pipe Bending, New Haven Clock, and all the others—contributed a major part of the wealth and corresponding opportunity enjoyed by those who live in the city today, and by those who live in its once quiet hinterlands. The generations of people drawn to New Haven's corona—Guilford, Madison, Cheshire, Woodbridge and all the rest—owe something of their identities and heritage to the manufacturing district that is the subject of this work, and to the generations that lived and toiled within.

REFERENCES

Chandler, A. D. 1977. *The Visible Hand: The Managerial Revolution in American Business*. Cambridge, Mass.: Harvard University Press.

Clark, G. B. 1914. *A History of Connecticut*. New York: Putnam.

David, P. A. 1991. "The Hero and the Herd in Technological History: Reflections on Thomas Edison and the Battle of Systems." *Favorites of Fortune: Technology, Growth, and Economic Development since the Industrial Revolution,* edited by P. E. A. Higonnet, 72–119. Cambridge, Mass.: Harvard University Press.

Edison, T. A. 1892. "The Dangers of Electric Lighting." *North American Review* 149:625–634.

Gibson, C. 1998. "Population of the 100 Largest Cities and Other Urban Places in the United States: 1790–1990," *U.S. Bureau of the Census Technical Papers, No. 27.*

Hounshell, D. A. 1984. *From the American System to Mass Production, 1800–1932*. Baltimore: Johns Hopkins University Press.

Mitchell, M. H. 1930. *History of New Haven County, Connecticut*. Chicago: Pioneer Historical Publishing.

Nye, D. E. 1998. *Consuming Power: A Social History of American Energies*. Cambridge, Mass: MIT Press.

Rae, Douglas W. 2003. *City: Urbanism and its End*. New Haven: Yale University Press.

Tyler, D. P. 1846. *Statistics of the Condition and Production of Certain Branches of Industry of Connecticut*. Hartford: State of Connecticut.

NOTES

1. See Chandler 1977.

2. From the statewide survey published in 1846. The facts displayed here are from Tyler 1846, 38ff.

3. It is very difficult to infer the actual average number of employees per firm, as some industries are listed without any reference to the number of firms. For example, some number of firms produced 17,766 pairs of boots, and employed a total of 373 men and 165 women. If we assume (almost certainly against the fact) that all such cases indicate a single firm, we find a global average for the city of 18.8 employees per firm. This is an upper limit, and the actual average is probably much closer to ten.

4. The combination of innovative technology and small scale in this period is suggested by this telling of the story: "Three workmen could take brass in sheets, press it out, level it under the drop, cut the teeth, and make the wheels for five-hundred clocks in a day." See Clark 1914, 357.

5. The Palladium Company. *New Haven of Today, Its Commerce, Trade and Industries* (New Haven, Conn.: Clarence H. Ryder, 1892), 42.

6. A fine overview of energy history in the U.S. is offered by Nye (1998).

7. See Tyler 1846, 193.

8. Ibid., 120.

9. These and subsequent horsepower figures are U.S. Department of Commerce estimates. See *Historical Statistics of the United States* (1975), Series S-14, and updates for later years available through *Statistical Abstracts of the United States*. It is difficult to suppose that these estimates are as accurate as they are precise for any one period. It is on the other hand probable that they give a good sense of the changes that occurred between periods.

10. State produced *Register & Manual of Connecticut*, for years in question.

11. Price & Lee (New Haven, 1913). This is the earliest directory to give both street and alphabetical listings.

12. Mitchell 1930, 813–814.

13. Edison 1892, 632.

14. See David 1991.

15. He had begun with three-wheelers.

16. Hounshell 1984, 224.

17. Taken from *Connecticut Fiscal Indicators* (1997). Per capita figures use 1990 population data.

18. All the data employed in this paragraph comes from table 23 in Gibson 1998.

19. Only five states have higher costs for industrial electricity on a per kilowatt basis (Hawaii, Massachusetts, New Hampshire, New Jersey, and Rhode Island). Connecticut's statewide average cost is 7.76 cents per kilowatt hour. United Illuminating, serving New Haven and its immediate region stands at 8.79 cents, higher than seven of the state's nine regional utilities (only Norwalk's tiny publicly owned utility was higher). Data for 1997. See U.S. Department of Energy, table 16, at www.eia.doe.gov)

DIANA BALMORI

Industry and Water in New Haven

lthough we have descriptions of industry that came to New Haven in the nineteenth century and we have descriptions of New Haven's natural systems, the two are rarely described together. The intent of this essay is to describe the city's industrial development and growth together with the transformation of its very important and visible water systems.

The history of New Haven revolves around water. The colonists, attracted in 1638 by the broad navigable harbor, the great tidal marshes, and the freshwater rivers, looked to these rich natural resources to provide food, transportation, drinking water, irrigation, waste disposal, and recreation.

In a 1748 map of New Haven, you can see its initial nine-square layout carefully tilted from a true north-south alignment as if to fit better between the West and East creeks (figure 1). In addition, there is the calm water of the harbor leading into Long Island Sound, providing the reason for the founding and continued survival of New Haven as a port. Not shown on this map are the Mill, Quinnipiac and West rivers.

Compared to the Housatonic, Thames, or Connecticut, New Haven's rivers— the West, Quinnipiac, and Mill—are small. Of the three, the Mill River is smallest but played the most important role in New Haven's development. Rivers running on tidal flats cannot generate waterpower; above tidewater, however, a small waterfall on the Mill River encouraged construction of the colony's first grist mill. At its site, Eli Whitney rebuilt the dam in 1798 and began using the waterpower to run machines for manufacturing muskets. Still later, his son built a higher dam and the city's first water supply system.

Downstream from Whitneyville, the banks of the rivers and the harbor itself were lined with broad tidal flats, common to Connecticut's shoreline. The Quin-

FIGURE I. *An early map of
New Haven.* (New Haven Col-
ony Historical Society, "A Plan of
the Town of New Haven," the
Hon. General Wadsworth, 1748.
Edward E. Atwater, ed., *History
of the City of New Haven* [New
York: Munsell, 1887], 300)

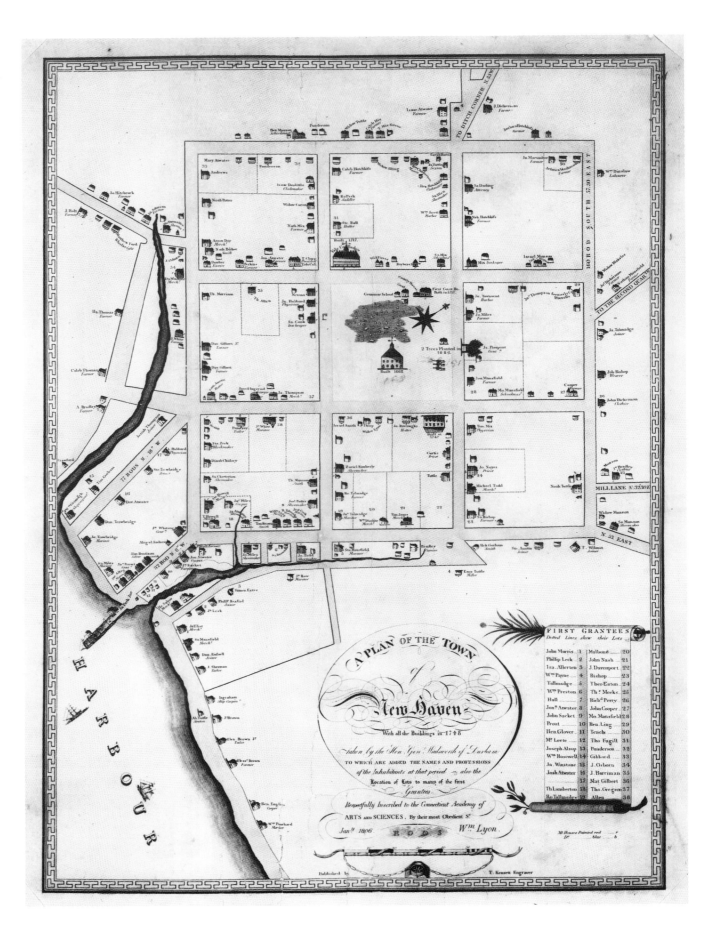

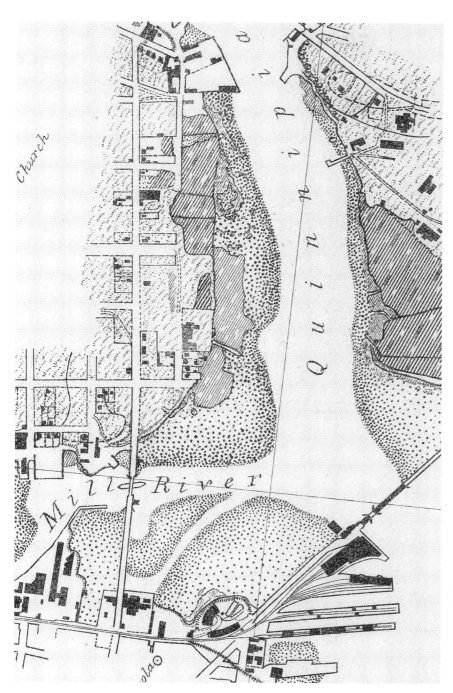

FIGURE 2. *The Quinnipiac and Mill marsh fill.* (New Haven Colony Historical Society. U.S. Coast Survey, New Haven Harbor, 1872; Benjamin Pierce, superintendent; topography by R. M. Bache [New York: Julius Bien, 1872], segment)

nipiac and Mill River marsh was originally the largest salt marsh in the state. Colonists harvested its native salt hay for their cattle. Less visibly, it nourished a productive estuarine ecosystem, including Long Island Sound, which became renowned for its fish, oysters, clams, mussels, and lobsters. In ignorance of ecology, New Haven grew by filling in tidal flats and the marshes, over a period of three hundred years. Historical maps of the area show the extent of the fill, which coincides nearly with the extent of the old marsh.[1] This salt marsh fill, then, precisely in the area around the confluence of the Quinnipiac and Mill rivers, is the area in which to observe the story of New Haven's acquisition of industry and of its growth from small town to city (figure 2). This story involves water in all ways.

From the beginning, New Haveners were manipulating their waterfronts for commercial advantage. Marshes were filled; docks and wharves were built to handle the coastal trading, fishing, and oystering that were early mainstays of the colony.

The Harbor

As early as 1644 New Haven colonists worried that their shallow harbor was silting in and would cut off their water access to the world, for exporting agricultural products and importing consumer goods. To allow docking of larger ships in deeper water, they began building what was later called Long Wharf, jutting into the harbor from the point between the East and West creeks where the Nine Squares met the waterfront.[2] Long Wharf was lengthened and widened repeatedly over the next two hundred years.[3] By 1820, it was the commercial center of New Haven, providing both docking for large trading vessels and warehouses for New Haven's successful merchants (figure 3).

Steamships from New York began arriving as early as 1815, and railroads reaching New Haven between 1838 and 1850 also proceeded to the harbor. The Hartford & New Haven Railroad built a major rail terminal in 1848 adjacent to Belle Dock, the site of important steamboat service to New York (figure 4).[4] By 1850, rail lines were built right down to the waterfront for the New York & New Haven rail line,

cementing the site as the shipping and trading center of the region. The railroad would grow to dominate shipping and commerce, yet the waterfront was still an important link for local industry.

The first dredging of the harbor took place in the 1880s.[5] The channel was widened to a depth of twenty feet right up to the Mill River. This allowed large shipping and trading activities concerned with New Haven's industries. Coal was now the major import, with lumber, copper, iron, and paper pulp coming in bulk. The practice of dredging and filling the harbor front would continue. In the 1960s, seven million cubic yards of fill were dredged from the harbor and used to fill in the Long Wharf mud flats, creating the platform for Interstate 95 and the Long Wharf industrial park.[6]

The Disappearing Creeks

The East Creek flowed adjacent to State Street, along the same course as the present-day railway cut. In earlier times it had many wharves and docks, for the most important merchants built their warehouses and shops here. It was the first creek to be altered. The mouth of the creek became the terminal basin for the Farmington Canal (dug largely by Irish immigrants from 1825 onward) and opened as far

as Farmington in 1828. This bold experiment to link New Haven to the interior by water reached its destination at Northampton, Massachusetts, by 1835, but failed after ten years of excessively expensive maintenance and growing competition by railroads. Meanwhile, the canal also served the growing city as a source of water for putting out frequent fires in the buildings downtown. In 1846 the canal stockholders voted to turn the canal into a railroad; within a few years the canal was drained, and a new rail line laid in its bed.[7] The canal and the railway that took its place reinforced State Street as an important commercial district for artisans and traders. By 1860 warehouses and shops lined State Street from Long Wharf north to Chapel Street.

West Creek also disappeared. Imagine for a moment you are standing at the corner of Church and George Street, near the present-day Knights of Columbus headquarters. In 1850, you would be in one of the densest and busiest commercial quarters of New Haven. There was water flowing here: the West Creek, deeper than East Creek, meandered to the harbor. Along the creek were situated the wooden docks and wharves where vessels unloaded raw materials and goods and loaded agricultural and finished products. The harbor itself was not far away, just two blocks east of here. Farther up the creek were newly built tenements; new immigrants were coming into New Haven and this was where they could find affordable housing and work. West Creek in 1850 was not very attractive; the water had a stench because it was polluted with sewage and effluent of the tanneries along this southwest side of the original nine squares. By 1872, when New Haven inaugurated its first sewer system,[8] West Creek was considered an open sewer, and in 1875 was filled in.[9] New housing built on top of the fill aged over the years, was declared a slum, and was removed for the Oak Street connector (Route 34) in 1965.

Water Street to Mill River

From earliest times, other wharves and docks carved up the marshes and the shoreline. Water Street (also known as Bankside) was an early site of commercial trading and later, intensive industrial development. In the postcolonial era, it held small wharves for traders and artisans. With the advent of the railroad, these sites became the locale of major dealers in bulk goods like coal, lumber, and wood products, including George Alling and Sons (wholesale lumber dealers) and J. Gibb Smith & Co. The Sargent Hardware Company, founded in the 1860s, grew dramatically along the waterfront on Water Street. To meet its expansion needs, Sargent's tall brick mills were built on piers right into the harbor. More waterfront was filled in to accommodate the growth of this major industry. By 1880, some two thousand workers were employed here. Further east, mills and warehouses sprang up between East Street and the railroad lines along the Mill River. The W. & E. T. Fitch Company, a major supplier of carriage hardware, moved in 1853 from a site in Westville to the corner of East and Water Street.[10] By 1875, the west shore of the Mill River was covered with warehouses and factories.

Mill River as Drinking Water

The growth of population in the wake of industry—nearly doubling from 10,678 inhabitants in 1830 to 20,345 in 1850—brought about a marked deterioration of the quality of life in the city, in terms of appearance and health. Many references to the creeks as sewers, to crowded tenements, and muddy streets appear in this period; so do reports of disease. By midcentury the growing recognition of a linkage of cholera and typhoid to contaminated well water brought about a demand for pure water.

After many disputes about whether a water company should be private or public, the private New Haven Water Company engaged Eli Whitney (son of Eli Whitney, the inventor and arms manufacturer) to transfer to New Haven several acres next to his Mill River factory, for the construction of a higher dam, reservoir, pumping station, and waterworks. Water from the resulting Lake Whitney was clean and began flowing through pipes to city houses in 1862.[11] But the intrusion of sewage into the groundwater and the continued use of well water by a good portion of New Haven's population meant no great change occurred in the number of illnesses (cholera, dysentery, and typhoid) caused by contaminated water. Eighteen to twenty-six cases per thousand were reported from the mid-1860s to the mid-1870s.[12]

The Sewer System

With the Mill River dammed for New Haven's water system, sewage disposal became the next priority. New Haven was the second city in the country to install sewers, only a year later than Chicago in 1872.[13] Chicago's engineer, Eliot Cheeseborough, planned New Haven's sewer system. But in 1872, sewage disposal meant collecting and removing wastewaters, not treating them. Connecticut State health reports in 1878 describe the general conditions succinctly: "The small brooks which are used as open sewers are often overtaxed and soil saturation is directly produced. The present outbreak of diphtheria commenced in one such locality. The maps indicate the volume of water that flows in the different streams proportionately; they also indicate the probabilities of the Quinnipiac providing a never failing volume of water for the proper dilution of sewage."[14] Concerning industrial pollution, the same report continues, "if the sewage and manufacturing waste can be rapidly removed and sufficiently diluted, the problem is solved. The manufacturing waste is, with the exception of that from the woolen mill, beneficial to the sewage, rather than otherwise."[15] Another report author agreed that "if diluted with the proper volume of water, sewage can be disposed of by water carriage without detriment to the health of any living near the stream."[16]

The Quinnipiac River and its Industrial Uses

From the late eighteenth century, fisherman, oystermen, and shipbuilders made their living along the banks of the Quinnipiac River in a place called Dragon, later known as Fair Haven. Small frame houses with raised cellars were built adjacent to their waterfront workplaces (figure 5).[17] By the 1820s both sides of the river were densely settled by an active seafaring community and the merchants that supported these businesses.[18] Yet the large tract of land, known as Grapevine Point,

that existed between the Quinnipiac River and New Haven was still undeveloped. The Grand Avenue and Chapel Street bridges did not yet span the Mill River.

Fifty years later, however, you could travel down Chapel Street and cross the Mill River into Fair Haven, where a new street grid had been laid out for future residential construction.[19] Fair Haven was a major oystering port, but other industries were moving to the southern shores of Grapevine Point where broad tidal flats still existed. Along the banks of the Quinnipiac and Mill rivers factories were being built (figure 6). First to locate here was the Bigelow Boiler Company, which moved here in 1869.[20] The National Pipe Bending Company, C. S. Mersick & Co., and Holcomb Brothers, carriage makers, followed by 1888.[21] Across Chapel Street new housing was built for workers, as speculators took advantage of the open land and the street trolley now running along Grand Avenue.

Steam engines were powering these industries. A waterfront location was important because an industry needed water access to bring in coal to fuel the steam engines. The manufacturers also needed waterfront access to ship in raw materials and ship out finished goods. The shore was modified to accommodate these needs. The large marshes, with their rich biota, were stripped down and filled in; the water edges were covered with wharves and piers. Manufacturers took water from the river and heated it in coal-stoked boilers to make steam for the engines to power machines. Industrial wastes were dumped out into the river. But these

FIGURE 6. *Factories were being built in the late 1860s and early 1870s along the banks of the Quinnipiac and Mill rivers.* (New Haven Colony Historical Society, "The City of New Haven, Conn, 1879" [Boston: O. H. Bailey and J. C. Hazen], segment)

industries were bringing prosperity to New Haven, attracting immigrants to work. New Haven was growing rapidly.

Across from Grapevine Point, on the east shore of the Quinnipiac River, other industries were taking root. The New Haven Wire Company and the New Haven Chemical Company located here before 1879.[22] New Haven Wire would expand greatly at this location over the next seventy-five years and fill in acres of marshland along the Quinnipiac.

New Haven's First Industry: Oystering

Water was without a doubt a most important ecological resource in the settlement of New Haven and its consequent industrial development. The combination of saltwater from the sea and freshwater in the highly productive tidal estuaries offered a rich biological opportunity. The relationship between man and oyster led to the development of New Haven's first and longest surviving industry: oystering. From their role as a food staple for Native Americans and the colonists alike, New Haven oysters became the most valuable oysters in the United States (by price per weight and volume).[23] These shellfish and the industry built around them reflect the dynamic relationship between humans and their biophysical environment.

The abundance of oysters along the Quinnipiac and the harbor from early times provided both a steady food supply and commercial endeavor for the colonists. So much oystering was going on that by 1766, while deeply involved in the West Indies trade, local government became alarmed enough to pass protective legislation. The act "Preservation of Oysters and Clams and Regulating the Fishery Thereof" addressed overharvesting by banning the dragging and harvesting of oysters during spawning season. This protection seems to have been successful; by 1836 most of the one thousand residents of Fair Haven and three hundred boats were employed in the oyster industry.[24] By the mid-1850s Fair Haven had three major shipyards building oyster boats, tinsmiths making tins to put oysters in, and lime producers processing the by-product of shells.[25] Meanwhile a second oystering center grew up at City Point (then Oyster Point), where conditions needed for the oysters' growth and survival were enhanced.[26] New Haven became the oyster capital of the country.[27]

In the 1870s, a major development in the industry took place: the Quinnipiac River was now used to seed oysters that were then transplanted across Long Island Sound to beds owned by local dealers, allowing for much greater cultivation.[28] At the same time a major shift from sail to steam technology also spurred the oyster industry. By 1874 steam-powered boats and dredges, working the breadths of Long Island Sound, made massive harvests possible.[29] By 1900, the oyster industry had peaked after a Connecticut harvest reached four million bushels, perhaps three-fourths of which came from New Haven (figure 7).[30] The export of thousands of barrels of oysters provided employment for hundreds of shuckers, mostly women and boys. They worked in oyster sheds built on wharves along the Quinnipiac River as well as in the raised basements of oyster houses on the Quinnipiac and at City Point.[31]

But the degradation of the water systems by domestic and industrial wastes eventually exceeded the rivers' natural capacity to dilute pollution. Although there is no direct evidence that the incidence of water-borne diseases such as diarrhea and typhoid was increased by ingesting contaminated shellfish, it is highly likely. In any case, in 1902 it was decreed no longer safe to harvest oysters for human consumption directly from New Haven's harbor or rivers, and in 1909 new regulations

FIGURE 7. *Oyster fishermen.* (New Haven Colony Historical Society Photo Archives)

of the industry were enacted for ensuring cleanliness of the oysters.[32] However, despite the clean water supply from Lake Whitney and the sewerage infrastructure that had been largely in place since 1890, downstream water quality continued to decline, and so did the popularity of oysters as a food. Storm conditions, burgeoning populations of the oysters' chief predators (starfish and oyster drills), disease, water pollution, overharvesting, diminished demand (or, more likely, a combination of all these factors) took their toll. The output of the industry steadily declined until it reached its nadir in 1970.

Since then, however, thanks to improved water quality, greater scientific understanding of shellfish biology, tidal marsh restoration programs, and intensive aquaculture, annual production has again risen from a low of 16,000 bushels in 1970 to 250,000 bushels. Baby oysters now must be removed from the harbor and transplanted to cleaner waters elsewhere in the Sound to cleanse themselves and fatten up for harvesting. In 1984 most of the Connecticut oyster crop originated in New Haven Harbor, one of the most productive oyster areas on the East Coast.[33] Although production is still lower than in 1900, New Haven's status as oyster capital of the country appears on its way to reinstatement.

A Plan for Postindustrial New Haven?

Piped-in water and sewerage systems, as well as city lighting and overall street improvements, became points of civic pride in the industrial city before the twentieth century. So did central parks to provide a breathing space and oasis of greenery for Sunday outings. In 1910, however, Cass Gilbert and Frederick Law Olmsted Jr. submitted a plan for New Haven that offered a much more complex vision of the city and its relationship to open space than just the nineteenth-century central parks.[34] The plan considered waterways as systems, not individual watercourses: it considered rivers as part of the city's infrastructure (which, in fact, rivers had become when used for piped-in drinking water and piped-out sewerage). But the Gilbert-Olmsted plan also added a citywide open-space program that protects rivers, giving them green parkland in which to flood and be cleansed, preserving its soft edges, and fostering their biota. It allowed for patterns of pools and riffles, as well as gradual modifications along the water's course.

Gilbert and Olmsted produced the plan for a civic commission and it imparted the image of a city ahead of its time. Unfortunately, it was never carried out. Commercial interests preferred a waterfront that supported industry and commerce. Additional wetlands and marshes were filled in for the large oil tanks and the highways of the twentieth century.

Though many parts of New Haven around its rivers have changed, it is still possible with some serious work to create a connective greenbelt for the recreation and health of its citizens and for the health of its rivers. The Gilbert and Olmsted vision is something we can admire today even more since it responds to our better ecological understanding of rivers as integral systems. Its only forerunner was the "Emerald Necklace" built in 1892 in Boston: a similar urban plan that created a continuous green belt around the Muddy and Charles rivers. That plan, by Frederick L. Olmsted Sr. and Jr., *was* built; Boston surged ahead while New Haven stepped back from civic glory. Boston's Emerald Necklace was, however, dismantled in the 1940s and 1950s. Still, in 2002 New Haven's and Boston's emerald necklace plans are the two best answers to the treatment of our water systems in modern ecological terms, particularly in response to water's role in the infrastructure of the city and its industries. It is time to dust off their covers and reconsider the radical transformation they intended.

NOTES

1. "Coastal Map of Harbor of New Haven, Connecticut, 1876," from a survey made of the City by R. M. Bache, U.S. Coastal Survey, 1876.

2. Penelope Sharpe, "A History of New Haven Harbor from Settlement to the Twentieth Century," *Bulletin of the Archaeological Society of Connecticut*, no. 42 (1980), 1–11.

3. Edward E. Atwater, *History of the City of New Haven* (New York: Munsell, 1887), 300–301.

4. Rollin G. Osterweis, *Three Centuries of New Haven, 1638–1938*, (New Haven: Yale University Press, 1953), 238 and 249.

5. Sharpe, 7.

6. Ibid., 8.

7. Floyd M. Shumway and Richard Hegel, "New Haven's Two Creeks," *Journal of the New Haven Colony Historical Society* 37, no. 1 (Fall 1990), 19 and 21.

8. Alice Davenport, "A City Ahead of its Time: Nineteenth-Century New Haven and its Groundbreaking Sewer System," Writing assignment for Yale College course "Urban Legal History," 18 June 1997, in collections of the New Haven Colony Historical Society library, 42; Atwater, 413–416.

9. Shumway and Hegel, 16.

10. Matthew Roth, *Connecticut: An Inventory of Historic Engineering and Industrial Sites* (Washington, D.C.: Society for Industrial Archeology, 1981), 178.

11. Karyl Lee Kibler Hall and Carolyn Cooper, *Windows on the Works: Industry on the Eli Whitney Site, 1798–1979* (Hamden, Conn.: Eli Whitney Museum, 1984), 48–49.

12. C. A. Lindsay, "Report of the Health Officer," in *City Yearbook of the City of New Haven, 1875–1876* (New Haven: Tuttle, Morehouse, and Taylor, 1876), 229–230.

13. Davenport, 22.

14. W. H. Brewer, "Pollution of Streams," in *First Annual Report of the State Board of Health of the State of Connecticut for the Fiscal Year Ending November 31, 1878* (Hartford, Conn.: Press of the Case, Lockwood, and Brainard Co., 1878), 58.

15. Ibid., 59.

16. C. A. Lindsay, " The Registration of Vital Statistics in Connecticut," in *First Annual Report of the State Board of Health . . . 1878, 70.*

17. See pages 24 and 55 of the essay section of the New Haven Historic Resources Inventory, Phase II: Eastern New Haven, produced by the New Haven Preservation Trust.

18. See pages 25–26 of the essay section of the New Haven Historic Resources Inventory, Phase II: Eastern New Haven, produced by the New Haven Preservation Trust.

19. "Map of the City of New Haven from Town Records and Survey," Frederick Beers, 1868.

20. Atwater, 595.

21. "Atlas of the City of New Haven, Connecticut, 1888" (Philadelphia: Hopkins, Griffith and Morgan, 1888).

22. "The City of New Haven, Connecticut, 1879," birds-eye map drawn and published by D. H. Bailey and J. C. Hazen, Boston, Massachusetts.

23. Personal communication with John Volk, director, aquaculture division, Connecticut State Department of Agriculture.

24. Osterweis, 104 and 243.

25. Doris B. Townshend, *Fair Haven, A Journey Through Time* (New Haven: New Haven Colony Historical Society, 1976), 22 and 45.

26. Osterweis, 243.

27. Gaddis Smith, "New Haven and the Sea," in Floyd Shumway and Richard Hegel, eds., *New Haven: An Illustrated History* (New Haven: New Haven Colony Historical Society, 1981), 71.

28. Townshend, 25–27.

29. Amy L. Trout and Julie P. Salathe, "A Brief Introduction to the Maritime History of New Haven," *Journal of the New Haven Colony Historical Society* 37, no. 1 (Fall 1990), 7.

30. Virginia M. Galpin, "New Haven's Seascape, 1815–1900, and the Relationship between Steam Packets and Trains," *Journal of the New Haven Colony Historical Society* 37, no. 1 (Fall 1990), 32.

31. Townshend, 21.

32. Virginia M. Galpin, *New Haven's Oyster Industry, 1638–1887* (New Haven: New Haven Colony Historical Society, 1989), 31.

33. Galpin, *Oyster Industry*, 66.

34. Cass Gilbert and Frederick Law Olmsted, *Report of the New Haven Civic Improvement Commission to the New Haven Civic Improvement Committee* (New Haven: Tuttle, Morehouse & Taylor, 1910).

SANDRA RUX

Interweaving Carpet and Community in New Haven, 1830–1842

In 1830 New Haven was a flourishing small city with a population of 10,678. Its civic life centered on the town green, the middle of the nine squares laid out almost two hundred years earlier; its intellectual life centered on Yale College; its economic life centered on the market and the harbor. Retail, wholesale, and import-export merchants were busy buying, selling, and shipping goods produced elsewhere, from luxuries to agricultural produce, as well as products of handcraft artisans living in town. The area across the creek to the east, known as the New Township, had the beginning of a street grid, but was still largely open farmland, with a fringe of elegant houses on Water Street overlooking the harbor, and along Wooster Street (figure 1).[1] In 1825 the City of New Haven had bought a plot of pastureland in the New Township that became Wooster Square, a secondary "green." Lots around it were laid out for the development of substantial houses. The character of the New Township changed only gradually, as both dwellings and manufactories began to locate there, for production of goods on a larger scale than handcraft manufacture.

What follows is the story, reconstructed from surviving fragmentary documentation, of one of the very earliest companies to establish a larger-scale manufacturing presence in the New Township. Unlike other companies highlighted in this book, the New Haven Carpet Manufacturing Company, also known as Galpin & Robertson, did not grow very large, last very long, or become famous in its field. It flourished in the 1830s, went bankrupt in 1842, and seems to have operated feebly through the 1840s. Although it ran one of New Haven's largest early factories, the enterprise was practically forgotten by the late nineteenth century, when it merited only a few sentences in Atwater's *History of New Haven*.[2] Its story, however, is illustrative of several features of infant industries' experience in taking root in

FIGURE 1. *The New Township area of New Haven in 1812, before any industrial development took place.* (New Haven Colony Historical Society)

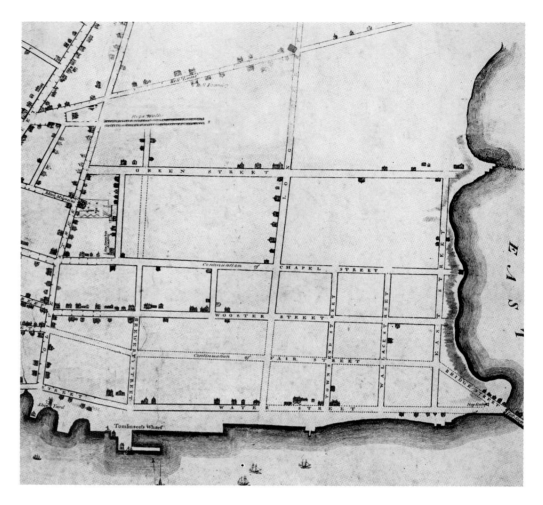

the new American republic: the importation of technology and technicians, the importance of family connections for financial support in the absence of a well-established banking system, the cushioning role of real estate investment, the frequency of holding public office and of contributions to civic amenities, and the eventual absorption of skilled labor into a larger pool of new industries. It was a time of challenges and flexible responses at the beginning of New Haven's shift of economic emphasis from commerce to manufacturing. Risks were taken; failures were frequent. The carpet factory pioneered in that shift and—despite its "failure"—left a valuable material, technical, and social heritage to the city in the development of physical plant and housing stock, in the skills of its workers, and in the civic contributions of their employers.

Water-powered textile manufacture in Connecticut had taken successful hold in the upper northeast corner of the state and in Humphreysville (later Seymour) but not in tidewater New Haven, whose waterpower sites were few and upstream from the city proper. A cotton mill established upstream in Westville in 1789 produced cotton cloth for a few years, then changed to woolen cloth, and shortly after was converted to a paper mill.[3] The New Haven town report of 1811 mentioned

the presence of "one cotton manufactory, containing all the usual machinery for spinning and twisting cotton," but its list of occupations and products omitted weavers and textiles.[4] Most textiles in New Haven were imported from overseas.

By 1830 the cotton-spinning factory was gone, but the musket factory that Eli Whitney had established upstream at Mill Rock in 1798 was thriving under his nephews' management. New Haven and environs also housed a wide variety of nontextile manufactures including shoes and other leather goods, pleasure carriages, hats, watches and clocks, bells, soap and candles, combs and brushes, paper, books and bookbinding, cabinetry and chairs, silver and gold ware, scythes, nails, axes, and tinware, rope, and ships' pulley blocks.[5] Very few of these manufactures used powered machinery.[6]

In this environment of low participation in the early textile industry but lively involvement in handwork manufacturing, Philip Galpin, a 36-year-old dry goods merchant, set up a factory in 1829 to produce ingrain carpets. Popular at the time, ingrain carpets were flat-weave (as distinct from pile) carpets with two layers interwoven, or, for more elaborate patterns, three layers interwoven. Both warp and weft contributed colors to the decorative patterns (figure 2). For two years Galpin leased space for his factory upstairs in a brick building on Chapel Street at an annual rent of $125;[7] he then also leased a sizeable piece of land with a building at the intersection of Brewery and Water streets in the New Township, for $175 per year.[8] A portion of the factory was probably located here, where proximity to the Northampton Canal and Canal Basin would have facilitated shipping the carpets.

Other manufacturers also began moving to the New Township. In 1830 Alexander Harrison built a stone building on upper East Street for use in manufacturing axes. James Brewster purchased thirteen acres early in 1832 and built a carriage works on East Street at the foot of Wooster Street. His acreage, stretching from Franklin Street to the Mill River and from the harbor to Wooster Street, included Brewster's own estate and housing for workers.[9] He built his factory not far from the elegant Pavilion Hotel, where southerners came for a summer respite from the heat, and the handsome houses on Water and Wooster Streets. Isaac Mix & Sons put up a large building for carriage manufacture farther inland on St. John Street later in 1832. When President Andrew Jackson visited New Haven in June 1833, he inspected the Brewster carriage factory and Harrison's axe factory.[10] He might have noticed construction of Galpin's new and larger carpet factory near the axe factory. Galpin's enterprise was expanding.

Unlike some other New Haven manufacturers at that time, such as carriage-maker James Brewster, Philip Smith Galpin (figure 3) did not begin as a handcraft artisan and work his way into ownership position. Instead, he branched out from a career in commerce, after working his way upward. A native of Berlin, Connecticut,[11] Galpin had begun his career in 1813 as a clerk for William H. Elliot, Esq., one of the leading dry goods merchants in New Haven. He did military service in defense of the city against the British in 1814 and apparently did well after the war. He also married well and was a landowner by November 1820. His wife, Ann Fitch, inherited land holdings including a dwelling house and other buildings on State Street that year, part of which Philip bought as a partner with Leonard Wales.[12] Such real estate acquisitions, which Galpin continued to make from time to time, added to his credit worthiness as a businessman; creditors knew what he was "worth" in terms of property as collateral.

Galpin became a dry goods merchant in 1822, forming a partnership with one Hervey Sanford. They purchased a store on the west side of Church Street for $400. This business apparently prospered, enabling Philip and Ann to buy a house and three-quarters of an acre of land from the David Tomlinson estate for $4500 in February 1824.[13] These land holdings added to his social status as well as his financial "worth." Galpin was first elected to public office in 1823 as a member of the New Haven Common Council, and was elected to the state legislature in 1829, 1834, 1835, and 1843,[14] during the lifespan of his carpet factory. He later twice became mayor of New Haven.

While there is nothing in Galpin's early history as dry goods merchant that would indicate a special interest in carpets, his experience selling them, among other textiles, must have made him aware that there was a demand for floor coverings and that the prices of imported ones were high. Domestic manufacture was encouraged by the tariff of 1824, which imposed import duties ranging from 25 to 50 cents per square yard on carpets. These duties increased in 1828.[15] Galpin

FIGURE 3. *Philip Smith Galpin.* (New Haven Colony Historical Society Manuscript Collection, MSS C-1, Box 87, Folder F)

began his ingrain carpet factory in 1829, when imported ingrain carpets carried a surcharge of 40 cents a yard, creating an advantage for domestic production by an "infant industry" such as his, and he seized it. His was Connecticut's third carpet factory.[16] The carpet factories in Tariffville (!) and Enfield, begun in 1825 and 1828 respectively, were larger than Galpin's, and constituted his closest competition. At that time power looms had not yet superseded handlooms for weaving carpets, so lack of waterpower was no drawback for locating in harborside New Haven. He hired handloom weavers.

By 1832, the year of a federal census of manufactures, the New Haven Carpet Manufacturing Company was still owned solely by Philip Galpin, who had a capital investment of $20,000 in it. He was employing twenty-six men at a dollar a day, eight women at 35 cents and two children at 25 cents.[17] He reported an output of 50,000 yards of carpet that year.[18] He was paying 45 cents a pound for wool, significantly more than his two large competitors in Connecticut paid, so it is possible that he was buying it already spun, while the others were spinning it on-site.[19] Galpin's operation devoted two pounds of wool to each yard, producing a high-quality carpet.[20] While the per-worker productivity for the New Haven factory was as good as or better than the competition, the cost of the wool made the business a losing proposition—at least by the numbers that Galpin provided to the government. When added to the $45,000 he paid for wool, his total expenses probably came to somewhat more than $56,000 per year,[21] while the value of the carpets manufactured was only $50,000.

Whether or not he was aware of losing money, in February 1833 Galpin embarked on an expansion of the business. He purchased a two-acre plot for a new carpet factory on the east side of East Street, extending from East Street to the Mill River, and a three-quarter–acre lot on the west side of East Street.[22] Presumably to gain capital and otherwise facilitate expansion, Galpin formed a partnership with John B. Robertson.

A Yale graduate (class of 1829), Robertson had recently moved his family to New Haven from his hometown of Charleston, South Carolina, where he had studied medicine and earned an M.D. degree. Although he was sometimes referred to as "Dr." in the New Haven records, John Robertson apparently never practiced medicine.[23] In 1830 he had married Mary W. Denison of New Haven. They had three children before she died in 1835.[24] His second marriage, to Mabel Maria Heaton in 1838, was socially and economically advantageous; she was the only child of Abraham Heaton, a prominent shipping merchant in New Haven.

By October 1833, when Galpin & Robertson purchased an additional small piece of land on Greene Street "a little north of the ax factory and a little west of the

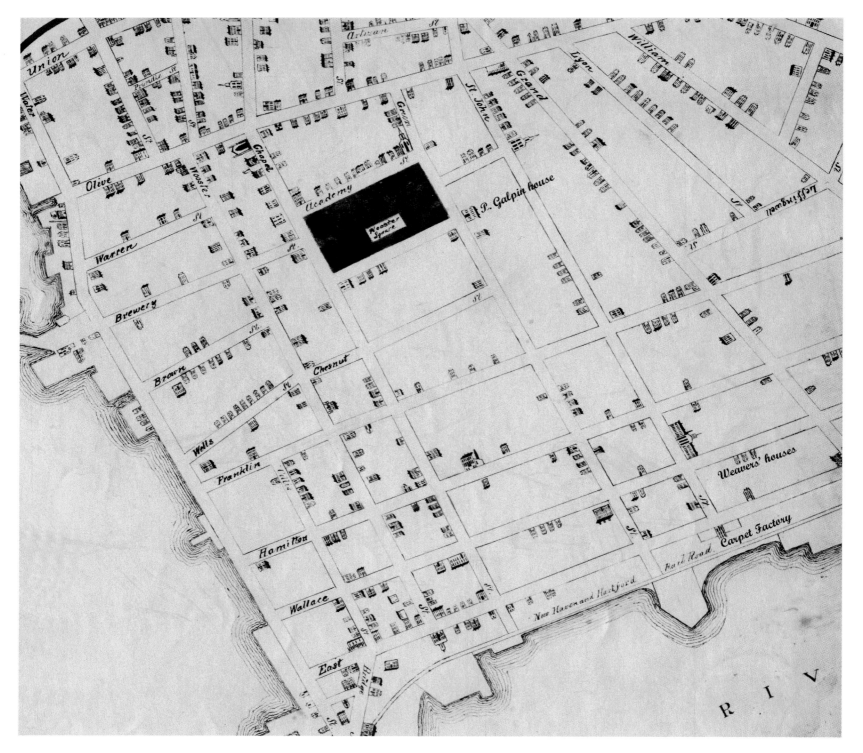

FIGURE 4. *The New Township area of New Haven as it appeared in 1847. The locations of the carpet factory, some of the weavers' houses and Philip Galpin's house have been added to this map.* (New Haven Colony Historical Society, with additions by Alan Haesche)

carpet factory,"[25] the partnership had been formed, the new factory built and, presumably, equipped with more looms than before—possibly as many as the thirty-eight recorded in 1842.[26] The factory must have been completed by July 1833, when the *New Haven Daily Herald* mentions it in an ongoing series about New Haven's scenery: "The New Township is the only designation we have for places as far distant as the carpet factory, the ax factory and the picturesque village springing up south of Barnesville."[27] The building remained the most northerly manufacturing site on East Street for over two decades. Only about an acre of land appears to have been used for the factory. The other land was used to build houses for the workers (figure 4).

The workers in the carpet factory, especially the skilled handloom weavers, were essential for creating a superior product. The looms they used were much more complicated than the ordinary household loom of the time: they interwove two or sometimes three layers of fabric, while also creating multicolored patterns more complex than just stripes or checks. While the workers in the early years of 1829–1833 are completely anonymous, the weavers employed from about the time Galpin built the new carpet factory are identifiable by name in records of land transactions and the early New Haven directories. Presumably many of them had already been working for Galpin. Most came from Scotland, as had weavers at other carpet factories in the region.[28] Scottish carpet weavers were viewed as a "new and most worthy class of artisans."[29] Unlike most overseas immigrants who later arrived in New Haven, the carpet weavers came not as young single men, but as mature, trained men with families. They had sufficient income to invest in business or dwellings and the foresight to plan for the future.

According to a later inventory, thirty-six of the carpet looms in the new factory were double looms for producing two-ply carpet, but only two were triple looms for making the more expensive three-ply carpet.[30] At an estimated $125 and $250 respectively, they accounted for $5000 of capital investment.[31] The dye house, the other major building located in the East Street carpet factory complex, contained kettles, pumps, wringers, soap, and dyestuffs for washing and dying wool. Other equipment included a turning lathe and tools and a blacksmith bellows and forge, probably used for making repairs. A six-horsepower steam engine built in New York powered "pumping and scouring" operations, and possibly also the forge bellows and the lathe.[32]

The 1842 factory inventory contains the entry "designs and cards for 220 patterns," which indicates a considerable degree of variety in the carpets offered by Galpin & Robertson.[33] It also listed 500 yards of carpet samples—certainly enough to represent a significant marketing effort. Although there is no record of an arrangement between Galpin & Robertson and any specific New York commission agent, they probably used either the New York auction houses or a commission agent for part of their sales. Packet sloops traveled from New Haven to New York three times a week, making it quite feasible to send carpets to New York. An alternative for distribution was with Robertson's father-in-law, Abraham Heaton, a shipping merchant with primary interests in Louisiana molasses. His ships made regular trips to Franklin and New Orleans in Louisiana. While the returning cargoes were usually molasses, the outbound cargoes consisted of variable "merchandise to order," when listed.[34] Given Robertson's personal connections both to Charleston and to Abraham Heaton and the markets developed in the South for other New Haven goods, such as carriages, it is likely that a portion of the carpets were sold through that channel.[35]

Because wool for carpets must be coarse, it was usually imported from less developed countries. In the 1830s and 1840s most of it came from South America and the Levant.[36] Galpin and Robertson apparently early identified the cost of wool as a problem for the business, as was apparent in the costs reported in 1832. They tried to remedy this by buying raw wool, cleaning it, and having it spun on a putting-out basis. In June 1834 they advertised:

> Employment for Females. Families where there are women and girls, who may wish employment at their own dwellings, may procure wool to have been hand picked, on application at the New Haven Carpet Factory. None need apply who cannot bring good recommendations for industry and honesty, from some person personally known to the subscriber.[37]

The longer-term solution was to card and spin yarn by machine. In April 1836 Galpin and Robertson paid $5000 for an eight-acre mill site including two mills, where the Cheshire Turnpike crossed the Mill River in Hamden. It was the closest available location with good waterpower.[38] They set up a carding and spinning mill, containing, according to the inventory in 1842, three sets of carding machines, three spinning jacks, and ancillary equipment.[39] The yarn produced at this mill was presumably carted down the turnpike to the main carpet factory in New Haven to supply weft for the thirty-eight looms worked by the Scottish carpet weavers. The inventory also showed worsted wool yarn, presumably for warp, but did not include equipment for processing worsted, so that would have still been purchased. Although their operations were separated geographically into two sites several miles apart, Galpin & Robertson now commanded an integrated process (except for the worsted) from raw wool to colorful woven carpet.[40]

New Haveners, as well as farther distant customers, bought carpets from Galpin & Robertson. Henry Huggins, New Haven dry goods and carpet merchant, advertised already in March 1833 that he had

> just received from the "New Haven Carpet Manufactory" an assortment of fine, double fine, super and double superfine Ingrain'd CARPETING, which, with those

previously received from New York, make the assortment more complete than can be found in this city. Purchasers are invited to call and examine them. Also Wilton and Brussels carpeting and rugs. No. 1 Central Row.[41]

S. Hughes & Sons, another dry goods and carpet dealer in New Haven, offered "70 pieces of imperial, extra fine and fine carpeting direct from the manufacturers" in May 1835.[42] While this does not say the manufacturer was Galpin & Robertson, an advertisement by Hughes the following March explicitly offered "New Haven Carpeting . . . 12 pieces New Haven carpeting, beautiful patterns—received and for sale by S. Hughes and Son."[43] The carpets were evidently viewed as equivalent to others available from New York merchants.

By estimating that each of their thirty-eight looms could be used to produce ten yards of carpet per day, we can calculate that the maximum possible production for Galpin & Robertson in a standard three hundred working-day year would have been 114,000 yards. While this is more than twice what Galpin reported producing in 1832, it was well below what their major domestic competitors were producing.[44] To put the production of Galpin & Robertson in broader perspective, it is necessary to look at the whole picture of carpet production and consumption in the United States. It has been estimated that the total domestic production of carpet in 1834 was 1,147,500 yards, 86 percent of which was ingrain carpet. Imported carpet averaged 616,000 yards per year for the years 1833–1835 and included ingrain.[45]

Thus Galpin & Robertson, with a product consisting primarily of two-ply ingrain, competed both with other domestic manufacturers and with the imports. Assuming, instead of maximum possible output, a more modest increase of 40 percent over their reported 1832 output, Galpin & Robertson would have produced about 70,000 yards of carpet in 1834, accounting for a respectable 6 percent of the whole domestic market for carpet, and perhaps as much as 7 percent of the domestic ingrain market, although less than their Connecticut competitors in Tariffville and Enfield.

The optimism with which Galpin and Robertson began their partnership is reflected in their personal investment in new dwellings on Wooster Square. In 1833 each built a double house on lots diagonally opposite each other.[46] They appear to have been the first manufacturers to settle on the square and the first to live in a neighborhood designed to be only residential. Other New Haven manufacturers in the New Township, including carriage-makers James Brewster, Solomon Collis, and Isaac Mix, lived close to their factories in what we would describe today as "mixed-use" neighborhoods. Most of the other early owners around Wooster Square were merchants such as Jonathan Nicholson, who owned a

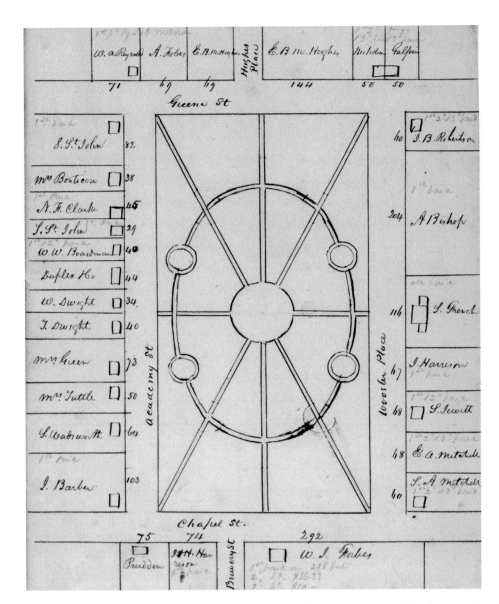

wholesale grocery business, and E. B. M. Hughes, who owned the largest hardware business in the city. Other early residents included Joseph Barber, owner of the *Columbian Register*, Samuel Wadsworth, one of the original organizers of the square, and Hannah Greene, widow of Daniel Greene, Captain of the *Neptune*.[47]

Galpin proved to be especially civic-minded, as the person most responsible for the beautification of Wooster Square. A small manuscript map (figure 5) provides a proposed plan for its improvement, along with assessments for each property owner for the years 1834–1838. The assessments show the need to replace trees several times and mention that maintenance of the square was paid for by the hay crop harvested each year.[48] Galpin was credited with the design of the fine fence that still surrounds Wooster Square, for which he persuaded the city to allot $4000 for construction and then supervised the work.[49] Both Galpin and Robertson were active members of Saint Paul's Chapel, a mission of Trinity Episcopal Church located near Wooster Square. During 1833 and 1834, Philip Galpin also served as the president of the New Haven Musical Society.[50]

Some of the carpet weavers also made a priority of investing in their homes. Weaver Archibald Leishman purchased his first piece of property from Ira Atwater in 1838, a lot with a dwelling house on Governeurs Lane.[51] Other weavers bought or leased property from Philip Galpin. Weavers Charles McGill, Charles Dawsett, and John Breckinridge acquired lots 40 feet by 130 feet on Wallace Street, each with a dwelling house, agreeing on 16 March 1839 to pay Galpin $120 a year for two years, with interest.[52] Weaver Hugh Brown apparently leased a house from Philip Galpin before buying it in 1839; it was on the south side of Grand Street, east of East Street, adjacent to the carpet factory.[53] Still other weavers rented houses from Philip Galpin that he had built on his property on both sides of East Street between the carpet factory and Grand Street.

In addition to investing in housing, Scottish carpet weavers seem to have collaborated in business ventures beyond Galpin & Robertson. The first record of these ventures occurred in 1836 when William Mix sold a quarter-acre piece of land with a building to a group of twenty Scottish carpet weavers.[54] It was located on Water Street, next to the Canal Basin, very close to the early carpet factory property.[55] It is possible that this was merely a joint real estate investment, but more likely that the weavers were setting up a small business of their own. Other financial transactions identify weavers acting as a group: when dry goods merchant Henry Huggins, suffering from the business panic of 1837, had trouble paying debts, four of the weavers—James W. Mitchell, David Daw, Archibald Leishman and Samuel Cleeton—loaned him $500 in March 1838, accepting a piece of property on Hancock Street as collateral until he repaid it.[56] Either the four had sold goods to Henry Huggins for which he owed them $500 or they had enough money to invest in helping Henry Huggins meet his debts. (As Henry Huggins owed payment to Galpin & Robertson for carpets, this aid could have been a prudent move on the part of the weavers.)

Collecting from their customers and getting a high-enough price to cover costs must have been a persistent problem for Galpin & Robertson even in good times, but good times ended. When President Jackson began in late 1833 to divert public funds from the Second Bank of the United States, sending shock waves through the country's banking system, Galpin was on a local businessmen's committee protesting to Congress "the unprecedented pressure in the money market."[57] The neighboring axe factory, for instance, "could not endure the financial storm which followed the removal of the public deposits from the United States Bank."[58] The subsequent bank panic of 1837 made financial survival difficult for many businesses. Retailer Henry Huggins became indebted in 1837 to a number of suppliers, among them Galpin & Robertson, to whom he mortgaged his own house in April.[59] He was declared an insolvent debtor in June; apparently he sufficiently covered his debts by January 1838 (when Galpin & Robertson transferred his property back to him),[60] but in March he had to borrow from four of the weavers, as mentioned above.

Though not all of their customers were in so much financial trouble as Henry Huggins, the panic of 1837 did produce a cash shortage for Galpin & Robertson, as it did for many manufacturers. While their debtors mortgaged property and even household furniture to Galpin & Robertson, in order to postpone paying cash, they in turn obtained cash by mortgaging the carpet factory that April and the spinning mill in July of that year, for $8000 from merchant William Bell in Charleston, South Carolina, and $3000 from the New Haven County Bank.[61] In 1839 they even mortgaged their thirty-six two-ply looms to John Rossiter, a farmer in Clinton, for $1250.[62]

Another problem, perhaps even more vexing than slow payment by customers, was the declining price of carpets, not only because of the general depression, but also in the longer run because of the greater availability and popularity of domestic Brussels and three-ply ingrain carpets. As the finer carpets became more available, the two-ply ingrain that was the bulk of Galpin & Robertson's business grew less desirable, and therefore no longer commanded a premium price. For instance, Henry A. Chittenden advertised a new carpet store in October 1841 with common ingrain carpeting for $0.58 a yard and better ingrain at $0.62½ per yard—a great reduction from the $1.00 a yard that Philip Galpin had reported receiving in 1832.[63] With only two looms to make the higher priced Imperial, or three-ply, carpet and no investment in making the cheaper Venetian, or cotton, ingrain carpeting, Galpin & Robertson were at a distinct disadvantage in the late-1830s marketplace. With little ability to reduce costs, they were not in a position to absorb price reductions.

The combined effect of the credit crunch of the late 1830s and the price reductions of ingrain carpet caused the failure of Galpin & Robertson on 3 March 1842.[64] Even though they were designated "insolvent debtors," Philip Galpin and John Robertson were appointed as agents for sale and disposal of the assets of their bankrupt partnership.[65] They transferred the factory property to William Bell of Charleston, South Carolina, to cover his $8000 mortgage.[66] They sold some of the East Street property to James Donaghe, Leverett Candee, and others for $3000 on the same day they were declared insolvent, presumably to repay the mortgage to the New Haven County Bank.

Candee, who had just failed in the papermaking business, began the manufacture of elastic suspenders in "a carpet factory on East Street." Later in the same year he received a temporary license from Charles Goodyear to use his vulcanization process in the manufacture of rubber shoes. Candee acquired more capital from Henry and Lucius Hotchkiss and began operations. It is not clear if he rented part of the main carpet factory for this endeavor or used another building that was on the land he had purchased. In either case, he was the first person to manufacture rubber overshoes under the Goodyear patents.[67] In 1843, Galpin and Robertson sold the spinning mill to Leverett Candee and Timothy Lester,[68] where the manufacture of rubber overshoes was continued and increased.

It is not certain that any carpet manufacture continued in the factory after 1842. Philip Galpin was clearly not involved with the manufacturing after the failure of the business. Atwater states that John Robertson continued in the business until 1849, when he turned it over to his foreman, whom Atwater dubiously names as Daniel Mitchell, a name unknown as weaver in New Haven.[69] Whether or not Atwater is correct, the number of carpet weavers in New Haven decreased after 1842, indicating at least a severe curtailment in the business.[70] Meanwhile, the two Connecticut competitors, already larger, merged in 1840, continued to expand their capacity far beyond the thirty-eight looms of New Haven's carpet manufacturing company, added production of other kinds of carpet that required different looms, and toward the end of the decade began installing the recently invented Bigelow power looms.[71]

What became of the owners and workers in New Haven's short-lived carpet factory? Philip Galpin was elected mayor of New Haven in June 1842, shortly after the bankruptcy of Galpin & Robertson. In 1844, he was instrumental in organizing the Mutual Security Insurance Company of New Haven, serving as its secretary almost until his death in 1872. He was again elected mayor in 1856, serving until 1860. During his second term as mayor he was responsible for spearheading the revision of the city charter, persuaded the railroad to replace an unsightly and unsafe wooden bridge over the railroad at Chapel Street with a sturdy and handsome iron one, and acquired land for the first city hall. He served on the committee to plan the city hall until the construction was under way.[72] He regained title to the Greene Street property and continued to live there. After Ann Galpin died in 1856, Philip married Sarah Hull of Waterbury.

John Robertson, a representative to the state legislature in 1841, was clerk of the probate court of New Haven in 1843. He became postmaster in 1849, serving in that capacity until 1853.[73] In the 1850s John and Maria moved to a new and grander house given to them by her father, Abraham Heaton, next door to Heaton's on Temple Street. They had six children, one of whom became a judge and candidate for governor. John Robertson served as mayor of New Haven from 1881 until 1883 and died in 1892.

While they did not become prominent in civic affairs, the weavers recovered in various ways from the demise of the carpet factory. Some continued weaving carpet: New Haven produced 10,200 yards of it in 1845, one-fifth of Galpin's 1832 output;[74] others engaged in different activities. James W. Mitchell, after acquiring three pieces of property to settle the $1508.54 debt he was owed by Galpin & Robertson,[75] parlayed several real estate transactions in the New Township into a handsome profit and in 1845 moved to Yonkers, New York, where there was a carpet factory. In contrast, Hugh Brown continued until 1851 to live, listed as a weaver, at the property he had purchased from Philip Galpin in 1839. During the early 1850s he lived and worked on Clinton Place as a coach-lace weaver.[76] In 1854 he purchased a lot on Home Street,[77] where he built a home and conducted his weaving business. By 1866 Brown was weaving rag carpet.[78] The land records show that he was able to upgrade his real estate modestly through the years, that he paid off his mortgages, and never needed to mortgage his weaving equipment.

Samuel Cleeton, unique among the carpet weavers in having come from England instead of Scotland, had married Phoebe Seeley of New Haven in 1836.[79] In 1840 he was one of the few carpet weavers who did not live in the immediate vicinity of the carpet factory, living instead at his mother-in-law's boardinghouse on Wooster Street.[80] The failure of the carpet factory caused some hardship to the Cleeton family.[81] He is listed as a carpet weaver in the city directory through 1844; by the 1850s, however, his profession is given as pie baker in the birth records of several of his children.[82] After living at several addresses on Wallace Street, he moved to Elm Street, where he died in 1892 at the age of seventy-eight.[83]

David Maud, James Craig, John Cunningham, Charles McGill, James Cunningham, and David Galt identified themselves as carpet weavers through 1850. After this period, most of the weavers are identified as coach-lace weavers, indicating that, like Hugh Brown, they had decided to migrate to that growing industry, accessory to New Haven's carriage industry.

Archibald Leishman (1789–1872) remained in the traditional carpet-weaving business the longest of the New Haven weavers, as an indirect small successor to Galpin & Robertson. By 1846, Archibald leased a shop at 97 East Street from Burr Andrews (who had bought the old carpet factory from William Bell),[84] and purchased another house and lot on St. John Street from James W. Mitchell.[85] The eight looms and warping and dyeing equipment for carpet manufacture that he mortgaged to Burr Andrews for $1700 in April 1848,[86] were probably a portion of the former Galpin & Robertson equipment. From the description of the inventory for the mortgage, it is clear that Leishman was weaving wool, and perhaps cotton, ingrain carpet. It is possible he employed the seven persons whose output of 10,200 yards of carpet was reported in 1845.[87] It is probable he was in the wholesale business, for there are no surviving retail advertisements. In 1857, Leishman purchased the buildings and lot at 170 East Street (later renumbered to 356 East Street) for $800[88] and moved the carpet-weaving business to this address. With occasional financial help from his daughters, Leishman managed to retain ownership of the three properties and continue to earn a living as a carpet weaver.[89] It is not clear when Leishman began to weave rag carpet, for which an advertisement by William Elder in 1873 states that he is successor to A. Leishman.[90]

While the New Haven Carpet Manufacturing Company failed after only a dozen years of existence, it left in New Haven a small lasting legacy of carpet manufacturing skills that ended only in the 1880s with the gradual dying out of rag carpet manufacture. No one had become wealthy from this enterprise, but neither was anyone ruined. The factory buildings and housing built for and by the carpet weavers contributed to the development of the New Township and set the stage for the next round of enterprises (primarily the manufacture of rubber goods and carriages) in New Haven's industrial era.

NOTES

1. Doris B. Townshend, *The Streets of New Haven: The Origin of Their Names* (New Haven: New Haven Colony Historical Society, 1984), 148. Townshend remarks that Benedict Arnold had lived on Water Street.
2. Edward E. Atwater, *History of the City of New Haven* (New York: Munsell, 1887), 535 and 556.
3. Atwater, 533. New Havener Abel Buell, William McIntosh of Scotland, and some New York City capitalists established the cotton mill.
4. Timothy Dwight, *A Statistical Account of the City of New Haven* (New Haven: Connecticut Academy of Arts and Sciences, 1811), 37 and 39–40.
5. This list comprises those manufactures that persisted over a span of thirty-four years before and after 1830. They are listed for New Haven both in Dwight, 39–40 and in Daniel P. Tyler, comp., *Statistics of the Condition and Products of Certain Branches of Industry in Connecticut, for the Year Ending October 1, 1845* (Hartford, Conn.: John L. Boswell, State Printer, 1846), 38–41. The list is of course not comprehensive for either year. The McLane Report of 1832 also lists ten manufactures, all of which are included in these 1811 and 1845 lists, except for a curious combination of "razor strap and marble." Louis McLane, comp., *Documents Relative to the Manufactures in the United States Collected and Transmitted to the House of Representatives in Compliance with a Resolution of January 19, 1832*, by the Secretary of the Treasury. House Executive Document No. 308. 22nd Cong., 1st Sess. Washington, D.C. 1833 (reprint, New York: Burt Franklin, 1969), vol. 2, doc. 9, #31, p. 1033.

6. In 1838 eleven steam engines were listed for New Haven by Levi Woodbury, "Letter from the Secretary of the Treasury, Transmitting in Obedience to a Resolution of the House of the 29th of June Last, Information in Relation to Steam Engines," House Document No. 21, 25th Congress, 3d sess. (Washington, D.C.: 1838), 66. Eight were ten-, eight-, or six-horsepower engines.

7. New Haven Land Records, 75:495. The block including Galpin's factory at 129 and 131 Chapel Street was home to several dry-goods stores.

8. New Haven Land Records, 75:506. This piece of land, about 90 feet by 300 feet, was located on the south side of Water Street. The building was described as a store; a term used to describe both warehouses and retail establishments. Atwater (556) states that the factory was located on Water Street from the start, seemingly unaware of its beginning on Chapel Street.

9. Brewster's estate had formerly been owned by sea captain and merchant Daniel Greene. Arnold Guyot Dana Scrapbook Collection, 56:51, unpublished scrapbook collection at the New Haven Colony Historical Society.

10. On his way to Hartford the next day, Jackson visited the Whitney gun factory at Mill Rock. Rollin G. Osterweis, *Three Centuries of New Haven, 1638–1938* (New Haven: Yale University Press, 1953), 308.

11. Philip was the only child of Benjamin Galpin and Nancy Smith Galpin, born 12 October 1795. William Freeman Galpin, *The Galpin Family in America* (Syracuse, N.Y., 1955), 57.

12. New Haven Land Records, 70:93 and 467.

13. New Haven Land Records, 69:324.

14. *New Haven City Year Book, 1864–65* (New Haven, 1865), 98–99.

15. The 1824 Tariff Act imposed a duty of 50 cents per square yard on Brussels, Turkey, and Wilton carpets and 25 cents per yard on Venetian and ingrain carpets. In 1828, the rates went up to 70 cents for Brussels and 40 cents for Venetian and ingrain. While the tariff of 1832 reduced these somewhat to 67 cents for Brussels and three-ply ingrain and 35 cents for Venetian and two-ply ingrain, the terms were still favorable. Arthur H. Cole, *The American Carpet Manufacture: A History and Analysis* (Cambridge, Mass., 1941), 21.

16. John S. Ewing and Nancy P. Norton, *Broadlooms and Businessmen: A History of the Bigelow-Sanford Carpet Company* (Cambridge, Mass., 1955), 35 and 37.

17. To put this in perspective, James Brewster's carriage factory, the largest of the establishments in the New Township at that time, employed one hundred men. See Brewster, *An Address Delivered at Brewster's Hall January 28, 1857: to the Young Men of New Haven, Connecticut* (New York: I. J. Oliver, 1857).

18. McLane Report, 2:930–931.

19. The Tariffville Manufacturing Company in Simsbury and Andrews, Thomson & Co. in Enfield were joint stock corporations chartered by the state of Connecticut and capitalized at $123,000 and $145,000, respectively. The factories in Enfield and Tariffville paid 32 cents and 27 cents per pound of wool, respectively. The wholesale price for common wool in New York City was 27½ cents in 1832. Elizabeth Hitz, *A Technical and Business Revolution: American Woolens to 1832* (New York, 1986), 393.

20. The Enfield company used only 1.38 pounds per yard, partly because it was also making cheaper carpets. Tariffville used 2.08 pounds per yard, comparable to Galpin's two pounds per yard.

21. If Galpin's employees worked full-time, which is likely for the men, but less so for the women and children, his labor cost for three hundred workdays per year would have been $8,790. His rent for the Chapel Street and Water Street locations was $300 per year, and he would have been paying for coal and possibly freight on the finished carpets.

22. New Haven Land Records, 82:150–152. In the 1840 *New Haven Directory* the address of the carpet factory is 81 East Street.

23. *Obituary Record of Graduates of Yale University deceased from June, 1890–June, 1900* (New Haven, 1900), 146.

24. *New Haven Daily Herald*, vol. 8, no. 28, 2:3.

25. New Haven Land Records, 83:273.

26. The inventory made in 1842 during bankruptcy proceedings showed thirty-six two-ply looms and two three-ply looms. New Haven Land Records, 104:299.

27. *New Haven Daily Herald*, vol. 1, no. 197, 1:3. On the 1830 Buckingham map of New Haven, the area north of Grand Street (now Avenue) where East Street was planned to continue but not yet cut through, was called Barnesville. See also the glossary compiled by Henry H. Townshend (Osterweis, 485).

28. Cole, 13. New Haven Land Records, 101:26–29.

29. Dana Scrapbooks, 143:31.

30. Details of the carpet factory are preserved in the inventory of 1842. This probably represents the equipment for most of the period between 1833 and 1842. The weaving equipment consisted of: 2 three-ply looms, 36 two-ply looms, 1 warping mill, 9 wheels, 9 swifts, 50 dozen shuttles, 50 dozen warping spools, and 500 dozen shuttle bobbins. New Haven Land Records, 104:299.

31. A similar inventory for the Thompsonville (Enfield) factory in 1846 gives these values for the two- and three-ply looms. Ewing and Norton, 41.

32. Pumping was necessary to obtain water—whether from a well or the Mill River—for "scouring," or cleaning, the raw wool. The steam engine was built by the Novelty Works in New York City and was five years old in 1838, so it was new when the carpet factory was built. Levi Woodbury, "Letter from the Secretary of the Treasury, Transmitting in Obedience to a Resolution of the House of the 29th of June Last, Information in Relation to Steam Engines," House Document No. 21, 25th Cong., 3d sess. (Washington, D.C.: 1838), p. 66.

33. Although the carpet looms were not Jacquard looms, they also used perforated "cards" to program the actions that created different patterns during weaving.

34. *New Haven Daily Herald*, 7, no. 142, 2:4.

35. Cargoes insured by the New Haven Insurance Company prior to 1832 included such items as clocks, weights, carriages, shoes, and hats going primarily to southern ports such as Mobile, Charleston, Savanna, and New Orleans. Index of the records of the New Haven Insurance Company, New Haven Colony Historical Society, cargoes. The New Haven Insurance Company ceased insuring vessels in 1831.

36. Cole, 21. The only record of Galpin & Robertson receiving wool comes in a weekly maritime report stating that the schooner Lexington had arrived from Boston on 24 November 1835 with wool for Galpin & Robertson, and departed for New York the next day. *New Haven Daily Herald*, 3, nos. 276 and 277, 3:1 and 2:4. It is probable that other shipments of wool arrived under the ubiquitous entry "merchandize to order."

37. *New Haven Daily Record*, 2, 2:4.

38. Eli Whitney's mill site on the Mill River was closer to New Haven, but already occupied. Galpin and Robertson's purchase farther up the river included the right to raise the dam one foot for more power. They also bought a nearby piece of property with a dwelling house for seven hundred dollars. Galpin owned two-thirds of these properties and Robertson one-third. Hamden Town Records, 18:21 and 24.

39. Besides the carding and spinning machines, the mill contained two reels, one picker, one waste cleaner, and one emery cylinder and frame. It was heated by two stoves with pipes.

40. A detailed inventory of equipment at both locations is in New Haven Land Records, 104:299. The inventory was made at the time of bankruptcy proceedings in 1842.

41. This advertisement gives us the most precise definition of the carpets produced by Galpin

& Robertson: four qualities of two-ply ingrain. Moreover, it provides a strong indication that three-ply looms were not yet in operation at their factory. *New Haven Daily Herald*, 1, no. 89, 3:3.

42. *New Haven Daily Herald*, 3, no. 102, 4:2.

43. *New Haven Daily Herald*, 4, no. 72, 3:1.

44. An output of 114,000 yards was already matched by Tariffville and surpassed by Thompsonville in Enfield (180,000 yards) in 1832. McLane Report, 1:981.

45. Cole, 31 and 44.

46. Philip Galpin's lot was on Greene Street, opposite Wooster Place. New Haven Land Records, 82:247. John Robertson's lot was on Wooster Place. New Haven Land Records, 83:272.

47. See Philip Galpin's plan of the square for the complete list of residents and the 1840 *New Haven City Directory* for their occupations.

48. Manuscript in the New Haven Colony Historical Society Library, "P. S. Galpin" on cover.

49. *City of New Haven—1864 Address of the Mayor and Annual Reports* (New Haven, 1864), 98.

50. *New Haven Daily Herald*, 1, no. 171, 2:1.

51. Ira Atwater was a builder and sash and blind manufacturer whose manufactory was on Water Street. Governeur's Lane was a street connecting Bradley and Franklin streets, above William Street. *Patten's New Haven Directory,* 1844–45; pp. 5 and 15. It no longer exists.

52. New Haven Land Records, 99:378. The buyers must have made substantial down payments, as Galpin had paid $720 for the land alone.

53. New Haven Land Records, 87:496; 99:445.

54. Isaac Davis, Joseph Clayton, Hugh Brown, Robert B. Wilson, John Cunningham, James Cunningham, David Galt, Patrick Joyce, Robert Maud, Patrick McNulty, John M. Wilson, John Flood, John Price, William H. Hoyt, John L. Sperry, John L. Mitchell, John McLean, Thomas Clinton, John Fisher, and William W. Polk.

55. New Haven Land Records, 92:317. The building had been used as a boat shop and was being used as a cooper's shop at the time of sale.

56. New Haven Land Records, 96:117, 94:515.

57. Osterweis, 295, citing the *Connecticut Journal*, 4, 11, and 18 February 1834.

58. Atwater, 535.

59. The mortgage of April 1837 covered a promissory note to Galpin & Robertson for $925.88. New Haven Land Records, 92:538.

60. *New Haven Daily Herald*, 5, no. 169, 2:4. New Haven Land Records, 94:374.

61. The manufactory, dye house and all other buildings on the East Street property were mortgaged to William Bell on 29 April 1837, with the principal due on 17 February 1839. New Haven Land Records, 96:13. The spinning mill was mortgaged to the New Haven County Bank in July 1837. Hamden Land Records, 18:225.

62. New Haven Land Records, 101:24.

63. *New Haven Weekly Palladium*, 12, no. 51, 4:3. While this ad does not refer directly to Galpin & Robertson carpets, it tells us what the retail prices were that they faced.

64. Abraham Heaton (Robertson's father-in-law) and Caleb Mix were assigned to take over the assets of the company, which included the factory on East Street, the spinning factory in Hamden and Philip Galpin's and John Robertson's dwelling houses. New Haven Land Records, 104:299.

65. *New Haven Weekly Palladium*, 13, no. 22, 3:7.

66. New Haven Land Records, 108:456.

67. Atwater, 591.

68. Hamden Land Records, 21:160.

69. Atwater, 556. The only Daniel Mitchell in New Haven at that time was a mason, living in West-ville. New Haven Vital Records, 12:173.

70. *Patten's New Haven Directory*, 1840–44.

71. The Thompsonville company, which bought the Tariffville factory in 1840, had 50 three-ply looms, 78 two-ply looms and 40 Brussels looms, plus numerous chenille and Venetian looms by 1846. The installation of power looms, to meet competition from the Lowell Manufacturing Co., took four years and more than $350,000 between decision in 1847 and actuality in 1851. Ewing and Norton, 41–44.

72. Dana Scrapbooks, 29:21.

73. Atwater, 379. Dana Scrapbooks, 48:30–31.

74. Tyler, 38. The 10,200 yards, valued at $6,930, were produced by five men and two women. It is uncertain whether these were employed at one small manufactory or operating separately.

75. New Haven Land Records, 106:37–38.

76. *Benham's New Haven Directory*, 1850–1854. Coach lace is the trim used on carriage upholstery and interiors.

77. New Haven Land Records, 154:399.

78. *Benham's New Haven Directory* [J. H. Benham, New Haven, 1866], pp. 103 and 251.

79. New Haven Vital Records, 4:171.

80. Dana Scrapbooks, 63:6.

81. Cleeton mortgaged his household furniture to Daniel Moore in May 1842. New Haven Land Records, 104:368.

82. New Haven Vital Records, 9:130 and 239.

83. New Haven Vital Records, 29:35.

84. New Haven Land Records, 119:32.

85. New Haven Land Records, 118:417.

86. The equipment included eight carpet looms with appurtenances, four copper boilers, one warp-ing mill, 1,200 yards of carpeting valued at sixty cents per yard, 800 pounds of worsted yarn at fifty cents per pound, 2,000 pounds of woolen yarn at thirty cents per pound and 500 pounds of cotton yarn at eighteen cents per pound. New Haven Land Records, 122:479.

87. Tyler, 1845; see note 74.

88. New Haven Land Records, 169:306.

89. At one point Leishman mortgaged the household furniture to his daughter Elizabeth for $106. New Haven Land Records, 105:270. At another time daughters Christiana and Margaret, who were working in Lowell, Massachusetts, paid off a $250 note for their father. New Haven Land Records, 114:179.

90. *New Haven County Directory for the Year Commencing 1873* (Boston: Briggs and Company, 1873), 13. See also William Elder's advertisement in the 1877 *New Haven City Directory*, 385.

PRESTON MAYNARD

Saving New Haven's Industrial Heritage

Old industrial buildings and sites exist throughout New Haven, yet their future is very uncertain. Some have been brought back to new uses but many have a sad, neglected quality about them, one that speaks to years of underuse and decay. Many younger residents do not realize the dominant role that these factories, warehouses, docks, and rail yards played in the economic and cultural life of the community. There remain however, older New Haveners who remember leaving the company gate from nationally recognized manufacturers such as the Sargent Hardware Company, the New Haven Clock Company, and the Winchester Repeating Arms Company. These workers walked shoulder to shoulder with hundreds of other workers, often to homes in neighborhoods a short distance from the factory.[1] Older residents remember New Haven's important role as a producer of cigars, corsets, hardware, guns, rubber products, paper boxes, metal wire, clocks, toy trains and erector sets, and more, and the thriving economy that manufacturing provided for them. Still other residents remember the bustling wharves and busy rail yards that lined the waterfront and riverbanks from where New Haven's diverse products were shipped the world over.

In this regard New Haven's past is similar to many cities in the Northeast, be it Worcester, Waterbury, Paterson, or Providence. These places grew quickly as manufacturing took hold in the mid-nineteenth century. They grew in population, in physical development, and in civic wealth and social standing. Yet their decline was almost as precipitous. Industries lost ground to competition. Residents lost jobs and left the city for more profitable locations.

Some of these cities, like New Haven, have reinvented themselves. Others struggle with the stigma of dying industry, blighted buildings and neighborhoods, and endemic poverty. Yet all these places have important buildings and sites that tell the story of America's industrial revolution. Many of these neglected buildings could be reused as centers of new economic activity, with new businesses creating jobs, providing goods and services, and generating tax revenues.

The future viability of many industrial buildings and sites in New Haven is very much in question. Without community intervention, there will be little to remind the public of the role these sites played in the development of Connecticut. Important buildings have already been lost, most notably the Eli Whitney gun factory at Lake Whitney, the Sargent Hardware factory, and the Brewster Carriage Company buildings. Other industrial sites are slated for demolition, including portions of the Winchester Repeating Arms complex and the W. & E. T. Fitch Hardware Company site. Still others, like the Bigelow Boiler Company and New Haven Clock Company, are in such poor condition that without some attention, they will deteriorate beyond repair.

What do these industrial buildings mean to us? What role can they play in this postindustrial era? Should they fall? Or can we reuse these structures in economically viable projects that bring new life to neighborhoods and the community?

New Haven has a rich and impressive architectural legacy. The post-and-beam frame houses that face the New Haven Green remind us of our colonial origins. The large brick and stucco Italian villas bordering Wooster Square speak to the wealth of New Haven as a mercantile city.[2] The historic factory and warehouse buildings that remain in New Haven remind us of the important role New Haven played as a manufacturing center.[3] These surviving structures are material symbols of the vivid yet untold story of industrialization in America. They reveal how the short-term rapid growth of industry shaped our concept of the city, be it New Haven or other northeastern centers. We are reminded of the ingenuity that led to inventions and technological changes, the diversity of businesses, the drama of commerce, and the chaotic and sometimes brutal social conditions that workers faced during this period. Beyond their association with the past, these sites create an irreplaceable urban-industrial context; a sense of place that is quickly disappearing in New England.

A good example of this is River Street, an industrial district in the Fair Haven section of New Haven (figure 1). This stark streetscape, complete with abandoned rail line and gritty brick and wooden factory buildings, is listed on the National Register of Historic Places. The New Haven Clock Company on Hamilton Street and the former Marlin Firearms plant at 85 Willow Street also evoke this power of place and association.

Industrial buildings, like those mentioned above, were located in the center of neighborhoods and the industries they housed were the lifeblood of the local

FIGURE I. *River Street in Fair Haven.* (Photo by Preston
Maynard)

economy. Industrial buildings were not attractive or romantic buildings in their day. Their tall smokestacks, noisy engine rooms, and machinery-filled workspaces were utilitarian structures and spaces built to facilitate production. As new technologies developed, spaces and layouts changed to meet the new requirements. If a complex was outdated, sections might be demolished for a new building. Some buildings were expanded and still others were adapted to new industries and uses over time.

No site demonstrates this better than the former Bigelow Boiler Company complex on River Street. This complex is made up of a succession of buildings, built from 1873 through 1930.[4] The earliest portions are brick and stone, the later glass and steel. The complex is a beehive of shapes and spaces, some dark and gloomy, others light and open. The River Street portion of the building is a typical nineteenth-century mill structure: the brick facade set close to the street rises three stories. The most unusual features in this facade are the large horseshoe-arch openings from which round boilers could be shipped from the plant. The use of materials is important too: brick and stone were used in the nineteenth century mill structure facing River Street, glass and steel in the early-twentieth-century additions at the back of the plant. All of these elements create an architectural ensemble rich in textures, materials, and associations.

The New Haven Clock Company mill complex is one of the largest of its kind remaining in the city. Started in the 1860s and expanded for almost sixty years, the multistory mill occupies nearly an entire block between Hamilton and Wallace Streets, connected around a large open courtyard.[5] The New Haven Clock Company is a site of great architectural and historical significance. It is only partially occupied and much of the complex is in poor condition. Its location next to the interstate, however, makes it an attractive site for renovation and adaptive reuse.

English Station, an electric power plant on Grand Avenue, is another complex built over several decades and is worthy of preservation. The original 1930s structure occupies a spectacular site in the middle of the Mill River.[6] The building has a medieval look with its massive brick and concrete facade and towering smokestacks. Although still capable of generating electricity, the day will come when a new use will be required that is more compatible with the surrounding neighborhood: perhaps a new housing development or a mixed-use facility with retail, office, and residential uses.

Adaptive Reuse and the Market Advantages of Old Buildings

Can older industrial buildings be brought back as centers of employment, commerce, and economic activity? Can they be rewoven into the fabric of their neighborhoods and the city too? Is there a prescribed method for redevelopment and reuse for these important, yet neglected structures? The answers are not simple, and depend on many factors. Two important ones are the location and condition of the property. It takes a creative developer to configure a successful redevelopment strategy involving these particular historic structures. An analysis of the structure, the site, and interior spaces as well as environmental issues, market factors, and financing need to be carefully evaluated. In other New England cities such as Providence and Lowell, creative property owners have redeveloped these structures in ways that create economic vitality and urban design synergy with their surroundings.

There are many advantages of reusing old industrial buildings, advantages not found in new construction. The rehabilitation of these structures offers a finished product that is very different from typical commercial buildings.[7] The unusual settings, unique spaces, and textures can attract tenants who do not want cookie-cutter commercial spaces. A former mill or foundry or brewery building can be reused to create new spaces that impress clients and motivate employees. These structures also make wonderful settings for artists' studios, professional offices, retail galleries, and restaurants.

Historic industrial buildings were built of durable and attractive materials, creating another advantage when brought back to new use. Walls were often constructed of load-bearing masonry supporting massive floor joists and roof trusses. Large wood or cast-iron columns were spaced at regular intervals to create work areas for machinery and equipment. Tall windows allowed light and ventilation into the workspaces. Later, steel and concrete columns were used to support still heavier equipment and material loads. These architectural elements can be featured in new offices or apartments.

Another advantage of reusing industrial buildings is an economic one: when divided into small work areas with inexpensive rents they are well suited as places to incubate new businesses. Woodworking and metal shops, artists' and design studios, furniture dealers and fulfillment companies all need flexible and inexpensive space. The interior floor areas can be modified and expanded to meet the needs of a growing business. This type of arrangement offers an advantage for the property owner: it is less of a financial risk to have many small tenants rather than one large one. New Haven has several successful buildings used in this way, including the former Marlin Firearms Company at 85 Willow Street, which houses numerous offices and studios of architects, designers, and artists. The former A. C. Gilbert Company building located at 315 Peck Street houses designers, artists, offices, and other small businesses. The small companies in these buildings employ hundreds of workers and add substantially to the city's tax base.

A second economic advantage is that historic rehabilitation is often less expensive than construction of a new building of comparable size and quality. Historic rehabilitation, although more labor-intensive, requires fewer materials. When the expense of demolition and subsequent cost of removing debris are factored into a project, the cost savings of rehabilitation are more significant.[8] In a historic urban setting like New Haven, rehabilitation will often garner public support and subsequent regulatory approvals faster than trying to win approval for demolition followed by new construction. Environmental remediation can add considerable expense to a rehabilitation project, however. Pollutants associated with previous use of a site have to be cleaned up whether new construction or rehabilitation. There are now loans and grants from the State of Connecticut and the federal government to help finance this clean-up.

Industrial buildings were traditionally constructed near the waterfront or near rail lines where raw materials could be delivered and finished products shipped to distant markets. These waterfront and rail locations were critical in the nineteenth century, but are less important today. Shipping has moved from the rail yard to highway. Industrial development has moved from urban locations to more spacious suburban settings. Small towns near a highway compete with urban areas for a limited number of manufacturing plants. Some former industrial sites in New Haven, like the Marlin Firearms complex on 85 Willow Street and the Seamless Rubber Company at One Long Wharf Drive, were successfully converted to new uses because of their proximity to the interstate highway. Other underutilized sites, such as the New Haven Clock Company, could use their proximity to the highway as a factor in attracting new businesses. These in-town locations provide a competitive advantage for companies searching for a strategic location for warehousing, distribution, or light industrial uses.

A waterfront location can be a very compelling amenity when the new use of the property is for a residential or retail project. Many historic industrial sites in New Haven are located near a river or the harbor. The former Quinnipiac Brewery on the corner of Chapel and Ferry Streets demonstrates the advantages of a waterfront location for residential uses. The Eli Whitney Museum, situated in a former factory building on Whitney Avenue, is dramatic because it is adjacent to Whitney Falls, the Mill River, and East Rock Park. Waterfront access and views can enhance the design and marketability of a reuse project.

Some former industrial buildings have site-specific advantages. The Strouse, Adler factory is in a prime location between downtown and the Wooster Square neighborhood. Part of this building was recently converted to up-scale housing. The C. Cowles and Company building on Water Street and other industrial buildings located on Chapel Street are on the edges of the Historic Wooster Square neighborhood. More could be done to tie these buildings into this upscale neighborhood as sites for housing or commercial development.

Successful Renovations of Historic Industrial Buildings

New Haven has witnessed the successful transformation of old industrial buildings for new uses over the last twenty-five years. Apartments, artist lofts, and architectural studios; medical offices and research facilities; and museum and gallery spaces now occupy these structures. One of the earliest examples of this type of adaptive reuse is the McLagon Foundry at 33 Whitney Avenue. This brick factory building was renovated in 1975 as multiuse facility. It features a bookstore, a coffeehouse, and gallery space as well as studios and offices. It serves as an anchor building in New Haven's lively Audubon Arts district (figure 2).

A second successful conversion is 85 Willow Street, the former site of the Marlin Firearms Company (figure 3). This structure houses a variety of tenants including photographic, design, and architectural studios; construction companies and woodworking shops; galleries and professional offices. Because of the configuration of the original factory, the rental spaces are all varied, creating unique options for large and small tenants. This building has proved to be a successful

FIGURE 2. (Top left) *McLagon Foundry at 33 Whitney.* (Photo by Preston Maynard)

FIGURE 3. (Top right) *The Marlin Firearms Company complex.* (Photo by Preston Maynard)

FIGURE 4. (Bottom left) *The Sealy Rubber Company building.* (Photo by Preston Maynard)

FIGURE 5. (Bottom right) *The A. C. Gilbert factory complex.* (Photo by Preston Maynard)

incubator for many New Haven businesses to operate and grow over the years.

The former Sealy Rubber Company, built in 1919, now called One Long Wharf Drive, is a 250,000-square-foot building on the flank of the Hill neighborhood (figure 4). When the company moved out in the 1970s, the building stood abandoned for years. The structure was transformed in 1988 as a multitenanted office complex.[9] Now comprising nearly 350,000 square feet, the building features dramatic atrium spaces rising to a glass ceiling. The building houses medical, social services, publishing, and technology-oriented firms. These businesses employ hundreds of people. With close proximity to the highway, plenty of parking, and modern appurtenances, the building serves as a major business center for the region.

The former factory complex at 315 Peck Street was once the home of the A. C. Gilbert Company, world-renowned maker of erector sets and electric trains. Now known as Erector Square, the complex has wonderful, light-filled spaces occupied with a diverse roster of small businesses (figure 5). Many artists have their studios here, diversifying the tenant roster. The complex is a vital economic generator, providing jobs and tax base for the city, while at the same time preserving an important industrial landmark.

Several old industrial buildings have been converted into successful housing complexes. The former Quinnipiac Brewery at Chapel and Ferry Streets in Fair Haven is the most dramatic example. This building was a derelict hulk when Boston-based developers bought it in 1984. Using the tax credits for historic rehabilitation, they transformed the structure into a complex of 101 housing units.[10] The building's rehabilitation spurred revitalization in the surrounding neighborhood, especially along Front Street where condominiums were built as well as a new waterfront park.

The former Strouse, Adler Company factory, once a maker of corsets and undergarments, is located at the corner of Olive and Chapel Street at the edge of downtown. Some sections of this large brick mill complex date from the 1860s.[11] Recently vacated by the corset maker, it has been converted into one hundred and fifty upscale housing units. The apartments have tall ceilings, large windows, and excellent views of the city. Its conversion to housing has added an important link between downtown and the Wooster Square neighborhood.

In the Fair Haven neighborhood at 277 Chapel Street, the factory of the former Henry G. Thompson Company, makers of hack and band saws, was renovated in 1984. Housing units with dramatic loft spaces, some with views of the harbor, were created in the 1917 industrial plant (figure 6). Across town in the heart of the West River neighborhood, is the Berger Brothers apartment building, located at 165 Derby Avenue. Built for the Berger Brothers corset makers in the 1920s, the complex was converted in 1979 into 144 apartments for elderly and disabled residents (figure 7).[12] In the Westville neighborhood, the former Geometric Tool Company factory now houses offices and a day-care facility. The dramatic smokestack was reused as an architectural focal point for this office complex.

Artists have coveted old industrial buildings as low-cost locations for their studios. The large, rough, open spaces and inexpensive rents make ideal working studios. As noted, the former A. C. Gilbert Company was originally used in this way. The former F. D. Graves cigar maker on State Street and other former warehouses in and around the Ninth Square also have been used as artists' studios. Several writers have documented the benefits of artists and other workers in the so-called creative industries in bringing back old industrial buildings and neighborhoods.[13]

The Charrette Company operated until recently an art and architectural supply

FIGURE 6. *The Henry G. Thompson Company building.* (Photo by Preston Maynard)

FIGURE 7. *The factory complex of Berger Brothers.* (Photo by Preston Maynard)

store in the former W. & E. T. Fitch Foundry at 127 East Street. The ventilator of the foundry flooded the retail showroom in natural light. This structure won recognition from the New Haven Preservation Trust for the creative reuse of a former industrial space. (Unfortunately, this building has been demolished for the new harbor bridge crossing.) In the Ninth Square district of downtown, there are many former manufacturing or warehouse buildings that have been converted to retail boutiques and loft-style apartments.[14] One of the few buildings remaining on the site of the Eli Whitney gun factory is now the site of the Eli Whitney Museum, a major educational and cultural center.

Community Linkages and Development Strategies

Saving neglected historic industrial buildings will not be successful without restoring the physical, economic, and social linkages to the neighborhoods in which they are located. A comprehensive neighborhood plan should document existing resources and assets as well as the needs for economic development, affordable and market rate housing, public improvements, and educational and recreational components. In urban communities, local historical and architectural assets should be identified. A good plan is driven by local residents in partnership with business owners, local officials, and institutional stakeholders. Consensus is built in the community around the proposed plan and the improvements that will follow. Once the plan is approved, specific projects can be identified and implemented. Financial resources can be secured to carry out the projects in the plan.

A neighborhood plan should have a strong economic development component that looks at market conditions, employment characteristics, the business sector, and the availability of housing and commercial real estate. Renovating old industrial buildings for new uses can provide strong economic benefits. New jobs and businesses can be attracted to the location with all the accompanying benefits.

One long neglected yet potential area for redevelopment is the River Street industrial district bounded by the Mill River and the Quinnipiac River in Fair Haven. The historic Bigelow Boiler Company, National Pipe Bending Company, and Flint Ladder Company are located here and create a nineteenth-century industrial landscape not often found in Connecticut.[15] The preservation and reuse of these historic structures could be the centerpiece of a riverfront revitalization strategy benefiting the entire community. The buildings could be used for light manufacturing, for offices, for galleries, furniture showrooms, or studio spaces. Public improvements, including a proposed linear trail along the riverfront, coupled with new housing built on adjacent vacant lots, would attract public and private investment. And just to the north of River Street is the Fair Haven neighborhood, consisting of many late-nineteenth-century houses, churches, and small businesses. If River Street became a mixed-use district with new businesses, recreation facilities, and housing, it would fuel additional revitalization and investment in other parts of the neighborhood.

Sound impossible? The City of New Haven conducted a similar project along Front Street in Fair Haven a decade ago. It relocated a messy scrap yard from the river's edge, demolished blighted housing, and created a riverfront park. Private investors developed hundreds of units of market rate and affordable housing.[16] One of the biggest private developments at this time was the rehabilitation of the vacant Quinnipiac Brewery into Brewery Square apartments. Additional private investment took place in the area as new homeowners bought "fixer-uppers" and renovated them.

The New Haven Clock Company building, a significant historic building on Hamilton Street, stands largely vacant in deteriorated condition. This nineteenth-century complex covers a good portion of the block. Much of the surrounding neighborhood was demolished during the urban-renewal era, yet because of its location near the highway, the reuse potential of the former clock company is promising. It could be developed as a distribution center for wholesale or fulfillment companies, bringing new jobs and tax base to the city. Or it could be used as an incubator for small businesses that could benefit from inexpensive rents and flexible spaces. A recent proposal called for artist housing on the site.

Financing Reuse Projects

Real estate developments are risky ventures. Construction costs, market fluctuations, and environmental issues are not easily managed. Financing from public and private sources is often needed to bring a project to fruition. Lenders and investors require a full analysis of a project before financing is approved and construction can begin. The more unknown variables can be clarified—the tenants identified, the construction costs determined—the better the chance of attracting financing from investors or lenders.

Real estate markets, especially in urban areas, have to be carefully assessed. Without an understanding of broader real estate markets and trends, a project will fail. Without finding a qualified tenant or end user, a project will be perceived as highly speculative. A low-rent district or a soft real estate market will not support a lavish renovation budget. On the other hand, underutilized industrial space can be retrofitted without great expense for small businesses that need only inexpensive rent and room for expansion. Some of the most successful industrial building conversions in New Haven have been those that offer tenants affordable rents and the ability to improve their space as they grow.

Whether new construction or adaptive reuse, urban real estate projects often require some type of public subsidy to make them feasible. Community Development block grants, HOME funds, low-income housing tax credits, historic rehabilitation tax credits, and other financing programs can provide capital or gap financing to make a project work. To gain this type of public subsidy, a project often has to meet certain government requirements such as creating employment, providing affordable housing, or removing blighted conditions.

The historic tax credit for the rehabilitation of certified historic buildings provides substantial incentives for investors interested in renovating former industrial buildings. The program allows a 20 percent tax credit against the rehabilitation costs for buildings that are listed on the National Register of Historic Places.[17] Most of the River Street industrial district, the Ninth Square, and the Wooster Square neighborhood are listed on the National Register. Many other sites are eligible for this listing. The rehabilitation tax credit can bring solid returns to investors who see the potential in these projects.

Direct public subsidy or gap financing from the local municipality or the state can make the difference in making a project work. These short-term public investments can have long-lasting returns in the form of neighborhood stability, generating new jobs, tax revenues, and improved services. The Empowerment Zone designation New Haven received provides tax-exempt bond financing for projects located in zone neighborhoods. Much of Fair Haven, the Hill, Dixwell, and Dwight areas are in the zone and would qualify for the financing.

Conclusion

The glorious nineteenth-century era of industry and commerce described in this book created much of the urban fabric we know today as the city of New Haven. This fabric is similar to that found in other small and medium-sized cities throughout New England. These old industrial buildings and sites can be put to economically viable new uses. Their strategic locations near the waterfront or in the center of interesting neighborhoods make them well suited for housing, office, or retail uses. Because some of the buildings described here are in poor condition, they will need special attention and an experienced development team to be successful.

Environmental contaminants and hazardous materials will need to be cleaned up before work begins. Fortunately, there is now money from state and federal sources to do this remediation work. Opportunities await experienced developers who see the potential in these unique structures and can bring them to new life. At the same time, each project will bring new vitality to New Haven's waterfronts and neighborhoods.

Preservationists, architects, neighborhood residents, and community leaders need to build support for the redevelopment of these structures instead of allowing their demolition. Local residents can play an important role in creating neighborhood plans that focus on the reuse of these structures as centers of economic or housing activity. Residents can then help market these properties to experienced developers.

One idea that would bring public attention to these structures and their unique position in the community is creating a National Heritage Corridor centered around New Haven's industrial history.[18] This federal designation by the National Park Service would include the buildings highlighted in this book—important symbols of our region's unique cultural heritage. The heritage corridor designation would provide some funding for planning and management of these resources. Similar designations in Lowell, Massachusetts, and the Blackstone Valley bordering Massachusetts and Rhode Island, have led to the preservation and reuse of many historic structures, bringing jobs and attracting tourism.

The time is ripe to move forward with the preservation and reuse of old industrial buildings in New Haven. Some will not survive another decade of neglect. I hope this book, as it highlights the unique qualities of these resources, at the same time serves as a catalyst for their renewal.

NOTES

1. See the 1880 *New Haven Directory* (Price and Lee Company, New Haven), which lists New Haven residents by street address and occupation.

2. For more about New Haven's architecture and neighborhoods, see Elizabeth Mills Brown, *New Haven, A Guide to Architecture and Urban Design* (New Haven: Yale University Press, 1976).

3. See Matthew Roth, *Connecticut: An Inventory of Historic Engineering and Industrial Sites* (Society of Industrial Archeology, 1981) for a good overview of Connecticut's historic industry.

4. See building profile for Bigelow Boiler in the second part of this book.

5. See building profile for New Haven Clock Company in the second part of this book.

6. Brown, 199.

7. See "Plus Factors of Old Buildings" by Giorgio Cavaglieri (FAIA), in *the Economic Benefits of Preserving Old Buildings* (Washington, D.C.: Preservation Press, National Trust for Historic Preservation, 1976), 53–57.

8. Donovan D. Rypkema, *The Economics of Historic Preservation: A Community Leaders Guide* (National Trust for Historic Preservation, 1994), 87–90.

9. City of New Haven, Building Department records for One Long Wharf Drive.

10. See City of New Haven Building Department records for One Brewery Square.

11. See building profile for the Strouse, Adler Company in the second part of this book.

12. See City of New Haven Building Records for 165 Derby Avenue, Berger Brothers Apartments.

13. One such author is Richard Florida who wrote *Rise of the Creative Class and How it is Transforming Work, Leisure, Community and Everyday Life* (New York: Basic Books, 2002).

14. For more information about the Ninth Square district, see the National Register of Historic Places Registration form for the Ninth Square Historic District, prepared by Matt Roth and Bruce Clouette, 1983.

15. For more information about the River Street historic district, see the National Register of Historic Places Registration form for the River Street Historic District, prepared by Matt Roth and Bruce Clouette, 1988.

16. See Fair Haven Renewal and Redevelopment Plan, New Haven Redevelopment Agency, City of New Haven, 1969.

17. For more information about the rehabilitation tax credit, see "Preservation Tax Incentives for Historic Buildings," published by the U.S. Department of the Interior, National Park Service, Heritage Preservation Services, 2001.

18. See Andrea Oppenheimer Dean, "Thinking Big, Heritage Areas Expand the Concept of Historic Districts," *Historic Preservation* (November/December 1995).

PROFILES OF
HARBORSIDE INDUSTRIES

Research by Sylvia M. Garfield; Text by Marjorie Noyes

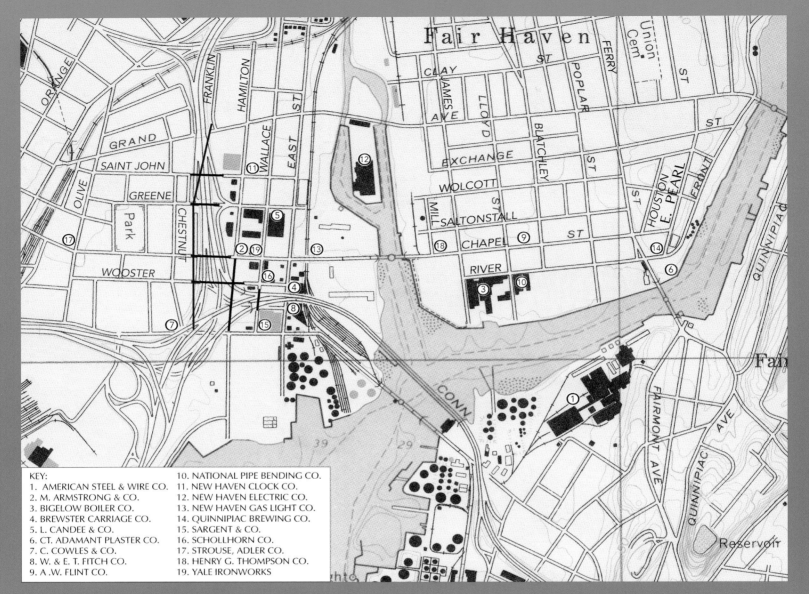

KEY:
1. AMERICAN STEEL & WIRE CO.
2. M. ARMSTRONG & CO.
3. BIGELOW BOILER CO.
4. BREWSTER CARRIAGE CO.
5. L. CANDEE & CO.
6. CT. ADAMANT PLASTER CO.
7. C. COWLES & CO.
8. W. & E. T. FITCH CO.
9. A .W. FLINT CO.
10. NATIONAL PIPE BENDING CO.
11. NEW HAVEN CLOCK CO.
12. NEW HAVEN ELECTRIC CO.
13. NEW HAVEN GAS LIGHT CO.
14. QUINNIPIAC BREWING CO.
15. SARGENT & CO.
16. SCHOLLHORN CO.
17. STROUSE, ADLER CO.
18. HENRY G. THOMPSON CO.
19. YALE IRONWORKS

In the late nineteenth and early twentieth centuries, several dozen industries were located in the Harborside area; manufacturing beer, boilers, and buttons, carriages and carriage parts, corsets, hardware, ladders, paper boxes, patent medicines and pipes, rubber boots, scissors, and wire rope. Industrial sites in the area are significant because they illustrate the relationship of location, transportation, and technology to the city's rise as a major industrial center in New England.

Some of the companies in the Harborside were large, their factories covering entire city blocks and employing a thousand or more workers. Others were small, one-building establishments with a few skilled workers. Most sold their products to other parts of the United States; several exported products throughout the world. The sixteen companies described on the following pages were chosen to illustrate the diversity of products made in New Haven, and the ingenuity and entrepreneurship that characterized the city's industries during the American industrial revolution.

Factory buildings in the Harborside also tell the story of New Haven's industrial heritage. As companies flourished, additions, and in some cases new buildings, were added to the original factory. As fortunes of the companies reversed, many of the buildings were vacated, becoming victims of decay and vandalism. Others were demolished for construction of highways or new buildings. Several were destroyed by fire. A few have been adapted for new uses.

Map above is a part of the U.S.G.S. topographic map, New Haven quadrangle. Filled lines show streets that were removed during construction of the interstate highways.

OVERLEAF. In the late nineteenth century, Mallory Wheeler & Company was one of the largest manufacturers of locks in the country. Their factory complex was in the Harborside area on the corner of St. John Street and Railroad Avenue. (New Haven Preservation Trust)

The Brewster Carriage Company

I n 1809, young James Brewster had recently completed an apprenticeship with a Massachusetts carriage-maker and decided to go into business for himself. He was on his way from Boston to New York City when the stagecoach broke down near New Haven. To pass the time while the coach was being repaired, he visited New Haven's first carriage-maker, John Cook, in his small shop on Chapel Street and was much impressed. A year later, Brewster set up his carriage-making shop on the corner of Elm and High Streets.

A Brief History of the Firm

Brewster began his carriage-making career by improving the design of the one-horse wagon, the vehicle of choice then, and soon manufactured the "Brewster wagon," which became very popular. Concentrating on building carriages that were better than those made in England, he eventually established an extensive business in the design and manufacture of high-style buggies, coaches, paneled carriages, and other "modern" vehicles of the day. A Brewster wagon or carriage in those days was considered as much a status symbol as a Packard automobile was a century later (figure 1).

For the next twenty-seven years, Brewster's business prospered. Andrew Jackson, Martin Van Buren, and Benjamin Silliman were reputed to be among his customers. In 1827, he and a partner, John Lawrence, opened a branch in New York City where they did a lively export trade, particularly with Cuba.

Brewster was a shrewd businessman. In 1832, after a succession of moves to larger buildings, he and Solomon Collis bought a sizeable tract of land on East and

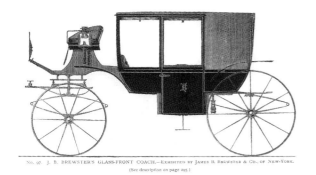

No. 97   J. B. BREWSTER'S GLASS-FRONT COACH.—EXHIBITED BY JAMES B. BREWSTER & CO., OF NEW-YORK.
(See description on page 295.)

FIGURE 1. *Brewster's elegant glass-front carriage was manufactured in the Brewster's New York plant.* (*The Hub*, 18, no. 18, November 1876, p. 295)

[Mr. Brewster] sought to raise the standard of workmanship by calling the best workmen to New Haven, by paying them good wages in cash, and seeking in many other ways to raise them to a greater sense of responsibility and to a higher grade of mental and moral culture.

—Atwater, ed., *History of the City of New Haven.*

Bridge streets at the foot of Wooster Street in an area known as "New Township" and built a large carriage manufactory on the site. "My business increased to correspond with the facilities of my new establishment, and more than equaled my expectations," Brewster wrote in his autobiography. At the same time, he invested large sums in improving the surrounding neighborhood, creating new streets, and upgrading existing streets and buildings. Known briefly as "Brewsterville," the area soon attracted other businesses related to the carriage industry.

Although he remained an owner of the factory and site, Brewster's attention for the next four years was almost completely consumed by a new interest: the building of the first railroad between New Haven and Hartford to connect with steamboats running between New Haven and New York City. Meanwhile, fire destroyed the factory on East Street on 25 February 1836. It was soon replaced by a more imposing brick manufactory with a figure of a phoenix on the roof to symbolize the factory's resurrection (figure 2).

Solomon Collis sold out his share of the factory to Brewster in 1837. Brewster retired from the railroad that year, and with his oldest son, James B. Brewster, established the Brewster and Allen carriage business across East Street from the former Brewster and Collis factory. James B. Brewster became the head of the company's New York branch, while his brother, Henry, was the senior member of Brewster & Company, also of New York. In the latter half of the nineteenth century, the Brewster sons were two of the leading carriage manufacturers in the United States.

FIGURE 2. *After the original Brewster Collis factory on East Street was destroyed by fire in 1836, it was replaced with this imposing brick building.* (Collection of Richard and Marianne Mazan; *Daily Graphic* [New York], 12 February 1875, p. 745)

In financial difficulty, James Brewster began to mortgage his buildings and to sell part of his land. Solomon Collis conducted the Collis and Lawrence Coach Manufacturer's business in the former Brewster and Collis factory from 1837 until 1842. In 1843, Brewster sold the entire factory site, between East Street and the Mill River to Hervey S. Hoadley.

Hoadley continued to manufacture carriages on the site until his death in 1852. The W. & E. T. Fitch Company occupied the axle and spring factory built by Hoadley next door to the carriage factory before purchasing it and all the land between the carriage factory and Bridge Street in 1863.

Rogers, Smith and Company manufactured silverplated ware in the carriage factory from 1863 to 1876. The Boston Buckboard and Carriage Company, manufacturers of wagons and carriages, occupied the building from 1879 to 1894, and enlarged the east wing. In 1904, it sold the parcel of land with the factory to the W. & E. T. Fitch Company, which then demolished all but the east wing before 1911.

REFERENCES

Atwater, Edward E., ed. *History of the City of New Haven*. New York: Munsell, 1887.

Babcock, James F. "James Brewster, the Recognized Father of New Haven's Light Carriage Industry." Excerpts from Memorial Address Before the Merchants Exchange, 1866. Dana Scrapbook, MS 1, vol. 127. New Haven Colony Historical Society.

Boston Buckboard Company. *Carriage Catalogue of the Boston Buckboard Company*. New Haven: Hoggson & Robinson, 1881.

Brewster, James. "Purchases in 1832 of New Township Property by James Brewster." Excerpts from James Brewster's autobiography. Dana Scrapbook, MS 1, vol. 142. New Haven Colony Historical Society.

Downing, Paul H. "The Brewsters and Their Carriages." *American Heritage* (October 1956); reprint from the *Carriage Journal*, n.d.

Hegel, Richard. *Carriages from New Haven: New Haven's Nineteenth-Century Industry*. Hamden, Conn: Archon Books, 1974.

Hoadley, Henry S. Estate Inventory, 17 April 1852. New Haven Probate Records, Microfilm 3, Roll 37. New Haven Colony Historical Society.

Hornstein, Harold, ed. *New Haven Celebrates the Bicentennial: Commemorative Book*. New Haven: Bicentennial Commission, 1976.

Kelley, Cassius W. "Atlas of New Haven, Connecticut." Bridgeport: Streuli & Puckhafer, 1911.

Map of the City of New Haven and Vicinity from Actual Surveys by Hartley and Whiteford. Cartographers: Hartley and Whiteford. Philadelphia: Collins and Clark, 1852.

New Haven City Directory. 1840–1879.

New Haven Land Records, 81:41, 90:475, 107:238, 109:29, 203:25, 204:16, 226:134, 286:414, 350:332, 436:307, 565:199.

"An Official Map Showing as in the 1840s New Haven's First Railway Terminus (The Hartford and New Haven Railroad Company) At Bridge and Water Sts. And Steamboat Dock." Dana Scrapbook, MS 1, vol. 134. New Haven Colony Historical Society.

Seymour, George Dudley. "New Haven." Privately printed, 1942, p. 738.

The W. & E. T. Fitch Company

William Fitch had intended to follow in his father's footsteps as a banker, but after a few years as a bookkeeper and teller, his interest turned to the hardware trade. In 1848, he and his brother Eleazer formed a partnership to manufacture carriage springs and cabinet locks in Westville. Five years later, the brothers moved their plant to the axle and spring factory next to the former Brewster and Collis carriage factory on East Street. Here in the heart of New Haven's carriage-making district, they had the advantages of steam power and easy access to rail and water transportation to Boston and New York City.

A Brief History of the Firm

As their business prospered, the Fitch brothers added new buildings to their site and new products to their line, including carriage springs, saddlery hardware, currycombs and other carriage-related specialty items (figures 1 and 2). Between 1863 and 1868, the W. & E. T. Fitch Company built a malleable iron foundry on the corner of East and Bridge streets and added malleable iron castings to its production line. Statements in its 1876 catalog, however, suggested a possible decline in the company's fortunes. "on the first of January of this year, we relinquished the manufacture of 'Carriage Malleables,' which will explain the disparity in size between this and previous catalogs. We insert a few cuts of Carriage Springs as a reminder that we continue this branch of manufacture."

This setback was only temporary. In 1889, about 130 skilled workmen were employed in Fitch's sprawling plant, well equipped with modern machinery and appliances operated by two steam engines. The W. & E. T. Fitch Company incor-

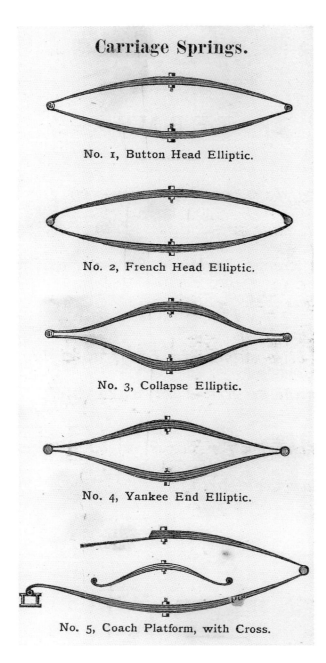

Carriage Springs.

No. 1, Button Head Elliptic.

No. 2, French Head Elliptic.

No. 3, Collapse Elliptic.

No. 4, Yankee End Elliptic.

No. 5, Coach Platform, with Cross.

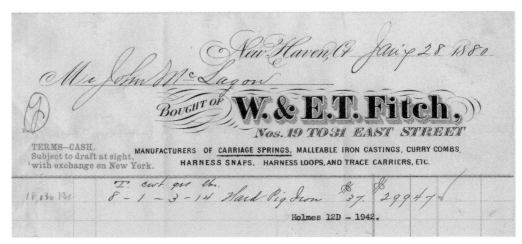

FIGURE 1. *Until the advent of the automobile at the turn of the century, the W. & E. T. Fitch Company specialized in carriage hardware including carriage springs, saddlery hardware, currycombs and specialty items in support of the carriage industry.* (New Haven Colony Historical Society; Dana Scrapbooks, 128:108)

FIGURE 2. *A W. & E. T. Fitch billhead.* (New Haven Colony Historical Society; Dana Scrapbooks, 128:110)

FIGURE 3. *The W. & E. T. Fitch Company's buildings on the north side of I-95 are among the few remaining buildings of this once-large complex still standing.* (Photo by Henry Lord)

porated in 1893 with John Brewster Fitch, son of Eleazer, as president and Frederick F. Brewster as secretary. At the time, it was one of the oldest hardware manufacturing companies in America in continuous operation without change of name or management.

As automobiles replaced carriages in the early 1900s, the fortunes of the company, like those of so many others in New Haven's once-vibrant carriage industry, declined. In 1905, the Fitch Company ceased manufacturing carriage hardware and began listing itself as "hardware manufacturers (saddlery and specialties)" in the *New Haven City Directory*. The W. & E. T. Fitch Company closed its doors in 1919. The North & Judd Manufacturing Company, manufacturers of harness hardware, bought the entire factory site with buildings in 1920. It ceased operations in 1925, marking the end of carriage-related manufacture on the Brewster site (figure 3).

The Plant

The industrial history of this site began on 14 February 1832, when James Brewster and Solomon Collis bought land in the New Township and built a large carriage manufactory on East Street at the foot of Wooster Street. The W. & E. T. Fitch Company acquired the building in 1904 and demolished all but the 1881 east wing by 1911. When the North & Judd Manufacturing Company bought the W. & E. T. Fitch Company plant in 1920, the following brick buildings were on the site:

1920   North (Chapel Street) end
- Boiler Shop, one-story, 1891 (at railroad tracks)
- Machine Shop, two-story, 1883 (on East Street)
- East wing of the Carriage Manufactory, three-story, 1880

Center
- Two factory buildings, 1854–1859, two-story (on East Street, built by the Fitch brothers in front of the Axle & Spring Factory)
- Axle & spring factory building, pre-1851, 1½-story (rear 1850s Fitch buildings; enlarged to three and four stories c. 1890 and to five stories c. 1906, architect Leoni Robinson)
- Axle & spring factory building, before 1851, 1½-story (center lot between brass foundry and East Street factories)
- Brass foundry, 1888–1897, one-story (at railroad tracks)
- Two factory buildings, 1890s, five-story (parallel to East Street, one or both designed by Leoni Robinson)

South (Bridge Street) end
- Malleable iron foundry, 1863–1868, one-story (on East Street, addition designed 1891 by Leoni Robinson on-site at East and Bridge streets by 1897)

1961   Construction of Interstate 95 cut through the middle of the Fitch complex, removing five and part of a sixth buildings on the site. The following buildings remain; malleable iron foundry; brick factory buildings (1854–1859); remaining wing of the Brewster and Collis factory (1880–1881); and shop (1891). Plans for expansion of I-95 include demolition of the malleable iron foundry.

REFERENCES

Beers, Frederick W. *Map of the City of New Haven and Fair Haven*. Beers, Hellis & Soule, 1868.
Connecticut Business Directory. New Haven, Conn.: J. H. Benham, 1851.
Connecticut Malleable Castings Company. *The Connecticut Circle* (November 1943).
Fitch, W. & E. T. *Illustrated Catalogues*, 1876, 1883. MS 1. Dana Scrapbook, vol. 128. New Haven Colony Historical Society.
[Fitch, William]. "Hon. William Fitch, Mayor of New Haven, 1869–1870." *City Yearbook for the City of New Haven*. 1878. Hartford, Conn.: Case, Lockwood and Brainard Company, 1878.
Fowler, Earl G. "Remains of Old Carriage Factory Center as Found in Cursory Survey in 1937." In

New Haven's Problems. Whither the City? All Cities? by Arnold Guyot Dana. New Haven: Tuttle, Morehouse & Taylor Co., 1937.

Hopkins, Griffith Morgan. *Atlas of the City of New Haven, Connecticut.* Philadelphia: 1888.

Kelly, Cassius W. *Atlas of New Haven, Connecticut.* Bridgeport, Conn.: Streuli & Puckhafer, 1911.

Kirby, John B., Jr. "New Haven Building Permit Records, 1882–1886." Vol. 2. New Haven, March 1983.

Map of the City of New Haven and Vicinity from Actual Surveys by Hartley and Whiteford. Cartographers: Hartley and Whiteford. Philadelphia: Collins and Clark, 1851.

New Haven Chamber of Commerce. *The Industrial Advantages of the City of New Haven, Connecticut.* New Haven: Jas. P. McKinney, 1889.

New Haven Directory. 1847–1894; 1902–1910; 1919–1934; 1964–1965.

New Haven Land Records. 122:393; 203:25; 204:16; 565:199; 887:519; 1096:382.

Robinson, Leoni W. (FAIA). 1852–1923. Architectural Drawings. MS AD5, New Haven Colony Historical Society.

Sanborn Map and Publishing Co. *New Haven, Connecticut.* 1880.

Sanborn Map Company. *Insurance Maps of New Haven, Connecticut.* 1886 (updated to 1897); 1901; 1923; 1923 (updated to 1931); 1965 (updated to 1973).

Searle, Silas W. *Map of the City of New Haven, Connecticut.* Philadelphia: W. H. Rease, 1859.

Underwood, A. B. "The Manufacturing Interests of New Haven." *The New England States*, ed. William T. Davis. Boston: D. H. Hurd & Co., 1897.

M. Armstrong & Company

"The production of this establishment has for many years been known as the finest and best work made, combining beauty of design, ease of riding, lightness of running, luxuriousness of finish and durability."

— *Leading Business Men of New Haven County* (1887)

Describing New Haven's carriage industry in 1887, local historian Edward Atwater wrote in *The History of the City of New Haven*, "There have been periods in its history in this city when more persons were engaged in it, when the amount of capital invested in it was greater, and its product more valuable than any other two branches of the industrial arts." M. Armstrong and Company was among the most prominent New Haven carriage-makers.

A Brief History of the Firm

In 1859, a blacksmith named Montgomery Armstrong established a carriage-making company on Temple Street with George and Thomas Alling, brothers who owned a lumber business. Two years later, the outbreak of the Civil War ended New Haven's important trade with the southern states. Dependent on the southern market, many New Haven carriage-makers found themselves in financial distress. The Armstrong company survived the Civil War and the depression that followed, and prospered largely because it maintained a significant foreign export business and obtained substantial United States government contracts for ambulances and other vehicles. After the war, business was going well, and Montgomery Armstrong decided to go it alone. He bought out the Alling brothers' interest in 1867.

M. Armstrong and Company moved to a new six-story brick building on Chapel Street in 1882. It was one of the best-organized carriage factories in the city. With forty experienced and skilled workmen in various departments, the company produced "heavier" luxury carriages known as landaus, coaches, coupes, broughams, victorias, cabriolets, and hansom cabs (figure 1). Much of its busi-

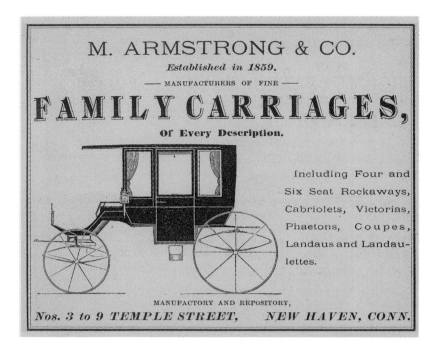

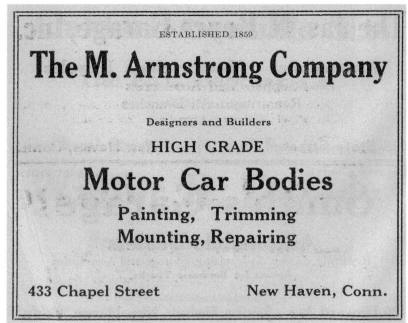

FIGURE 1. *Advertisement for M. Armstrong & Company.* (New Haven Colony Historical Society; *New Haven City Directory*, 1878, xxiii)

FIGURE 2. *This advertisement in 1917 was a desperate, last-ditch effort to remain in business.* (New Haven Colony Historical Society; *New Haven City Directory*, 1917, 22)

FIGURE 3. *The Armstrong factory was one of the best-organized carriage factories in the city.* (New Haven Colony Historical Society; Dana Scrapbook, 127:77)

ness in the 1880s was devoted to making luxury carriages for upscale hotels in New York City: by the late 1890s, its superior-quality, heavy carriages were sold throughout the United States.

At the beginning of the twentieth century it became evident that the automobile was here to stay, and M. Armstrong & Company added high-grade automobile bodies to its line of fine landaus and coaches. The company discontinued carriage production entirely by 1917. In the *New Haven City Directory* that year, Armstrong advertised itself as "Designers and Builders of High Grade Motor Car Bodies, Painting, Trimming, Mounting, Repairing" (figure 2). It was a desperate, last ditch

effort to remain in business. As the center of the automobile industry shifted to the Midwest, business dropped off dramatically, and this once-prominent manufacturer of luxury carriages closed down in 1927.

THE PLANT

1882   M. Armstrong and Company moved to a new 100 × 150 ft. six-story brick building on the north side of Chapel Street, next to the Yale Iron Works foundry that stood on the corner of Chapel and Wallace streets.

1897   Armstrong organized the plant at 433 Chapel Street with a blacksmith shop in the basement, office and repository on the first floor, fitting-up and storage on the second floor, woodworking and trimming on the third floor. Paint and drying rooms occupied the fourth floor. Gas provided light, and steam provided heat. There have been no major additions or changes to the original footprint of the plant.

1928   The John P. Smith Company, wire goods manufacturer[s] and dealer[s], moved into the building.

1990s   Connecticut Courier, Inc. moved into 433 Chapel Street and later shared the building with several other businesses.

The Armstrong building is the sole survivor of the New Haven carriage manufactories. This factory remained a single building with no major additions (figure 3).

REFERENCES

Atwater, Edward E., ed. *History of the City of New Haven*. New York: Munsell, 1887. 556.

Dana, Arnold Guyot (1862–1947), comp. *New Haven Old and New, 1641–1947*, Vol. 127. MS 1. New Haven Colony Historical Society.

Hegel, Richard. *Carriages from New Haven: New Haven's Nineteenth-Century Carriage Industry*. Hamden: Archon, 1974.

Kirby, John B., Jr. "New Haven Building Permit Records." Vol. 1 (permit 20, February 1882). New Haven, December 1982.

Leading Business Men of New Haven County. Boston: Mercantile Publishing, 1887.

New Haven Directory. 1858–1883, 1891, 1910–1928, 1990, 1998.

New Haven Land Records. 239:123 and 523; 347:538; 1143:29.

Hopkins, Griffith Morgan. *Atlas of the City of New Haven, Connecticut*. Philadelphia, 1888.

Kelly, Cassius W. *Atlas of New Haven, Connecticut*. Bridgeport: Streuli & Puckhafer, 1911.

Sanborn Map Company. *Insurance Maps of New Haven, Connecticut*. 1886 (updated to 1897); 1923 (updated to 1931, 1961).

Underwood, A. B. "The Manufacturing Interests of New Haven," in *The New England States*, vol. 2, ed. William T. Davis. Boston: D. H. Hurd, 1897.

C. Cowles & Company

"The output of this company comprises almost everything novel and desirable in carriage trimmings, and among the patrons of the house are numbered some of the largest jobbers in this line of merchandise, and many of the most extensive coach and carriage manufacturers in the United States."

—*Leading Business Men of New Haven County* (1887)

C. Cowles and Company has survived three wars, two depressions, and a multitude of changes in industry for more than 150 years. Two young men, William Cornwall and Chandler Cowles, founded the company in 1838 with little experience and barely two nickels to rub together. They rented a shop on York Street and began making carriage hardware with no capital, no assets, no employees, and no machinery other than their own tools—but they were inventive and hard-working, with a talent for things mechanical.

A Brief History of the Firm

The partners picked an opportune time and place to start their business. In a few years, New Haven would become one of the most prominent carriage-making cities in the nation and the world. More than thirty carriage manufacturers in the area at that time gave rise to dozens of specialty manufacturers who supplied them with springs, wheels, axles, malleable castings, lamps, hardware, and almost everything else needed to make carriages.

Cowles and Cornwall made their lamps from tin, with silver or copperplate for the reflectors and inside parts. They put plate glass in their high-end lamps and common window glass in the cheaper ones. Candles, rather than oil, provided the light. Soon their lamp-making business became so successful that they were encouraged to add other coach hardware products to their line: bolts, locks, and other parts needed by New Haven carriage-makers. In 1844, they took on Lewis Judson as a third partner.

Eventually, Cornwell and Judson left the firm: in 1855, Chandler Cowles, together with his half-brother Ruel Cowles, a coach-maker, and Louis Babcock, an accountant, incorporated under the name of C. Cowles & Company. Their combined knowledge of finance and carriage hardware made a good partnership. Within two years they moved the business to a five-story brick building on Orange Street "to manufacture, buy, sell, and deal in all articles used in the manufacture of carriage hardware, harness and saddlery."

Carriage-makers in New Haven survived the depression of 1857, but many were hard-hit a few years later when the Civil War deprived them of their southern market. After the war the carriage industry moved westward, leaving fewer manufacturers in New Haven. Those that remained prospered briefly, making mostly luxury carriages rather than inexpensive models. As it would do in decades to follow, C. Cowles & Company met the postwar challenge by seeking wider markets, technological innovations, and product improvements, and by extending its product lines (especially in iron forgings and patent carriage lamps).

By 1882, C. Cowles & Company had become one of the largest manufacturers of carriage trimmings in the country. Its plant on Orange Street was humming, equipped with the most up-to-date machinery and tools powered by a 70-horse-power engine. With about one hundred and fifty employees, it had the capability, the equipment, and the facilities (including a foundry) to "forge, melt, cast, mold, bend, stamp, cut and enamel materials like iron, brass, silver, ivory, glass, rubber and wood." It held patents for important improvements in making button backs, knobs, slat irons, saddle clips, and other hardware components; in 1880, it was the first company in the country to build a telephone switchboard. With a capacity of thirty-five simultaneous connections and plug-in jacks, it became standard equipment everywhere. But carriage lamps remained its specialty, and the company produced "a larger variety than any house in this country, averaging over a thousand pairs a month by 1887." Its market had expanded beyond New Haven to reach manufacturers throughout the United States as well as in Canada, South America, Great Britain, continental Europe, Mexico, the West Indies, and Australia. C. Cowles & Company products won awards in the 1876 Philadelphia Centennial Exhibition, the 1880 Melbourne Exhibit, and the 1893 Colombian Exposition in Chicago.

Even as its stake in the carriage-making business was booming, C. Cowles & Company was preparing for the emerging automobile industry. In 1891, it moved to a newly built five-story brick plant on the corner of Water and Chestnut streets. (Architect Leoni W. Robinson drew a site survey for the 1890 factory at the corner of Water and Chestnut streets, and is the probable architect for that building.) The workforce increased to about two hundred men and women whose Irish, Scot-

FIGURE 1. *Frank Hill, Superintendent supervising workers in the Cowles factory early in the 20th century.* (New Haven Colony Historical Society Manuscript Collection. MS B59, box 1, folder G)

FIGURE 2. *Women in the "Girls Lamp Cleaning Department."* (New Haven Colony Historical Society Manuscript Collection, MS B59, box 1, folder K).

tish, German, English, and occasionally French backgrounds reflected the ethnic makeup of the city at that time (figures 1 and 2). The new modern facility allowed Cowles to expand hardware production, add new styles and price ranges to its carriage and coach-lamp lines, and to introduce automobile hardware and trimmings production. Its 1900 catalog lists a variety of automobile lamps: electric, gas, oil or candle, and even offers to put new electric lights into customers' old lamps. The catalog features Cowles's latest innovation: electric lamps run by its dry battery system called "Climax," a three-candlepower lamp "with no oil, grease or dust—no smoke, smell, no changing batteries each night or week . . . no trouble. The Climax will throw light for 200 feet for a half to four hours a night, or 100 hours total."

Within seven years, Cowles was producing a full line of automobile parts from bolts and strap buckles to interior dome lights, tire holders, clock cases, and electric cigar lighters. The 1907 catalog introduced an early prototype of rear signal lights: a brake light, plus right- and left-turn signals.

During the next two decades, the company continued to expand its plant and improve its line of automobile parts, while phasing out production of carriage parts. Just before the Great Depression, it specialized only in motor vehicle parts and accessories. The Depression years were hard on most of New Haven's industrial firms, but Cowles survived by ingenuity and diversification. In 1938, it received government orders for military truck hardware and military airplane parts, signaling the end of the Depression. Cowles mobilized a workforce of between four hundred and five hundred men and women to make war materials and to continue production of automobile hardware for export.

Cowles saw no letdown after the war. Propelled by a postwar auto sales boom, it added a $65,000 building on Chestnut Street to its plant in 1949, and continued to expand its line to include hardware for furniture, refrigerators, switch gears, and meters. In 1963, the board of directors adopted modern articles of incorporation initiating a period of unprecedented expansion that continued into the mid-1980s, during which time it acquired several manufacturing companies and again expanded the plant (figure 3).

In 1997, about one hundred employees produced lighting and automotive products in the Water Street plant. More than a century and a half after its founding, C. Cowles & Company is the sole significant survivor of the local carriage industry and the oldest New Haven manufacturing concern under continuous management.

FIGURE 3. *The 1969 addition to the C. Cowles & Company factory.* (New Haven Colony Historical Society Manuscript Collection, MS B59, box 1, folder V)

THE PLANT

1890–97   C. Cowles & Company bought land on the corner of Water and Chestnut streets in 1890 and built a state-of-the-art, five-story brick factory. Equipped with hot-air heat, electric lights, and freight and passenger elevators, the 40 ft. × 175 ft. building was designed to be as fireproof and "modern" as possible. This building housed brass working, finishing, plating, buffing, stamping, and glass-bending operations, a cycle manufactory, coach-lamp department, and storage areas (architect: Leoni W. Robinson).

A two-story brick building housing the dynamo connected the main factory with a one-story forge shop and boiler building on Water Street. A one-story machine shop was attached behind the forge shop. Sometime between 1891 and 1897, an addition was built on the northwest corner of the factory to house polishing operations and japan ovens.

1912   Building 3, a two-story 22 ft. × 60 ft. brick factory building, replaced the brick forge and machine shops.

1914   Building 4 on Water Street, a new five-story 61 ft. × 116 ft. structure of fireproof materials, with reinforced concrete floors, frame, and roof (architect: Leoni W. Robinson).

1916   Building 5, built of fireproof materials, with reinforced concrete floors, frame, and roof, on Chestnut Street.

1949   A new building on Chestnut Street for plating operations.

1958   Construction of Interstate 91 and Interstate 95 claimed several Cowles Company sites and the underside of I-91 is within eleven inches of the factory's upper stories.

1969   A new 50,000 sq. ft. steel-frame addition on the Water Street plant nearly doubled the company's production capacity.

REFERENCES

Atwater, Edward E., ed. *History of the City of New Haven.* New York: Munsell, 1887.

Beach, Randall. "Q Bridge Expansion: Neighbors Not Happy. Dirt, Noise, Traffic Among Their Concerns." *New Haven Register,* 13 October 1997.

Commerce, Manufacturers and Resources of New Haven, Connecticut. New Haven: National Publishing, 1882.

Cowles, C. & Company. "Makers of Lamps for All Vehicles." Catalogue 18. New Haven, 1907.

———. Records, 1873–1964. New Haven Colony Historical Society Manuscript Collection, MS B59.

Hogan, Neil. *A Certain Distinction: C. Cowles & Co., 1838–1988.* New Haven: S. Z. Field, 1988.

Leading Business Men of New Haven County. Boston: Mercantile Publishing, 1887.

Mercantile Illustrating Company. *New Haven and Its Points of Interest,* 1895.

New Haven. "Report of the Building Inspector." In the *City Yearbook of the City of New Haven for 1914.* New Haven: Ely Printerie, 1915.

New Haven. "Report of the Building Inspector." In the *City Yearbook of the City of New Haven for 1916.* New Haven: A. J. Ely, 1917.

New Haven. "Report of the Fire Marshal." In the *City Yearbook of the City of New Haven for 1890.* New Haven: O. A. Dorman, 1891.

New Haven Chamber of Commerce. *New Haven Industry on Parade: C. Cowles & Company, Automotive Hardware.* New Haven Chamber of Commerce, April 1955.

New Haven Directory. 1840–1891, 1924–1930, 1989, 1990.

New Haven Land Records: 420:52; 516:404; 2305:272 and 275; 2343:288; 2359:576 and 622–624.

Robinson, Leoni W. (FAIA). 1852–1923. Architectural Drawings. New Haven Colony Historical Society Manuscript Collection, MS AD5.

Sanborn Map and Publishing Company. *Insurance Maps of New Haven, Connecticut.* 1886, updated to 1897; 1923 and 1923, updated to 1931; 1965, updated to 1973.

Sargent & Company

The history of one of the country's hardware giants began in New Britain in 1857, when Joseph B. Sargent bought out the New Britain firm of Peck and Walter Manufacturing Company, a bankrupt hardware manufacturer. With his brothers, Edward and George, he re-established the business as J. B. Sargent and Company, and with shrewd business acumen, soon brought the company up to speed. By 1863 business had increased to such an extent that the Sargents needed more space (figures 1 and 2).

In early March 1863, dismayed by dim prospects for his firm's continued success in New Britain, and aware of the advantages New Haven offered, J. B. Sargent purchased a two-acre site in the Harborside area on Water Street between Hamilton and Wallace streets for $22,210. The site included a tract of land across Water Street extending to the harbor front.

A Brief History of the Firm

Sargent lost no time in building his new plant and "contracted for a year's capacity of all the active brick yards in New Haven and Hartford counties; bought all of the other necessary building material; and proceeded to cover said land with an up-to-date 'slow burning' manufacturing plant," according to his grandson Ziegler Sargent. On 1 May 1864, with about 150 employees, many of whom had followed the company from New Britain, hardware production began in the new brick, timber, and plank plant.

The site on the harbor-front offered J. B. Sargent several advantages. Ships bringing coal and other supplies for manufacturing unloaded nearby, enabling him

157

J. B. Sargent converted the former Pavilion Hotel in the block east of the factory to house the employees and their families who followed the company from New Britain to New Haven. "Operating the made-over hotel became an increasing headache. It was difficult to please the tenants' wives, who had plenty of squabbles among themselves. So in 1879, the building was converted for factory use."

—Ziegler Sargent

FIGURE 1. *The machinery that powered equipment in the Sargent plant.* (New Haven Colony Historical Society Photo Archives)

FIGURE 2. *The original Sargent factory complex.* (New Haven Colony Historical Society; *1910 Sargent & Co Mechanics Tool Catalog*)

to move them quickly to storage areas on his site. Railroad tracks close to the Sargent and Company properties provided easy access to other markets, and to New York City, where goods could be distributed rapidly by rail and sea to markets throughout the United States and Europe. The city's water system provided the huge quantities of water required for the plating process of hardware production.

Ownership of land on the waterfront had one other advantage for Sargent and Company. Mud flats across the street from the main building on Water Street were barely covered at high tide and exposed at low tide. "As soon as the company operations in New Haven were begun in 1864, scrap and other materials not otherwise usable were dumped on the flats to make new land," according to Ziegler Sargent. The first building was constructed on this site in 1869, and like all other Sargent buildings south of Water Street, was built on piles.

The company made only a few products when it started operations; by the turn of the century, however, Sargent and Company's catalog contained more than seven thousand products. An important factor in this expansion was J. B. Sargent's decision in 1884 to add locks to the company's product line (figure 3). By the end of the nineteenth century, Sargent and Company was one of the two most important manufacturers in New Haven. Its expansion had extended to every phase of its operations: sales, workforce, physical plant, and product line had all increased several times.

In 1870, J. B. Sargent purchased another lot west of the Water Street site for

For Outside of Door
Knob and Escutcheon

FIGURE 3. *Sargent's "Lock sets for front doors" from the 1910 Sargent & Company catalog.* (New Haven Colony Historical Society)

$15,000 and within the year, expansion of the plant began in earnest with construction of two new buildings. More buildings were constructed in 1872, 1880 and 1885, the last for the production of locks (see Rae, "Technology, Population Growth and Centered Industrialism," figure 3). Products included locks and lock trim, padlocks, door closers, marine hardware, carpenters' tools, farm equipment, food choppers, wire goods, and casket hardware to name a few.

As production increased, so did the workforce. From 160 men in 1864, the workforce increased to almost 400 the next year; by 1873 the figure had risen to nearly 650. By the turn of the century, Sargent and Company was one of the largest employers in New Haven, with a workforce of 1,600, many of whom were Italian or Irish immigrants.

During the early twentieth century, the company continued to prosper. It operated one of the largest factories of its kind in 1914, with sixty thousand items of hardware listed in its catalog. But gradually Sargent and Company began to lose its preeminence in the industry. In an agonizing reappraisal to reverse this trend, it weeded out obsolete and unprofitable lines, developed new products, and reengineered some of the old ones. In 1925, as one of the leading producers of "shelf hardware," including hardware for doors, windows, and other parts involved in building, the company had capital, surplus, and undivided profits of more than $8,000,000, including its subsidiary merchandising concerns in New York and Chicago.

In 1949, Sargent and Company bought William Schollhorn & Company and its factory. Established in 1863, Schollhorn manufactured a fine grade of Star brand scissors and shears, the Bernhard pliers, and other hardware specialties. In 1887, it moved from its original factory on State Street to a newly built five-story brick factory on the corner of Wooster and Wallace Streets. The building had elevators and "all the most improved machinery and tools." In 1889 some one hundred men operated the factory. The building still stands and has been converted to offices.

Sargent family ownership of the company ended in 1967, when it was acquired by Kidde, Inc., a New Jersey–based firm. It soon became evident that product development had outstripped the production facilities, and the twenty-five brick buildings spread over twenty-one acres with a maze of corridors, bridges, and elevators at various levels were no longer adequate to turn out quality products with maximum efficiency and at competitive prices. The company, with 950 employees, moved to a one-story contemporary building at 100 Sargent Drive; all but one of the buildings and the Schollhorn building were demolished during the construction of Interstate 95.

REFERENCES

Commerce, Manufacturers, and Resources of New Haven, Connecticut: A Historical, Statistical and Descriptive Review. New Haven, Conn.: National Publishing, 1882.

"Executives purchasing Sargent Co." *New Haven Register*, 15 July 1987.

"History of Sargents' Fifty Years Manufacturing Here is Just Like Gripping Tale from A Story Book." *New Haven Sunday Union*, 25 October 1914.

The Industrial Advantages of the City of New Haven, Connecticut. New Haven Chamber of Commerce. New Haven: Jas. P. McKinney, 1889.

"Joseph Bradford Sargent." Transcript of a talk by Ziegler Sargent at the meeting of the New Haven Colony Historical Society, 19 October 1953.

New Haven Directory, 1885–1892 and 1923.

Purmont, Jon E. "Sargent Comes to New Haven." *Journal of the New Haven Colony Historical Society.* 1976.

Sanborn Map and Publishing Co. "New Haven, Connecticut." 1880.

Sanborn Map Company. "Insurance Maps of New Haven." 1886, updated to 1897; 1901; 1924; 1937; 1965, updated to 1973.

Sargent, David E. "Joseph Bradford Sargent, 1822–1902, Captain of Industry." West Hartford, Conn.: *News Press*, August 1973.

Singer, George. "The Sargent Company." Typed manuscript for American Studies Program, Yale University, 5 May 1970. New Haven Colony Historical Society.

"Times Change and We Change With Them." Pamphlet, Sargent Company, 1966.

Wright, Mark. "Factory, Neighborhood and Workers: Sargent Company, Wooster Square and Italian Immigrants in 1890." Typed manuscript for Yale University, 14 December 1982. New Haven Colony Historical Society.

The Bigelow Boiler Company

"One of the best known and most justly celebrated concerns engaged in this branch of industry (steam power) is The Bigelow Boiler Company of New Haven, whose steam boilers of special and most practical design are known and used the world over."

— *New Haven and Its Points of Interest* (1895)

When a plant foreman named Hobart Bigelow bought his boss's machine business on Whitney Avenue in 1861 to start his own company, his friends and colleagues thought he was either foolhardy or naive. The company would never survive, they predicted: the nation was on the brink of civil war, which they believed would inevitably be followed by a crushing depression. Nevertheless, Bigelow proceeded to found a company that would be one of New Haven's major industries for more than a century (figures 1–3).

A Brief History of the Firm

Far from being an impediment, the Civil War was an opportune time for Bigelow to start his manufacturing business. Responding to the wartime demand for arms production, he negotiated contracts to provide the government with specialized machinery for making rifles. With a workforce of two hundred, the company also produced some of the rifle parts to arm Lincoln's troops and fabricated portions of the Union's famous ship, the Ericsson *Monitor*. To increase capital for his company's rapidly expanding production, Bigelow reorganized the Bigelow Manufacturing Company under the Connecticut joint stock laws in 1863–1864.

After the war, with civilian contracts for gold-mining machinery from the far West and for portable engines and drilling apparatus from the newly opened oil fields in Pennsylvania, the Bigelow plant was running full speed. To add further to their success, Bigelow contracted with Ohio capitalists to manufacture the James Leffel Patent Turbine Water Wheel—which proved to be a very lucrative venture. During the same period, the company also began to manufacture boilers, which

"Not withstanding the general unrest that pervaded business circles in consequence of the war, which was then fully upon us, the business of the Bigelow works assumed proportions far in excess of all expectations."

—George Bigelow, in "The History of The Bigelow Company"

FIGURE 1. *Workers and machinery in Bigelow plant.* (New Haven Colony Historical Society Manuscript Collection. MS 54, box 3, folder D)

FIGURE 2. *Boilers coming out of the Bigelow plant.* (New Haven Colony Historical Society Manuscript Collection. MS 54, box 3, folder D)

were soon in such demand that, even with the addition of a boiler department, the plant on Whitney Avenue was not large enough to meet production needs.

When Yale University offered him a three-acre site at Grapevine Point in Fair Haven in 1869, Bigelow seized the opportunity to expand. The site, a former training camp for Civil War soldiers, included several frame buildings, which were converted for manufacturing. The company moved to a new 100 ft. × 50 ft. frame building at the site and quickly geared up for production of dozens of models of boilers, as well as portable and stationary steam engines. An early morning fire— the city's most disastrous fire that year—nearly destroyed the building in June 1873. Given the delay in raising the alarm, the limited number of available hydrants and the fierce headway made by the fire, "it was, to use the owner's expression, surprising to him that even a vestige could have been saved." Bigelow rebuilt the plant within the year. In 1889, the Chamber of Commerce noted that "the facilities of the company for the receipt of the raw material and the shipment of the finished product are particularly favorable both by rail and vessel, the works being contiguous to the water and connected by tracks with the railroad system."

At the time of the move to Fair Haven, the Bigelow Manufacturing Company dissolved and soon reorganized as a partnership under the name H. B. Bigelow & Company. With a workforce of one hundred employees and ever-increasing sales of engines and boilers, the partnership incorporated as The Bigelow Company

FIGURE 3. *Boilers in the Bigelow factory yard.* (New Haven Colony Historical Society Manuscript Collection. MS 54, box 3, folder D)

in 1883. Eight years later, it ceased production of stationary engines and general machinery to concentrate solely on making large boilers. Bigelow boilers had gained a reputation for producing maximum steam power combined with minimum fuel consumption. In 1905, the company acquired exclusive rights from an English firm to manufacture Hornsby Water Tube Boilers in the United States, and to sell them in this country and Mexico. The deal was such a success that stockholders voted to modernize the entire plant for greater efficiency in handling the new line of boilers.

During both world wars, the Bigelow Boiler Company devoted almost full production to the war effort. It supplied boilers for the nation's emergency fleet in the first war, and in the second war, as a subcontractor to the Electric Boat Company, it built foundations for submarine engines, escape trunks, and many other component parts.

After World War II, with a workforce of 150 employees, the company continued to improve the design and production of its boilers. Bigelow boilers powered mines in South Africa, oil wells and pipelines in Mexico, sugar mills in the West Indies and the Peter Paul candy company's coconut-shredding plant in the Philippines. The boilers were installed in wineries and distilleries, universities, foundries, and electric power plants. In 1955, the company built a 65-foot long, 85-ton furnace for the Tidewater Oil Company of Delaware; it was believed to have been the largest piece of equipment ever built in New Haven.

Despite advances, the end was near for one of New Haven's oldest manufacturing firms. With only seventy-six employees, the Bigelow Boiler Company was sold in 1963 to the Grapevine Point Company, an affiliate of the Malleable Iron Fittings Company in Branford, Connecticut. Four years later, the new company merged with the Superior Materials Company of Wilkes-Barre, Pennsylvania; in 1971, it produced another huge packaged boiler for installation at the Bayonne Military Terminal: a self-combined water tube boiler weighing seventy tons, designed to produce more than 100,000 pounds of steam per hour.

Recently imposed federal economic controls took their toll on the company now called Bigelow Superior Industries. In August 1974, insufficient funds to meet future payrolls forced the company to shut down. A month later, it filed for bankruptcy, and resumed production with its remaining forty employees. Within a year, the Etherington Companies bought the company for $700,000.

THE PLANT

1869	Hobart Bigelow moved his company from its original location on Whitney Avenue at the Farmington Canal to a new 100 ft. × 50 ft. frame factory on the south side of River Street at Grapevine Point.
1873	Fire destroyed the factory in 1873. Bigelow replaced it in the same year with another wood frame factory that fronted 200 feet on River Street.
1881	Bigelow made large additions to its factory including the three-story 100 ft. × 40 ft. brick factory with five unique round-arched openings on the streetside ground floor to allow passage of giant assembled boilers and other large equipment.
1884	Two more brick factories were built on River Street: 41 ft. × 97 ft. and 108 ft. × 97 ft. The larger of the two was likely the brick boiler shop with five-foot monitor added to the south side of the three-story factory building.
1886	The company added a one-story, 206 ft. × 43 ft. brick plate-iron building to the west side of the boiler shop. The 1888 atlas shows a block of brick additions on the west side of the complex attached to the 1873 block of wood-frame structures.
1889	The Bigelow plant included machine, plate iron, boiler, and blacksmith shops, a foundry and other buildings. A second major fire severely damaged a large two-story wood building on the east side of the complex along River Street. It was quickly replaced with a 100 ft. × 56 ft. one-story brick machine shop. By 1897, all of the principal factory buildings in the complex were of brick construction.
1902	The company built a two-story brick building on the corner of River and Lloyd Streets in 1902 to house a machine shop and company offices.
1906	The brick factory plant was upgraded at a cost of $24,000. The power plant was reorganized and updated with new boilers and engines powered by electricity. Renovations transformed the boiler shop into two erection shops: a one-story brick building, 122 ft. × 78 ft. with a three-foot roof monitor for lighting; and, attached on the south, a new 53-foot wide structure extending 342 feet toward the harbor. One 42-foot-story high with a near flat roof, this building has a steel frame sheathed in corrugated metal siding to a height of 20 feet. Above the siding, the walls are entirely steel-framed windows.
1918–21	Some $10,000 in factory additions at the Bigelow plant were made in 1918. By 1921, Bigelow widened and lengthened the plate-iron building and extended the boiler erection shop another 100 feet toward the waterfront.

The Bigelow plant (figure 4) is an example of an intact late nineteenth- and early-twentieth-century industrial complex, one of the most interesting such com-

FIGURE 4. *The Bigelow Factory today has potential for adaptive reuse but is deteriorating rapidly.* (Composite photo by Henry Lord)

plexes in New Haven. It features typical two- and three-story late-nineteenth-century brick machine shops together with early-twentieth-century steel-frame erection shops at the rear. Note the distinctive and unusual horseshoe-arch openings in the front facade (now enclosed) used for the transport of large equipment from the plant. This building has neat dentil work at the eaves, above rhythmic segmental arched window and door heads. This complex is a major architectural landmark contributing to the dense, urban industrial character of River Street.

REFERENCES

Atwater, Edward E., ed. *History of the City of New Haven.* New York: Munsell, 1887.

"Bigelow Boilers Serve Industry." *Connecticut Industry* (October 1958).

Bigelow, George W. "History of the Bigelow Company" [1906]. MS 54, Bigelow Company Records, 1852–1967. New Haven Colony Historical Society.

The Bigelow Co., New Haven, Conn. Site plan, 22 August 1912. Boston: Underwriters Bureau of New England, 1912.

———. Site plan, 16 May 1961. Hartford: Factory Insurance Association, Eastern Regional Office, 1961.

Chamber of Commerce. *The Industrial Advantages of the City of New Haven, Connecticut.* New Haven: Jas. P. McKinney, 1889. 61.

Connecticut Development Commission. *Register of War Production Facilities in Connecticut.* Hartford, Conn.: n.p. [1951].

"Fires & Alarms from January 1, 1873–January 1, 1874." "Report of the Chief Engineer." *City Year*

Book of the City of New Haven for 1873–4. New Haven: Tuttle, Morehouse and Taylor, 1874. 218.

"Fires & Alarms in the City of New Haven for the Month of August, 1889." *City Year Book of the City of New Haven for* 1889. New Haven: O. A. Dorman, 1890.

Hopkins, Griffith Morgan. *Atlas of the City of New Haven, Connecticut.* Philadelphia, 1888.

Kirby, John B., Jr. "New Haven Building Permit Records." Vol. 3 (permit 104, April 1884). New Haven, May 1983.

Mercantile Illustrating Company. *New Haven and Its Points of Interest,* 1895.

New Haven Chamber of Commerce. "The Bigelow Company Since 1833. What New Haven Makes, Makes New Haven." April 1953.

New Haven Directory. 1860–1869, 1881–1884.

New Haven Journal Courier. 10 December 1955 and 30 April 1963.

New Haven Register. New Haven Now and Then, Series 42, 1931, 6 July 1971, 3 August 1974, 14 September 1974, 12 March 1975.

"Records of the Bigelow Company, July 11, 1882–March 4, 1923." MS 54, Bigelow Company Records, 1852–1967, New Haven Colony Historical Society.

"Report of the Building Inspector." *City Year Book of the City of New Haven for 1906 and 1981.* New Haven: S. Z. Field, 1907 and 1919.

"Report of the Fire Marshal." *City Year Book of the City of New Haven for 1881.* New Haven: O. A. Dorman, 1882.

Roth, Matthew. *Connecticut: An Inventory of Historic Engineering and Industrial Sites.* Hartford, Conn.: Society for Industrial Archeology, 1981.

Sanborn Map and Publishing Co. *New Haven, Connecticut,* 1880.

Sanborn Map Company. *Insurance Maps of New Haven, Connecticut.* 1886 (updated to 1897), 1924.

The National Pipe Bending Company

"In supplying some of the prime essentials and requisites for manufacturers, plumbers, and gas and steam fitters' purposes, the National Pipe Bending Co. have for six years filled an important place among the industrial concerns of New Haven, and in a wide field of operations they developed a trade which is a large item in the great aggregate of business centering here."

—Leading Business Men of New Haven County (1887)

In the late nineteenth and early twentieth centuries, in addition to producing consumer goods, New Haven factories made products for use by other industrial manufacturers in the city and the state. One such company was the National Pipe Bending Company. This company typifies the specialized manufacturing that historically developed to service a particular industry and began to specialize in a way that could service several industries. Its development parallels—not perfectly—the evolution of machine-tool industry that originally grew in response to the needs of textile, carriage, and other manufacturing in New Haven and other localities.

A Brief History of the Firm

Throughout its long history, the National Pipe Bending Company specialized in the manufacture of metal coils for heaters and in making heaters for industrial boilers. With this strong focus and its close alliance with the Bigelow Boiler Company, it prospered from the late nineteenth century until late in the twentieth century. Hobart Bigelow's boiler-manufacturing firm used coiled pipes in making its water-tube boilers. To have ready access to these special pipes, he joined with several partners to found the National Pipe Bending Company in 1882 and deeded a part of his land, with a new factory building, to the company. The factory stood on the north side of River Street near Bigelow's boiler factory.

The Bigelow Boiler Company and the National Pipe Bending Company each incorporated in 1883. By 1887, experienced workmen in the Pipe Bending factory were turning out large quantities of iron, brass, and copper bent in coils, angles,

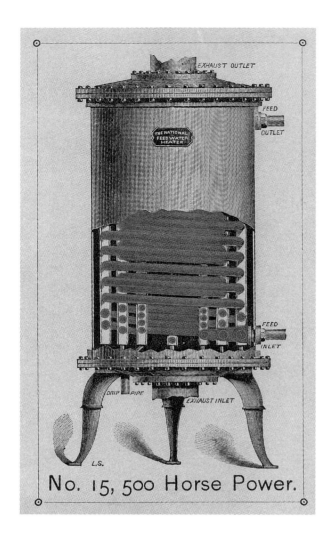

FIGURE 1. *The Feed-Water Heater.* (Collection of Richard and Marianne Mazan)

FIGURE 2. *Giant coils, components in the manufacture of custom-engineered heat transfer systems.* (New Haven Colony Historical Society, Dana update, vol. 123)

and return bends for Bigelow and other manufacturers, as well as for plumbers and gas and steam fitters. The company was also the sole manufacturer of the National Feed-Water Heater. One of the most popular appliances in use in the country for heating feed-water for boilers, it was made of a series of coiled-metal piping in a cast-iron shell (figure 1). The company eventually expanded its line to include heaters specifically for use in hotels, hospitals, breweries, and dye houses. At the turn of the century, the National Pipe Bending Company's product pamphlet listed more than one thousand establishments in America and some foreign nations that used the National Feed-Water Heater.

The National Pipe Bending Company continued to perfect its products and maintained a steady business through two world wars and the Great Depression. In 1950, with a workforce of only thirty-two people, the company added storage,

FIGURE 3. *The National Pipe Company Building today.* (Composite photo by Henry Lord)

feed-water, and instantaneous heaters to its World War II production of fuel oil preheaters, coils, and bends. Twenty years later, it began phasing out multiple-stock items to specialize in the manufacture of custom-engineered heat transfer systems and components for those systems (figure 2). Custom work generated growth for a few years; in 1983, however, the National Pipe Bending Company sold its plant and in the following year merged with the Bigelow Company, which had been owned by the Etherington Company since 1975 (figure 3).

THE PLANT

1890–93   The National Pipe Bending Company purchased a site on the southeast corner of River and Lloyd streets in 1890, across the street from its original factory. Six one-story attached brick buildings were built on Lloyd Street that year to house a testing room, stock room, iron storage, engine and boiler rooms and an iron shop. A three-story brick factory and office building was completed on the corner of River and Lloyd streets in 1893.

        The river was bulwarked and much of the land in the area south of River Street was fill on top of tons of oyster shells. Between 1900 and 1911, the company added seven more buildings.

1900   Addition of one-story brick brass and copper shop; one-story brick brass foundry and one-story wood garage.

1906   Addition of one-story brick building for iron pipe racks; one-story brick iron shop and one-story brick welding room.

1911   Addition of two-story steel and glass machine room and pattern and heater shop.

1911–23   A few small additions completed the factory complex between 1911 and 1923. The company built four small one-story wood buildings and added a second story to the brick building adjoining the large three-story factory at River and George streets.

REFERENCES

Atwater, Edward E., ed. *History of the City of New Haven.* New York: Munsell, 1887.

Connecticut Development Commission. *Register of War Production Facilities in Connecticut.* Hartford, Conn.: n.p., 1951.

The Industrial Advantages of the City of New Haven, Connecticut. New Haven Chamber of Commerce. New Haven: Jas. P. McKinney, 1889.

Leading Business Men of New Haven County. Boston: Mercantile Publishing, 1887.

The National Feed-Water Heater. New Haven: National Pipe Bending Company, c. 1890s.

New Haven Directory, 1883 and 1884.

New Haven Land Records. 366:251, 422:37, 3058:284, 3243:27.

New Haven Register, 13 September 1971.

Plot Plan of the National Pipe Building Co., New Haven, Conn. 21 January 1926.

Price List of the National Feed Water Heater. New Haven: National Pipe Bending Company, January 1891.

"Report of the Building Inspector." *City Yearbook for the City of New Haven for* 1906. New Haven: S. Z. Field, 1907.

"Report of the Building Inspector." *City Yearbook for the City of New Haven for* 1911. New Haven: A. D. Steinbach, 1912.

"Report of the Fire Marshal." *City Year Book for the City of New Haven for* 1890. New Haven: O. A. Dorman, 1891.

Sanborn Map Company. *Insurance Maps of New Haven, Connecticut.* 1901 and 1923.

Townshend, Doris B. *Fair Haven, A Journey Through Time.* New Haven: New Haven Colony Historical Society, 1976.

The New Haven Clock Company

Chauncey Jerome, founder of the New Haven Clock Company, started his career in 1816 working for Eli Terry, the well-known Connecticut clockmaker. Terry was just beginning mass production of his famous thirty-hour wooden-movement clock that revolutionized the clock-making industry. Jerome's job was to make the elegant wooden cases that housed the clocks. Two years later he went into business for himself, making cases that he traded to Eli Terry and others for wooden movements.

A Brief History of the Firm

In 1822, Jerome built a small shop in Bristol, Connecticut, and with his brother Noble, a skilled mechanic, he produced thirty-hour and eight-day wooden clocks. Although production of wooden clocks was difficult and slow, the business was a success until the panic of 1837, which paralyzed business, temporarily closed banks, and virtually shut down the Connecticut clock industry, including the Jerome Clock Company.

"While thinking over my business troubles and disappointments, I could not help feeling very much depressed," Jerome wrote in his autobiography. "That minute, I was looking at the wood clock on the table and it came into my mind instantly that there could be a cheap one-day brass clock that would take the place of the wood clock. I at once began to figure on it: the case would cost no more; the dial, the glass, weights and other fixtures would be the same, and the size would be reduced. . . . I knew there was a fortune in it." Soon after, he began to apply mass-production techniques and the magic of interchangeable parts to making clocks in

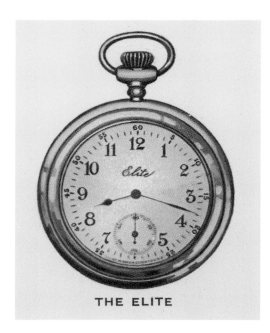

THE ELITE

FIGURE 1. *Pocket watch, early twentieth century.* (New Haven Colony Historical Society; *New Haven Clock Company Catalog* 171, page 1)

FIGURE 2. *Wall clock, early twentieth century.* (New Haven Colony Historical Society; *New Haven Clock Company Catalog* 171, page 1)

Bristol. He replaced wooden movements with those made of stamped brass, which was readily available and inexpensive.

The result was a thirty-hour brass-movement clock that could be manufactured in large volume and therefore could be profitably sold at a very low price. Compared to a one-day wooden clock that cost thirteen dollars, Jerome's thirty-hour metal clock cost only four dollars. It rejuvenated the faltering clock-making industry and stimulated the Connecticut brass industry. Business grew rapidly and Jerome began to export his clocks to England and later, to the European Continent (figures 1–3).

In 1842, with overseas sales increasing, Jerome bought a bankrupt carriage factory on St. John Street in New Haven to be near a shipping harbor, and moved the case-making and finishing works there in 1844. When fire destroyed his brass-movement factory in Bristol a few months later, he enlarged the New Haven plant and moved his entire operation into it. With his nephew Hiram Camp as superintendent of manufacturing operations, the company soon became the largest industrial employer in the city, with about 250 workers producing 150,000 clocks annually. In the clock face department, dials were stamped out by machinery; letters and figures were printed on them (figure 4). The cost of labor was about 20 cents a clock, and the cost of materials about 50 cents a clock, which sold for $1.50 to $2.00.

In 1850, Jerome formed the Jerome Manufacturing Company as a joint stock company, with the Benedict and Burnham Company, brass manufacturers in Waterbury. Three years later, the company's production had increased to 440,000 clocks and timepieces. With demands for his clocks at an all-time high, Chauncey Jerome was at the peak of his career.

Hiram Camp, frustrated with the increased volume of work and his antiquated tools, struck out on his own. He built a small wooden workshop in 1851 near the Jerome Manufacturing Company plant to make brass movements, which he supplied to Jerome. In 1853, Camp's business incorporated as the New Haven Clock Company "to manufacture, sell and deal in clocks and timekeepers of every description." In addition to Camp, principals in the new firm included James E. English and H. M. Welch, partners in a prosperous lumber and shipping business.

By his own admission, Chauncey Jerome was a better inventor than businessman. As his company became more successful, he overextended its operation. In 1855, he made the fatal mistake of buying out a failed Bridgeport clock company controlled by showman P. T. Barnum. Barnum was completely devious, according to Hiram Camp, and the deal left the Jerome Manufacturing Company bankrupt and Chauncey Jerome with more than 250 creditors, including the principals of the New Haven Clock Company. Jerome never recovered from the loss.

"I have not the least doubt but that my taking the job of making Mr. Jerome's clocks from 1847 to 1850 saved the clock business to New Haven people."

—Hiram Camp, "A Sketch of the Clock Making Business"

PLANT OF
THE NEW HAVEN CLOCK COMPANY

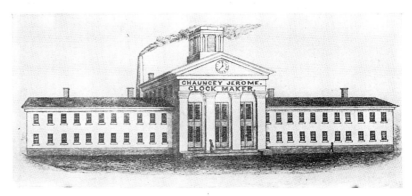

1845

1860

Present Plant, 133 Hamilton Street, New Haven, Connecticut

FIGURE 3. *An illustration from the New Haven Clock Company's catalog in 1916 shows the development of the company's factory complex.* (New Haven Colony Historical Society)

The New Haven Clock Company bought the Jerome Manufacturing Company plant, its tools, clocks, and parts for $40,000. Under the leadership of James English, with the same workforce and machinery, the company became the largest clock manufactory in Connecticut, and one of the largest in the world. The company prospered for the next fifty years, as it aggressively pursued the tradition

FIGURE 4. *The clock face department.* (Courtesy Carolyn Cooper; *New Haven Clock Company Catalog* 169)

of innovation established by Jerome. The nickel-plated alarm clock, the "dollar watch," and the wristwatch are early examples. In 1929, the company first produced synchronous electric clocks that were superior to handwound timepieces and led to the development of time switches for stoves, radios, and refrigerators, as well as car clocks.

In the mid-1930s the New Haven Clock Company plant covered most of two city blocks and its fifteen hundred employees produced more than three million timepieces a year. During World War II, with more than two thousand employees, its entire operation was devoted to the design and production of timing devices for anti-aircraft shells, bombs, and naval mines.

In 1945, Paul V. Eisner and Max Taussig, co-owners of the Rensie Watch Company, which represented prominent Swiss watch-manufacturing companies, were elected to the board of directors. Within a year, the company was reorganized under the name New Haven Clock and Watch Company. Richard Whitehead, president for sixteen years, resigned, disheartened by the erosion of his once-proud company. The new company's financial difficulties began almost at once and increased steadily. In 1956, it filed for bankruptcy and never recovered. A report by P. H. English, former treasurer of the New Haven Clock Company and the New Haven Clock and Watch Company, included the following reasons for the company's decline: "increasing Swiss competition in the watch field; loss of watch-worker skills caused by the drafting of the plant facilities for 100 percent war production in 1940–1945; the attempt by new management to expand the total sales from $6 million to $9 million without adequate bank credit, and domination of the clock field by new electrical models for home and automobile by aggressive new competitors such as Borg-Warner and General Electric." In March 1960 all of the manufacturing facilities, including five hundred machines, tools, dies, jigs, and works in progress, were sold at auction for half a million dollars. The Hamilton Development Company acquired the land and buildings in December 1960 for $250,000.

THE PLANT

1842–45   Jerome purchased the c. 1834 three-story factory on the north side of St. John Street, between Hamilton and Wallace Streets. A large cupola topped the building, flanked

FIGURE 5. *The remaining New Haven Clock Company Buildings have been sadly neglected and vandalized.* (Composite photo by Henry Lord)

by long two-story wings. The Neoclassical wood facade had pilasters, entablature and pediment in the Doric style.

1851–53   Hiram Camp built a wooden shop on the west side of Hamilton Street for making brass movements.

1856–60   A third floor was added to the two original wings of the clock company building and the cupola was removed.

1861–80   All but the northern wing of what would become "Clock Square" was completed by 1880. Three brick mills completed the south wing on St. John Street The west wing facing Hamilton Street appears to have been built in four sections between 1860 and 1880, in much the same style as the south wing, with flat arched segmental window and sash details, brick dental at the cornice and a stone belt course at the first floor line.

1885   A four-story brick mill was built on Wallace Street and a large one-story brick foundry partially filled the north wing. A four-story brick mill was built on the north side of the complex.

1889   The New Haven Clock Company plant occupied nearly two city blocks by 1889: the former Hiram Camp movement works on the west side of Hamilton Street, and the former Chauncey Jerome case works on St. John Street.

1905–14   Two four-story factories were added to the north wing, and other new buildings filled in to form Clock Square.

1960   When the New Haven Clock and Watch Company sold the plant in 1960, its eighteen factory buildings stood on four acres of industrial land. All of the buildings were of brick, heavy joist, or slow-burning mill construction.

1961–73   During the 1960s the former movement works on the west side of Hamilton Street were demolished for the Interstate 91 right-of-way. The east plant, known as Clock Square, survives.

The surviving plant (figure 5) is a good example of New England industrial architecture from the last quarter of the nineteenth century. It is one of the few surviving factory complexes of its period in the Wooster Square area, which was dominated by complexes of this type by the end of the nineteenth century.

REFERENCES

Atwater, Edward E., ed. *History of the City of New Haven*. New York: Munsell, 1887.

Barr, Leonard. "The New Haven Clock Company." *Bulletin of the National Association of Watch and Clock Collectors, Inc.* 71 (December 1957).

Beers, Frederick W. *Map of the City of New Haven and Fair Haven*. Beers, Hellis & Soule, 1868.

Camp, Hiram. *A Sketch of the Clock Making Business, 1792–1892*. [1893].

Jerome, Chauncey. *History of the American Clock Business for the Past Sixty Years and Life of Chauncey Jerome, Written by Himself*. New Haven: F. C. Dayton, Jr., 1860.

Kelly, Cassius W. *Atlas of New Haven, Connecticut*. Bridgeport, Conn.: Streuli & Puckhafer, 1911.

Kirby, John B., Jr. "New Haven Building Permit Records, 1882–1886." Vol. 4. New Haven, February 1984.

Map of the City of New Haven and Vicinity from Actual Surveys by Hartley and Whiteford. Cartographers: Hartley and Whiteford. Philadelphia: Collins and Clark, 1851.

New Haven Chamber of Commerce. *The Industrial Advantages of the City of New Haven*. New Haven: Jas. P. McKinney. 1889.

New Haven Clock Company. "A Century of Manufacturing, the New Haven Clock Company." *Illustrated Catalogue of Clocks Manufactured by the New Haven Clock Company*. Bristol: American Clock and Watch Museum [1976]. Reprint of 1880s catalogue.

——. *History of the New Haven Clock Company—Clock Makers for more than a Century—Established 1817*. New Haven, [1938].

——. Illustrated catalogues: No. 168 (1911–12), no. 169 (1914–15), no. 171 (1920–1921), no. 173 (1923), no. 174 (1924), and no. 72 (1935). New Haven Colony Historical Society.

——. Records, 1853–1946. MS 4, New Haven Colony Historical Society.

——. *The Story of the New Haven Clock Company*. New Haven [1945].

New Haven Journal Courier. 23 December 1960.

New Haven Land Records. 105:240, 123:421, 132:379, 161:114, 184:237, 1501:270, 2074:431.

"Report of the Building Inspector." *City Yearbook of the City of New Haven for 1911*. New Haven: A. D. Steinbach, 1912.

"Report of the Fire Marshal." *City Yearbook for the City of New Haven for 1905*. New Haven: Samuel Z. Field, 1906.

Roth, Matthew. *Connecticut: An Inventory of Historic Engineering and Industrial Sites*. Hartford, Conn.: Society for Industrial Archeology, 1981.

Sanborn Map and Publishing Co. *New Haven, Connecticut*. 1880.

Sanborn Map Company. *Insurance Maps of New Haven, Connecticut*. 1886 (updated to 1897); 1923; 1923 (updated to 1961); 1965 (updated to 1973).

Searle, Silas W. *Map of the City of New Haven, Connecticut*. Philadelphia: W. H. Rease, 1859.

Tilney, Bradford S. "The Architecture of Clock Square and a Brief for its Preservation." Typescript, February 1982. New Haven Colony Historical Society.

The Quinnipiac Brewing Company

Early settlers in New Haven considered a brewhouse as essential as a kitchen in the homestead. They believed the water in New Haven wasn't fit to drink, although they thought it safe enough for brewing beer. As a result, the entire family, including children, drank beer at meals as well as for refreshment. Most beer in New Haven was made at home or in taverns until the mid-nineteenth century, when four breweries were built. By 1885, there were eight significant breweries in the city, including the Quinnipiac Brewing Company, which was one of the foremost breweries in New England before Prohibition.

A Brief History of the Firm

In 1881, Peter Schleippmann, a New Haven laborer, and William Spittler, a brewer from New York City, bought land on River Street in Fair Haven overlooking the Quinnipiac River. Three months later they built the Quinnipiac Brewery, bought adjacent land, and by year's end began producing lager, which they sold locally.

In trouble financially but encouraged by the success of their lager, Scleippmann and Spittler bought more land in 1884, and added new machinery to produce ale and porter in addition to lager. Their products were doing well in a widening distribution, but the partners were not savvy businessmen and were soon mortgaged to the hilt and so deeply in debt that they were unable to obtain malt. They were forced to declare bankruptcy in June 1885, and to sell their real and personal property for the benefit of their creditors.

Nathaniel W. Kendall, a shrewd New York businessman, bought the brewery—its land, buildings and most of the equipment—for five thousand dollars

FIGURE 1. *Interior of the Cooper Shop at the Yale Brewery.*
(New Haven Colony Historical Society Photo Archives)

and incorporated it as the Quinnipiac Brewing Company. The new company was soon off and running, producing thirty-five thousand barrels of ale, lager, and porter a year—twenty-five thousand barrels more than the rival Fresenius Brewery, one of the city's earliest breweries. "The equipment is of the latest improved character, and embraces all the most modern appliances for the perfection of the product," boasted the New Haven Chamber of Commerce in 1889 (figure 1–3). A 200-horsepower steam engine powered the equipment and an electric dynamo furnished light to the entire plant. The brewery installed two twenty-five-ton refrigerating machines, and pioneered the successful storage of beer in steel casks.

By 1892, with an enlarged plant and thirty skilled laborers, some of them recent immigrants from Germany, the Quinnipiac Brewing Company had increased production to fifty thousand barrels of high-quality beer a year. Distribution expanded

FIGURE 2. *An electric train in the Quinnipiac Brewery transported goods from department to department and finally to a loading dock outside.* (New Haven Colony Historical Society Photo Archives)

from New Haven and nearby towns to all of New England. In 1896, encouraged by the brewery's continued success, Kendall commissioned Leoni Robinson, architect of numerous public buildings in the area, to design additions and a grand new facade to the plant. Kendall also had Robinson design his castlelike home in Fair Haven overlooking the harbor. The house is said to have cost one hundred thousand dollars, reputedly from the brewery's coffers. With Kendall as president, the company reorganized in 1902 as the Yale Brewing Company, Inc., with six hundred thousand dollars capital. The plant was again enlarged, as the beer industry in New Haven continued to flourish.

The good times came to a sudden halt in 1919 with the passing of the Volstead Act, and the beginning of Prohibition a year later. Christian Feigenspan, owner of brewing companies in Newark and Albany, refused to believe the country would

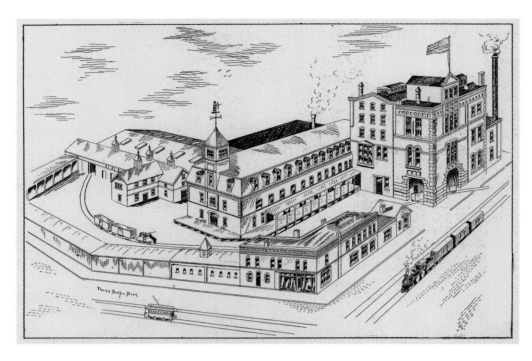

FIGURE 3. *A loading dock outside the building where kegs of beer were put on wagons or trucks for delivery.* (New Haven Colony Historical Society, Dana Scrap Book, vol. 123, folder 2, p. 21)

go dry and bought the Yale Brewing Company in 1919. Along with many other brewers, he thought he could survive Prohibition by producing "cereal beverages"—2.75 percent "near" beer—and adapted the Fair Haven plant for its production. The product was a complete failure. Production was reduced to a trickle compared with the thousands of gallons that had flowed from the brewery just a few years before. In 1922, the plant was virtually shut down for the duration of Prohibition.

When Prohibition ended in 1933, the Yale Brewing Company was reincorporated as The New Haven Brewing Company with Feigenspan as president. The company modernized the plant and produced beer there for another ten years before the brewery was shut down for good.

THE PLANT

1881 Peter Schleippmann and William Spittler built the Quinnipiac Brewery on River Street in Fair Haven. The brewery was approximately 50 ft. × 185 feet.

1892 The brewery now included the original three-story 100 ft. × 185 ft. brick brewery plus a 100 ft. × 185 ft. addition and a four-story 38 ft. × 48 ft. ell; a brick office and bottling shop; frame cooper shop; wash house; stables; and keg, wagon, and storage shed.
The brewery buildings occupied the entire block bounded by Ferry, River, East Pearl, Chapel, and Houston streets. They were a typical mix of industrial construction of the era: brick bearing walls, cast-iron interior supports and spanning members, with heavy nonsparking timber used in the dry-grain handling areas.

1895 Plant improvements designed by Leoni Robinson enlarged the four-story ell to the original building, added an additional story and created a new facade that conformed to the oblique angle of River Street. A square archway cut diagonally across the corner of the new facade to accommodate the railway line that led from the brewery to a loading dock in the courtyard.

1897 The section of the plant on the corner of River and East Pearl streets was rebuilt varying in height from three to six stories, housing the cooler, mash, and malt mill. The attached two-story building on the north was doubled in size, to house the ale department, storage, fermenting, malt, and filling rooms. A large one-story frame wash house and keg shed were joined on the north.

1906 Architect Otto Wolff designed further additions in 1906 and 1911, including two extra floors on part of the 1881 building, an elevator tower, and a large garage.

1913 A $34,000 bottling works was added on adjacent property.

1945–76 The property was used for various wholesale and storage purposes.

1986 The brewery site was vacant from 1976 until 1986, when it was converted to condominiums.

The brewery is an example of an intact late-nineteenth-century light manufacturing complex. This major Fair Haven landmark features a large manufacturing building encircled by smaller wings and outbuildings. The whole complex is

FIGURE 4. *The brewery was converted to condominiums in 1986.*
(Photo by Henry Lord)

unified by a brick perimeter wall that gives it a medieval effect. The front facade of the main building served to embellish a rather utilitarian main block that had been built fourteen years earlier. Note how the new facade conforms to the oblique angle of the street (figure 4).

REFERENCES

Atwater, Edward E., ed. *History of the City of New Haven.* New York, Munsell, 1887.

Baron, Stanley Wade. *Brewed in America: A History of Beer and Ale in the United States.* Boston: Little, Brown, 1962.

Greater New Haven Chamber of Commerce. Records, 1794. MS 34. New Haven Colony Historical Society.

Hopkins, Griffith Morgan. "Atlas of the City of New Haven, Connecticut." Philadelphia, 1888

Kelley, Cassius, W. *Atlas of New Haven, Connecticut.* Bridgeport, Conn.: Streuli & Puckhafer, 1911.

Kirby, John B., Jr. "New Haven Building Permit Records, 1882–1886." 4 vols. New Haven, December 1982, March 1983, May 1982, February 1984.

Malley, Richard C., and Michelle E. Parish. "Beer and the Brewing of Beer in Connecticut." *Connecticut Historical Society Bulletin* 56, nos. 3 and 4 (Summer–Fall 1991).

New Haven Chamber of Commerce. *The Industrial Advantages of the City of New Haven, Connecticut.* New Haven: Jas. P. McKinney, 1889.

New Haven Directory. 1880–1886.

New Haven Land Records. 349:25 and 184, 370:135, 375:335, 380:266, 836:38, 1295:176, 1484:57.

The Palladium Company. *New Haven of Today: Its Commerce, Trade and Industries.* New Haven: Clarence H. Ryder, 1892.

"Report of the Building Inspector." *City Yearbook for the City of New Haven for* 1913. New Haven: S. Z. Field, 1914.

Robinson, Leoni W. (FAIA). Architectural Drawings, 1896, 1907, & 1911 (Otto Wolff). MS AD5. New Haven Colony Historical Society.

Sokal, Diane, et al. "The Fair Haven Brewery." Typed manuscript, 28 October 1979. New Haven Colony Historical Society.

Sanborn Map and Publishing Company. *Insurance Maps of New Haven, Connecticut.* 1886 (updated to 1887); 1924; 1924 (updated to 1931); 1924 (updated to 1961).

L. Candee & Company

Leverett Candee had been involved in a series of successful dry goods busi-nesses with numerous partners and an ever-changing cast of characters, when he ventured into making book paper. It was a bad decision: his com-pany failed in 1842. Candee was forty-seven years old and bankrupt but, undaunted by failure, he started a modest business making elastic suspenders in the former Galpin and Robertson carpet plant on East Street. Then he met Charles Goodyear, who after years of frustration and disappointment in efforts to transform rubber tree gum into a usable product, had applied for a patent for his process to vulcanize rubber. The two struck a deal: Goodyear gave Candee a temporary license to try out his invention in making rubber shoes. With a loan of three thousand dollars from lumber merchants Henry and Lucius Hotchkiss, Candee started the world's first firm to manufacture rubber overshoes under the Goodyear patent.

A Brief History of the Firm

In 1843, the Hotchkiss brothers provided another six thousand dollars to become special partners in the newly formed Leverett Candee Company to make rubber overshoes. Candee managed the entire operation in a small spinning mill in Ham-den. It was a shaky beginning. For one, people were skeptical about the usefulness of rubber shoes that were ugly and uncomfortable and became discolored when exposed to the elements.

Things changed in 1848 when Goodyear's patent was finally validated; after many costly experiments, the discoloration problem was solved with the invention of an elastic varnish. Business picked up; products became popular and sold well.

Candee hired more employees and enlarged the plant several times. When business outgrew the capacity of the Hamden plant in 1850, he established a branch plant in a factory on a site on Greene Street in New Haven. Two years later, the partnership reorganized as L. Candee and Company, a joint stock corporation with two hundred thousand dollars capital. As business continued to increase, Candee built additional buildings on the site and in 1859, moved the entire operation there. He retired from the company in 1863 and sold his interest to Henry Hotchkiss, who with his son, Henry L. Hotchkiss, led the company for many years.

In November 1877, a disastrous fire destroyed the plant. Three men were killed and many employees were injured trying to escape the blaze. Not a pattern, a last, or a tool was saved. It was at the height of the company's busiest season of the year. Within a few days, management leased an unoccupied factory in Middletown, and arranged for the New York and Boston Railway to run special trains between New Haven and Middletown so that the several hundred employees could return to work. Lasts were made, new patterns cut, and tools and machinery purchased and set up. Three weeks after the fire, boots were again produced and delivered.

The company bought adjacent land on Greene Street, and within eight months a large factory, with twice the capacity of the one destroyed, was built and in operation. It was a showcase of new manufacturing technology, yet in no time at all, more space was needed to meet the demands of increasing sales. With new additions, the plant soon occupied the entire block on Greene Street between Wallace and East Streets. The plant contained twelve substantial brick buildings, separated by roadways to prevent the spread of fires. The main buildings were three-and-a-half-stories high; machinery was driven by five large Corliss engines, and twenty-one boilers provided the enormous amount of steam power needed for production. In 1890, the company acquired the G. F. Warner Company's Malleable Iron works

FIGURE 1. *The "Boot Room" in the Candee factory.* (New Haven Colony Historical Society; Candee Catalog, 1910, p 27)

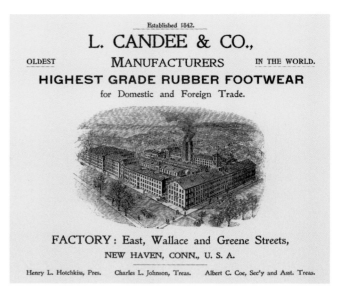

on East Street and built two new four-and-a-half story factories on the approximately four-acre site.

Candee produced a wide variety of rubber boots, sandals, shoes, and arctic rubbers. Most of the two to three million pounds of raw material was imported from Para, Brazil; other rubber gum was imported from Africa, eastern India, and Central America. At the end of the nineteenth century, fifteen hundred employees made about nine million pairs of shoes a year. The workers, including five hundred women, were paid an average of ten dollars a week. Wages were competitive and by standards of the late nineteenth and early twentieth centuries, employees were treated fairly and working conditions were good (figures 1–3).

Candee sold its products directly from the factory, eliminating the "middle man." Its products, waterproof and more stylish than the early models, sold well. Then, early in the twentieth century, a Boston firm, the United Shoe Machinery Company, invented a way to make leather shoes and boots that were relatively waterproof, yet resilient and more comfortable than rubber boots and shoes. By 1920 all leather shoes and boots produced in the United States were made by this method. Candee's sales plunged almost overnight; layoffs and reduced workhours followed. Things went from bad to worse until 1917, when the company was merged with the United States Rubber Company. In the next five years, the Candee Manufacturing Company, under United States Rubber Company ownership, expanded the plant to twenty-nine buildings. By the time all remaining operations moved to U.S. Rubber Company's Naugatuck plant in 1928, the Candee site occupied the entire block enclosed by Wallace, Greene, East, and Chapel streets.

In November 1936, a second spectacular fire roared through and reduced to a pile of ashes and rubble a large section of Candee's plant on East Street, damaged other plant buildings, and threatened to ignite the New Haven Gas Light Company's huge gas and oil tanks across the street. The remaining buildings on the block fell prey to urban renewal.

FIGURE 2. (Above left) *A Candee Company advertisement card at the turn of the century.* (New Haven Colony Historical Society Manuscript Collection 73, box I, folder L)

FIGURE 3. (Above right) *An 1897 Candee advertisement.* (New Haven Colony Historical Society; advertisement in *Las Industrias de New Haven*, 1897)

REFERENCES

"Articles of Association, 7 June 1852." Leverett Candee Papers, 1843–1864. MS 73. New Haven Colony Historical Society.

Atwater, Edward E., ed. *History of the City of New Haven*. New York: Munsell, 1887.

Candee, L., and Company. *Catalogue and Price List, Rubber Boots and Shoes,* 1898–99. New Haven: L. Candee & Co., 1898.

———. *Catalogue of the Celebrated Candee Rubber Boots and Shoes*. New Haven, Conn.: L. Candee & Co., 1878.

Hamden Land Records. 21:160.

"The L. Candee Company." *Commerce, Manufacturers and Resources of New Haven, Connecticut*. National Publishing, 1882.

New Haven Evening Register, 28–29 November 1936.

New Haven Land Records. 130:540, 322:156, 324:446–448, 325:291, 343:455, 422:350, 797:14, 500:477, 803:199, 812:234, 862:258, 863:455, 867:167, 869:119, 876:12, 884:151, 1227:35, 2153:429.

"Partnership List, 1832–1843." New Haven City and County Documents, 1648–1976. MS 28. New Haven Colony Historical Society.

"Report of the Fire Department." 1877. "Fires and Alarms from January 1, 1877 to January 1, 1878." In the *City Yearbook for the City of New Haven for 1877*. Hartford: Case, Lockwood & Brainard Company, 1879.

Sanborn Map and Publishing Company. *Map of New Haven, Connecticut,* 1880.

Sanborn Map Company. *Insurance Maps of New Haven, Connecticut*. 1886 (updated to 1897); 1923 (updated to 1931).

Wiedersheim, William A. "New Haven Industry Since 1920." *Journal of the New Haven Colony Historical Society* 33, no. 1 (Fall 1986).

Underwood, A. B. "The Manufacturing Interests of New Haven." In *The New England States*, ed. William T. Davis. Boston: D. H. Hurd, 1897.

The American Steel & Wire Company

With the most modern equipment and the largest capacity of any plant in the world for the production of wire rope, the American Steel & Wire Company played an important role in New Haven's industrial scene in the first half of the twentieth century. It produced steel wire cords, strands and ropes from $\frac{1}{32}$ inch to $2\frac{1}{2}$ inches in diameter for dozens of uses in the construction, mining, fishing, and lumber industries, as well as for ships, planes, elevators, bridges, and cars. American Steel & Wire shipped its products to industries throughout the United States, to Central and South America, Europe, Africa, and Asia.

A Brief History of the Firm

Alternate periods of success and bankruptcy marked the early history of this company. In 1871 Charles Atwater and Edwin S. Wheeler, partners in the Charles Atwater & Company iron, steel, and metal business, established the New Haven Wire Company as an independent joint-stock enterprise. The New Haven Wire Company bought a Fair Haven site in 1871 between the east bank of the Quinnipiac River and the present Fairmont Street from the American Chemical Company. There it produced a wide range of iron and steel wire products, sold to manufacturers throughout New England. After Charles Atwater declared bankruptcy in 1877, Edwin S. Wheeler acquired his interest in the New Haven Wire Company. The company incorporated in 1881, with $150,000 capitalization and Wheeler as president.

In 1887, the New Haven Wire Company declared bankruptcy, a failure Wheeler

blamed on switching from iron to steel wire production. After three years in receivership, the company sold its assets to the newly incorporated New Haven Wire Manufacturing Company, with E. S. Wheeler again president.

Local control of the wire works ended in 1899 when the National Wire Corporation, organized by a group of Boston executives, acquired the New Haven Wire Manufacturing Company. The National Wire Corporation rebuilt and enlarged the plant after fire destroyed it in 1901, and gradually expanded the original three-acre site to almost forty-one acres (figure 1). With five hundred to six hundred employees, National Wire manufactured telephone and telegraph wire, wire rope and fencing, barbed wire and nails at its New Haven plant until 1907. In that year, bankruptcy again forced the sale of the New Haven plant, this time to the American Steel & Wire Company, a subsidiary of United States Steel Corporation, for $650,000.

The new management converted the plant to specialize in making wire rope and cables and reopened for production with twenty-nine employees in 1908. After a slow start, the company finally gained a firm footing and production increased rapidly, reaching a total of 27,000 tons by 1913. Four years later, in 1917, World War I military demand for wire rope required significant enlargement of the plant. After the war, it claimed to be the largest wire rope–manufacturing facility in the world.

The company continued to prosper, developing new products and seeking new markets even as the Great Depression of the 1930s gripped the nation. When the

United States entered World War II, American Steel & Wire again put most of its production into making steel cables for military uses. Cables "scarcely thicker than a baby's little finger," released bombs from U.S. warplanes, and slender hemp-covered and steel-centered cables hoisted 300-ton locomotives onto liberty ships bound for overseas duty and launched planes from aircraft carriers.

Maintaining production during the war had its problems. "Wire Factory Paralyzed by 100% Walkout," headlined the *New Haven Register* on 16 October 1943, as a strike called by the CIO threatened to halt vital war production. Work resumed within a day, but even with fourteen hundred employees, the company lacked enough workers to man the machines, maintain the plant, and meet increasing demands for its products. The shortage prompted the hiring of women for the first time. "Women are also working in this plant on lighter machines and have proven able and willing workers on jobs formerly done only by men," the *Register* reported in 1945.

After the war, American Steel & Wire's production of wire rope and wire shattered all-time production records. Company engineers concentrated on finding new uses for wire rope to serve changing customer needs (figure 2). They developed cables to operate the largest dredges in the world and to drill lines capable of reaching oil 15,000 feet below the earth's surface. The company pioneered construction of overhead tramways for transporting materials to difficult building sites, building more than six hundred in the United States, Canada, South America, the Philippines, and France. A tramway in France was built in 1948 to haul sand and gravel to make concrete for construction of the giant Chastang Dam. The project used more than 100,000 feet of wire rope and cable and 500 tons of structural steel. All of the components—cables, rope, mechanical and electrical equipment, and structural steel products—were designed and fabricated in the New Haven factory and shipped to France.

In 1960, with about six hundred employees, the plant was still a major force in the New Haven industrial scene—but the end was near. American Steel & Wire continued to convert high-carbon steel rods from United States Steel's Philadelphia works into wire and wire rope (a very labor-intensive process). The cost of the finished product reflected the high cost of labor in New Haven. Then less-expensive high-carbon steel wire and rope made in Japan and Korea, where the cost of labor was a fraction of that in the New Haven plant, was introduced to the American market. American Steel & Wire could not compete with the import's lower price.

Even with modern equipment, there was no way to increase productivity enough to compensate for the high cost of labor. The employees refused to com-

FIGURE 2. *A worker braiding steel wire into rope at the American Steel and Wire Company works in 1952.* (New Haven Colony Historical Society; New Haven Chamber of Commerce, *New Haven Industry "On Parade,"* 1952)

FIGURE 3. *The New Haven Terminal adapted the remaining American Steel and Wire Company buildings for warehousing and distribution purposes.* (Photo by Henry Lord)

promise on pay rates. United States Steel, left with little choice, closed the plant in 1980. In an effort to save jobs for six hundred New Haven men and women, Mayor Biaggio Di Lieto and the city administration offered property tax and other concessions, and begged United States Steel to reconsider. The company refused, and closed the plant for good. The City of New Haven purchased the United Steel Corporation property and transferred the land and buildings to the New Haven Terminal, Inc., the following year (figure 3). This plant was typical in the New Haven industrial scene. Although old, the buildings were adequate for "straight-line" production.

THE PLANT

1871	The New Haven Wire Company occupied a wood frame building on a three-acre site between the east bank of the Quinnipiac River and Ferry Street (later Fairmont Avenue). The original 50 ft. × 160 ft. two-story structure housed office, boilers, and drawing wire and annealing areas.
1882	Fire destroyed the frame factory in 1882 or early in 1883. The company rebuilt it in a combination of brick and wood. When the National Wire Corporation took over in 1899, the plant included an engine room, machine shop, wire room, annealing room, rod mill, two-floor nail shop, tempering room, and cleaning house.
1901	On 3 February 1901, fire broke out in the rod mill, destroying most of the buildings. The company constructed a new brick plant within a few months at the same site with its excellent water facilities for shipping and receiving. Most of the buildings date from this period.
1907	The National Wire Corporation enlarged the three-acre site to almost forty-one acres before bankruptcy forced its sale to the American Steel & Wire Company in 1907. American Steel & Wire inherited the expanded plant of thirteen manufacturing buildings, nine storage sheds, two dwellings, and an office building, with docks on the riverfront and tracks connecting with the New York, New Haven & Hartford Railroad.
1917	American Steel and Wire enlarged the plant to meet war production needs. Significant 1917 additions included two factories, a fireproof storehouse, and other alterations. Although several of the factory buildings were two stories high, most were one-story brick structures. Two buildings were of corrugated iron- and steel-frame construction. A large 50 ft. × 500 ft. frame storage shed stood near the riverfront, and small frame sheds were scattered throughout the site.
1922	Alterations to the New Haven works in 1922 and in 1925 included another large iron and steel wire-storage building and crane-way at the north end of the site.
1980	Shortly after United States Steel closed the plant, fire gutted one of the large buildings. After 1984, the New Haven Terminal adapted the remaining buildings for warehousing and distribution purposes.

REFERENCES

Atwater, Edward E., ed. *History of the City of New Haven*. New York: Munsell, 1887.

"Fires and Alarms in the City of New Haven for the Month of February, 1901." *City Yearbook for the City of New Haven for* 1901. New Haven: "Mac" Printing Corporation, 1902.

Gallivan, Marie Campbell, ed. *New Haven, 1638–1938*. New Haven: Committee for School Tercentenary Plans, 1942.

Kelly, Cassius W. *Atlas of New Haven, Connecticut*. Bridgeport, Conn.: Streuli & Puckhafer, 1911.

New Haven Chamber of Commerce. *New Haven Industry "On Parade": Products of American Steel & Wire; Division, United States Steel Company*, April 1952.

New Haven Directory. 1869–1908.

New Haven Land Records. 346:419, 397:540, 417:301, 516:547 and 549, 528:70, 612:531, 3066:277, 3222:161.

New Haven Register, April 1929, June 1942, 16 October 1943, 8 February 1945, 2 July 1948, 29 April 1956. *New Haven Evening Register*, 4 February 1901.

"Report of the Building Inspector." *City Yearbook of the City of New Haven for* 1917. New Haven: S. Z. Field, 1918.

"Report of the Building Inspector." *City Yearbook for the City of New Haven for* 1922. New Haven: S. Z. Field, 1923.

"Report of the Building Inspector." *City Yearbook for the City of New Haven for* 1925. New Haven: Columbia Printing, 1926.

Sanborn Map and Publishing Co. *New Haven, Connecticut, 1880*.

Sanborn Map Company. *Insurance Maps of New Haven, Connecticut*. 1924 (updated to 1931, 1961).

Townshend, Doris B. *Fair Haven: A Journey Through Time*. New Haven: New Haven Colony Historical Society, 1976.

Wiedersheim, William A. "New Haven Industry Since 1920." *Journal of the New Haven Colony Historical Society* 33 (Fall 1986).

The Strouse, Adler Company

The Strouse, Adler story began in 1862, when Isaac Strouse, a tailor and owner of a dry goods store, started making corsets in a shop on Chapel Street. From this modest beginning he established the first, and one of the most successful, corset-making companies in the United States.

Until then, fashionable American women wore corsets imported from France and England, or had them made by "loving hands at home." In 1861, two New Haven bankers, Alexander McAlister and Joseph Smith, set up a factory to make corsets on a production basis. In less than a year, they sold out to Isaac Strouse, who combined his skills as a tailor with a basic instinct for constructing the complex undergarments. Strouse sewed his corsets—the first of this kind ever made. His corsets proved so popular with New Haven women that he had to move to larger quarters twice within the first five years.

A Brief History of the Firm

In 1866, Strouse founded Isaac Strouse and Company with young Max Adler, who had been store manager of his dry goods store, and started a corset-making busines. Two years later, the company moved to a new factory on Oak Street (figure 1). Two hundred employees worked in the factory, equipped with the latest labor-saving machinery, including hundreds of sewing machines powered by a 75-horsepower engine. Other work was farmed out to as many as three hundred local families, who worked in their homes using sewing machines bought from the company.

Isaac Strouse retired from the company in 1871. After an interim partnership, the firm, renamed Mayer, Strouse and Company, moved in 1877 to the large factory

FIGURE 1. *In 1870, workers posed for a photograph in front of Isaac Strouse's corset factory on Oak Street.* (New Haven Colony Historical Society Photo Archives)

FIGURE 2. *The C/B corset.* (New Haven Colony Historical Society; *Las Industrias de New Haven,* 1897, p. 112)

FIGURE 3. *This advertisement appeared in* Harper's Weekly *in 1889.* (New Haven Colony Historical Society; *New Haven City Directory*, 1888, p. 698)

on Court Street that Oliver Winchester and John M. Davies had built for manufacturing shirts. The corset company remained there until it closed more than a century later. Its products were wildly popular, and the new plant was soon buzzing with activity as employees (mostly women and young girls) sewed, pressed, and packed thousands of corsets. Working on specially designed Singer sewing machines, they produced the C/B à la Spirite corset, made with one hundred whale bones and eight yards of lacing to give fashionable women a waist of between eighteen and twenty-two inches (figure 2). The C/B trademark would become known worldwide.

The company was again reorganized in 1886, and renamed Strouse, Adler and Company. While S. I. Mayer and Abraham Strouse managed the company's warerooms in New York City, Max Adler was in charge of the plant in New Haven. With 1,200 to 1,500 employees, the company was the largest employer of its kind in the city.

Strouse, Adler was a pioneer in corset engineering. At the turn of the century, to replace whalebones, which were fragile and broke easily under the pressure of whittling down "milady's waist," the company developed the "Watchspring" corset, using sliding detachable steel watchsprings guaranteed never to break (figure 3). "Watchspring" corsets in several styles were soon the rage throughout the United States, Canada, and South America. They won gold medals at the 1889 Paris Exposition and the 1893 Chicago World's Fair.

Resourceful and inventive throughout its operations, Strouse, Adler designed and produced machinery for making wire and clasps for the "Watchspring" corset, and sold the wire to competitors as far away as Australia and New Zealand. The company devised labor-saving electric ironing machines (the first of their kind) to replace the hard, hot work of heating heavy cast irons and ironing as fast as possible, before the iron cooled. The company designed and made boxes for its own products, and equipped with the most modern machinery, was soon producing boxes of all sizes and shapes for retailers and other manufacturers.

The firm's success then and in decades to follow, was the result of its ability to adjust to changing times. It remained at the forefront of corset design from the pinched waist of the 1860s to the "kangaroo" straight front-laced corsets of the early 1900s, to the boyish flapper figure of the 1920s. During these years, Strouse, Adler employed about two thousand workers who produced twelve thousand corsets a day—between two and three million a year.

In the mid-twentieth century, two products, Latex and Lycra, reshaped the undergarment industry. Latex, developed in the 1930s, was a rubber thread that, when knitted or woven, created elastic fabrics far lighter and more flexible, and for

FIGURE 4. *The Strouse, Adler factory as it looked in 1909.* (Collection of Richard and Marianne Mazan; drawing from *Industries and Opportunities of New Haven, Connecticut,* 1909)

the first time, a true two-way stretch. Strouse, Adler used this technological breakthrough to create an entirely new line of foundation garment called "Smoothie"—a trademark that became an enduring company symbol. When the DuPont Company developed spandex fiber, known as Lycra, elastic mills testing the use of the product in garments turned to Strouse, Adler. As a result, the company was the first to produce an assortment of styles made with Lycra, a synthetic material with all of the desirable qualities of rubber and many other advantages.

In the 1980s, after more than a century of continuous progress and success, Strouse, Adler began to experience production problems, as well as fierce competition from abroad. By 1990, the workforce had dwindled to two hundred. Only 87,000 square feet of the immense 150,000 square-foot factory was in use, as much of the sewing was done in the Caribbean, where labor was cheaper.

In spite of diminished local labor force and space, the assembly process remained essentially the same as it had been for more than a century. "Workers, many of them older women, sit in rows, hunched over metal sewing machines, spools of thread whirling. Bins of bras and other silky garments are scattered about the factory's old wood floors," reported an article in the *New Haven Register* in 1994. "Bundle girls" moved stacks of finished pieces from operator to operator, until the garment was finished, inspected, and packed by hand. As a result of this production method, the company was able to fill only about half of its orders.

In 1994, the Aristotle Corporation, a holding company, took over Strouse, Adler; in 1998, the Sara Lee Corporation purchased it for $21.5 million. A year later, after one hundred and thirty-three years as one of the world's leading manufacturers of women's undergarments, the Strouse, Adler Company closed its doors.

THE PLANT

Oliver Winchester and John M. Davies built the original buildings on Court Street between 1850 and 1859 for their shirt-manufacturing business. Mayer, Strouse and Company leased the plant in 1877 and purchased the factory complex in 1886.

1850
: The original building [A] is a four-story (including basement) brick factory fronted 40 feet on Court Street and extended southward 78 feet. A 40-foot-wide brick ell [A], also four stories, extended eastward 118 feet from the south end of the factory.

1851–59
: The size of the plant was tripled in 1859 with the addition of a five-story block on the south side of the original factory. Building [B], approximately 30 ft. × 62 ft., adjoined the southwest corner of building [A]. The largest building on the site [C], 40 ft. × 192 ft., ran from east to west south of building [B]. A thirteen-foot square tower rose six stories at the Olive Street end of the building, and a two-story brick addition [D] extended north from its northeast corner to form an interior courtyard with buildings [A, B, & C]. With the exception of the addition of several small structures, the plant remained relatively unchanged from 1859 until the early twentieth century.

1906–09
: Between June 1901 and January 1906, Strouse, Adler acquired five parcels of land on Olive Street adjoining the factory site. Its $50,000.00 brick factory additions in 1906 were among the largest New Haven building operations of the year. Factories [A] and [C] were extended east to Olive Street. Further additions fill in the spaces to form a solid brick facade, four stories tall, in the center of the Olive Street block between Court and Chapel streets.

FIGURE 5. *A recent photo of the Strouse, Adler factory complex. A portion of the factory was renovated and converted to apartments in 2002.* (Composite photo by Henry Lord)

The Strouse, Adler Company, corset-makers, was one of New Haven's premier and longest running manufacturers. The existing mill complex is one of the largest in the city, covering almost one full block, with portions dating back to 1861 (figure 5). It is also one of the most successful examples of adaptive reuse.

REFERENCES

Atwater, Edward E., ed. *History of the City of New Haven.* New York: Munsell, 1887.

Beers, Frederick W. *Map of the City of New Haven and Fair Haven.* Beers, Hellis & Soule, 1868.

Dalpe, Peter. "A New Foundation: Strouse, Adler Still Makes Women's Undergarments, But Old Ways No Longer Bind." *New Haven Register,* 15 June 1997.

———. "Stamford Firm to Buy 30% of Strouse, Adler's Parent." *New Haven Register,* 24 October 1997.

Hessekiel, David. "French Lace is New Venture for Firm Built on Bone." *New Haven Register,* 20 April 1986.

Hopkins, Griffith Morgan. *Atlas of the City of New Haven, Connecticut.* Philadelphia, 1888.

Hogan, Neil. "New Haven Corsets Held American Women Tightly." *New Haven Register,* 22 March 1987.

Kane, Kevin. "Strouse, Adler Part of Sara Lee," *New Haven Register,* 2 July 1998.

Kelly, Cassius W. *Atlas of New Haven, Connecticut.* Bridgeport, Conn.: Streuli & Puckhafer, 1911.

Map of the City of New Haven and Vicinity from Actual Surveys by Hartley and Whiteford. Cartographers: Hartley and Whiteford. Philadelphia: Collins and Clark. 1851.

"Modern Woman's Hustle Put Quietus on the Bustle." *New Haven Register,* 27 October 1946.

New Haven Chamber of Commerce. *The Industrial Advantages of the City of New Haven.* New Haven: Jas. P. McKinney, 1889.

———. *Industries and Opportunities of New Haven, Connecticut.* New Haven: New Haven Chamber of Commerce, 1909.

———. *Now Showing: The Strouse, Adler Company.* New Haven: Greater New Haven Chamber of Commerce, 1961.

New Haven Directory. 1850, 1851, 1859–1869, 1871, 1872, 1876, 1896, 1897, 1926, 1927.

New Haven. *City Yearbook for the City of New Haven,* 1906. New Haven: S. Z. Field, 1907.

New Haven Land Records. 135:39, 136:247–249, 215:8, 236:550, 261:31, 320:243, 387:377, 537:495, 569:317 and 318, 579:570–572, 584:343, 1152:258, 3958:231.

"Oldest Corset Factory Still Sewing Up Profits." *New Haven Register,* 6 March 1994.

Sanborn Map and Publishing Company. *New Haven Connecticut,* 1880.

Sanborn Map Company. *Insurance Maps of New Haven, Connecticut.* 1886 (updated to 1897); 1923 (updated to 1931, 1961).

Searle, Silas W. *Map of the City of New Haven, Connecticut.* Philadelphia: W. H. Reese, 1859.

The Strouse Adler Story, 1861–1961. New Haven: Strouse Adler Company, 1962 (anniversary paperback publication).

Travers, Wayne E., Jr. "146 to Lose Jobs When Sara Lee Closes Shop." *New Haven Register,* 29 January 1999.

A. W. Flint Company

As a youth, Adelbert W. Flint was determined to make his fortune as the owner of a livery stable. He scrimped and saved the wages he earned as a salesman for a Hartford ladder company; by 1885 he had enough to lease the Elm City Livery on Chapel Street in New Haven for $1,682. The deal included among other things, a white horse named George; a black mare called Molly; a bay mare named Lady Mansfield; an assortment of carriages and wagons and a sleigh, lap robes, blankets, harnesses, and "the goodwill of the livery business now carried on by me at the Elm City Stables." Before long, Flint realized he could make more money by turning his livery stable into a ladder and furniture shop. For the next one hundred years, the A. W. Flint Company was widely known for the production of high-quality ladders and staging for contractors, utilities, industries, and households.

A Brief History of the Firm

In his livery stable, Adelbert W. Flint made and sold everything from basket seats, rattan and folding chairs, lawn furniture, clotheshorses, and worktables to washbenches, sleds, snow shovels, and wagon jacks, but his specialty was commercial ladders for fire departments, painters, carpenters, and masons. His "poleside" ladder—a lightweight, exceptionally strong ladder made from a whole native spruce tree—became a best-seller.

Flint moved his business out of the livery stable in 1890; by 1903, he owned a shop on Elm Street where he continued to manufacture a full line of ladders, as well as furniture and household goods, which were sold in the shop on Elm Street

FIGURE 1. *An early Flint delivery wagon.* (New Haven Colony Historical Society Manuscript Collection, MS 269, 100th Anniversary Flyer, 1980, Flint Ladder Company)

FIGURE 2. *The step ladder assembly room in the Flint plant.* (New Haven Colony Historical Society Manuscript Collection, MS 269, photo)

and distributed by horse-drawn wagons. Every April, a dozen or so wagons laden with lawn and porch furniture, racks for drying clothes, swings and ladders, set out on an eight-month trek to visit homes, farms, factories and building contractors throughout New England, Long Island, and the Hudson River Valley (figure 1). When necessary, Flint replenished the stock from New Haven. The wagon routes were eventually phased out in the early 1900s when permanent wholesale outlets were established.

When Adelbert Flint died in 1921, his son, William, acquired the business, moved it to larger quarters in Fair Haven, and dropped production of furniture to concentrate on improving production of ladders and staging. It was a wise decision. By the early 1930s the company was shipping products to all parts of the United States. As demand for Flint ladders and staging increased, more space was needed for production facilities. In 1937, Flint bought the Kilborn and Bishop plant at 196 Chapel Street, and renovated and equipped it to produce six thousand feet of ladders a day (figures 2 and 3). Soon, large orders began to roll in: Western Electric Company, Western Union and Postal Telegraph Companies, Boston Elevated Railway, New York Central and New Haven Railroads, Connecticut Light and Power Company, Westchester Lighting Company, Brooklyn Edison Company, United Illuminating Company, and several other companies bought high-quality ladders and staging.

A.W. FLINT COMPANY

Manufacturers of
Ladders and Scaffolding

THE WORLD'S FLINT *ladders* SAFEST LADDERS

P. O. BOX 1598
NEW HAVEN 6, CONN.
TELEPHONE 5-6167

FIGURE 3. *The Flint letterhead included a bird's-eye view of the factory.* (New Haven Colony Historical Society Manuscript Collection, MS 269, letterhead, c. 1940)

Until 1940, most of the Flint ladders were made from New England spruce; as this supply of trees was gradually depleted, however, Flint began using spruce wood from the West Coast. The lumber, cut to work lengths, was shipped from Oregon, Washington State, and British Columbia in railroad freight cars to A. W. Flint's mill yard, where it was stored until properly seasoned.

In the 1950s, with twenty-six workers, the A. W. Flint Company added lower-priced equipment for home and farm use to its line. To improve production, it developed a number of specialized machines for mass production, including high-speed saws and moulders, to turn out softwood rails, stepladder treads, and special hardwood parts. Other innovative machines bored twenty holes at a time, and hopper-fed saws and chuck machines cut rungs to exact length.

As metal ladders and staging replaced ones made of wood, the company's business declined, and in 1989 the A. W. Flint Company went out of business. Lynn Ladder and Scaffolding, Inc., occupied the plant at 196 Chapel Street the following year.

THE PLANT

The history of the property at 196 Chapel Street began in 1873, when Hobart B. Bigelow purchased land bounded by Chapel, Lloyd, and River streets and began to develop it for industrial use.

1882	Bigelow built a two-story 40 ft. × 140 ft. factory building for the National Pipe Bending Company on River Street. This old brick factory still stands on the north side of River Street, east of Lloyd Street.
1888–97	The National Pipe Bending Company enlarged the factory with two one-story additions: a brick structure at its northeast corner and a frame structure at the center of its east side.
1896–1910	The Kilborn and Bishop Company, manufacturers of special drop forges and forged hardware, purchased the tract of land on the corner of River and Lloyd streets and subsequently acquired two adjoining sites, including the former National Pipe Bending factory. By 1910, Kilborn and Bishop occupied almost the entire west half of the city block bounded by River, Lloyd, and Chapel streets.
1911–24	Kilborn and Bishop developed the site, constructing two frame buildings, two brick buildings, a large foundry with a five-foot frame monitor on the corner of River and Lloyd streets in 1917, and a two-story brick office building at 196 Chapel Street in 1924. Kilborn and Bishop also added two frame buildings and further enlarged the 1881 National Pipe Bending building as its factory.
1937	William A. Flint bought Kilborn and Bishop land, buildings and other improvements. The A. W. Flint Company renovated the plant, which covered about two acres and included an office building, large manufacturing building, and four storage buildings.
1953	The A. W. Flint Company built a 80 ft. × 158 ft. cinder block building on leased prop-

erty at 178 Chapel Street for manufacturing, assembling, storing, and selling ladders and staging.

1961   A two-story steel-frame addition on the north doubled the warehouse space in the old brick factory and extended it through to Chapel Street. Additions to the foundry (now used as a factory) joined it to the office building on the southeast corner of Chapel and Lloyd streets. With these additions and alterations, the Flint plant occupied the length of Lloyd Street between Chapel and River streets.

The building at 196 Chapel Street is an example of an early-twentieth-century manufacturing complex, utilitarian in form and detail. It relates strongly to the nineteenth-century industrial buildings one block south of here on River Street. Both have characteristic brick masonry and utilitarian construction.

REFERENCES

"A. W. Flint Company." Advertisement, *New Haven Register*, 26 November 1937.

The Consolidated Illustrating Company, comp. *Connecticut, 1639–1895*. Newark, N.J.: Consolidated Illustrating Company, c. 1895.

Flint, A. W., Company. *Catalogue* 21 of Ladders and Woodenware, Painters' and Builders' Staging, Revolving Yard Clothes Dryers, Garden Furniture. New Haven: A. W. Flint Company, c. 1930.

————. *Catalogue* 30, Ladders and Staging. New Haven: A. W. Flint Company, c. 1950.

————. *Catalogue No.* 78. New Haven: A. W. Flint Company, c. 1960.

"Flint & Co. in Fine New Plant." *New Haven Register*, 23 January 1937.

Flint, William A., Jr. 100 Years Ago This Is How We Sold Flint Ladders. 100th Anniversary Flyer, 1880–1980.

Hopkins, Griffith Morgan. *Atlas of the City of New Haven, Connecticut*. Philadelphia: 1888.

Kelly, Cassius W. *Atlas of New Haven, Connecticut*. Bridgeport, Conn.: Streuli & Puckhafer, 1911.

Kirby, John B., Jr. "New Haven Building Permit Records, 1882–1886." Vol. 1. New Haven, December 1982.

Leading Business Men of New Haven County. Boston: Mercantile Publishing, 1887.

New Haven Chamber of Commerce. *Now Showing A. W. Flint Company—A Good New Haven Citizen*. New Haven: New Haven Chamber of Commerce, 1952.

————. Manufacturer's Division. *What New Haven Makes, Makes New Haven*. New Haven: New Haven Chamber of Commerce, 1951.

New Haven Directory, 1880–1910, 1922–1925, 1936, 1937, 1990.

New Haven Land Records. 283:370, 366:251, 380:202, 420:320, 463:298, 485:328, 549:82, 642:219, 984:128, 1356:241, 1781:475, 4216:240.

New Haven. "Report of the Building Inspector." In the *City Yearbook of the City of New Haven for 1917*. New Haven: S. Z. Field, 1918.

Sanborn Map Company. *Insurance Maps of New Haven, Connecticut*. Updated to 1897; 1924; 1924 (updated to 1961).

"The Story of the A. W. Flint Co." Reprint from *Connecticut Industry* (May 1940).

Henry G. Thompson & Son Company

"Henry Thompson was a prototype of the shrewd and ingenious Yankee industrialist who gave direction and impetus to our nation's industrial growth with typical application of administrative skill, imagination, sales acumen and ample energy," recalled the Hon. Robert N. Giaimo of Connecticut, in the United States House of Representatives on the occasion of the country's Bicentennial observance and the 100th anniversary of the William G. Thompson Company.

Henry Thompson served his apprenticeship in his father's carpet mill, where his fascination with the flying shuttles and intricate looms led to a lifelong interest in things mechanical. When Hartford Carpet Company took over his father's business in the panic of 1857 he became the company's sales agent in New York City. He was a good salesman, but his curiosity and inventiveness led him to several outside ventures—some successful, others disastrous. In 1870, Thompson, then fifty-two, retired from the carpet business to pursue his interest in inventing and making things. This pursuit eventually led to the founding of the Henry G. Thompson Company in New Haven—a manufacturing company that endured for almost one hundred and twenty-five years.

A Brief History of the Firm

Henry G. Thompson moved his family from New York City in 1870, to a grand estate on the Milford, Connecticut, shore. Six years later, he founded the Henry G. Thompson Company with his son Harry in a small Milford shop known as the "Steam Power Factory." There he developed a pamphlet wire stitching machine

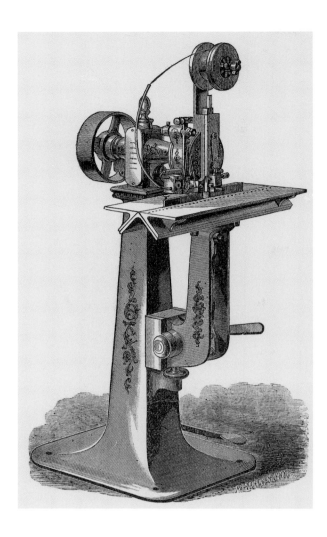

FIGURE 1. *A pamphlet wire stitching machine.* (New Haven Colony Historical Society; *The Industrial Advantages of the City of New Haven*, New Haven Chamber of Commerce, 1889, p. 188)

that replaced thread with wire staples for bookbinding (figure 1) and a shoe-lasting machine for attaching shoe uppers to innersoles. The little company had a few initial successes, but patent litigations and bad deals forced them out of business after only a few years.

Thompson was determined to continue. With his son and Samuel E. Mower, an excellent industrial designer, he moved the business to a small machine shop in New Haven in 1880. New ventures followed in rapid succession: an improved wire stitching machine, pin-tickets, prepayment gas meters, and tramcar motor gearing. The company had high expectations for its invention of the unique spiral hair pin, but this innovation was not a success; it failed because of "a regrettable lack of mechanical sense in women."

The invention and production of saw blades of many kinds, however, propelled the Henry G. Thompson & Son Company to worldwide recognition. With business improving, the company moved to a large brick building on the corner of Elm and State streets. In 1885, Thompson bought a patent for a "hard-tooth, soft back" hacksaw blade that, with its safety features, was superior to other comparable saw blades. Samuel Mower, now head of the manufacturing department and designer of its most successful products, developed a new process and an automatic machine for manufacturing these hacksaw blades under the trade name Eureka.

By 1887, with thirty to forty workers, the company manufactured and held patents for an expanded line of products. In addition to the pamphlet wire stitching machine and the Eureka saw blade, these included band and butcher saws, butcher and extension hacksaw frames, malleable iron tool handles, pin-tickets, and other valuable invented specialties, which it shipped throughout the United States and to some European countries. The New Haven Chamber of Commerce called the wire stitching machine "one of the most important revolutions in the book binding trade, since the inception of the art." The metal cutting band saw was considered a "great and growing success . . . which has proved itself to be one of the most useful tools that can be placed in any machine shop." Both were in great demand.

With sound policies and a never-ending quest for inventing new products or improving existing ones, Henry G. Thompson set the stage for the company's continued success for almost a century after his death in 1903. That year, the company bought a Springfield, Massachusetts, factory that manufactured a popular "all hard" type of hacksaw blade and adopted the trademark Milford for these blades. The Milford name eventually achieved international recognition and included the entire line of saw blades manufactured by the company (figure 2). A few years later it invented the first machine for milling saw blade teeth that produced a sharper,

"Go By The Name"

MILFORD

THE SUN NEVER SETS ON
"MILFORD" HACK SAW BLADES
NORTH, EAST, SOUTH, WEST, THEY ARE KNOWN
IN EVERY CIVILIZED COUNTRY IN THE WORLD.
MANUFACTURED BY
THE HENRY G. THOMPSON & SON CO.
New Haven, Conn., U. S. A.
38

FIGURE 2. *A 1913 advertisement.* (New Haven Colony Histoical Society; advertisement in *New Haven and Vicinity*, New Haven Manufacturers Exhibit Association, 1913, p. 38)

more accurately formed tooth. The result was longer blade life and more precise cutting.

In 1916, the Henry G. Thompson & Son Company bought land on the corner of Chapel and Mill streets and built a new 55,000 square-foot plant (figure 3). Here it made numerous innovations to metal cutting saw technology, for which the company became well known. For example, its hard-tooth, soft-back saw patent led to invention of the Flexible Back Metal Cutting Band Saw Blades. The company also invented a narrow metal cutting band saw that was widely used in industry. In 1922, the first Flexible Tungsten Alloy Hack Saw Blades were put on the market, and in 1928, Thompson & Son acquired a patent for the Easy-Starting Teeth for hack saws.

In 1937, the Henry Thompson & Son Company was the world's largest manufacturer of flexible back metal saw blades, which it exported worldwide. The only imported raw material was tungsten powder from China, which was needed to roll sheet metal for the saw blades.

As it had in World War I, the company supplied hack and band saw blades to aircraft- and tank-building industries during World War II. During the war effort, with three shifts and sometimes four, production increased so that every twenty days, it equaled the entire 1938 output. In 1943, Henry G. Thompson & Son Company received the Army-Navy "E" flag for high achievement in war-material production.

After the war, with two hundred and forty workers, the company continued to make hack [saw] and band saw blades, as well as compass saw blades and tool bits. In 1953, it introduced the "Rezistor" High Speed Steel Band Tool, designed for production "cut off" sawing of all metals, including stainless steel, die steels, titanium and other hard-to-machine alloys.

In 1966, the Henry G. Thompson & Son Company became a subsidiary of the Vermont American Corporation, a diversified manufacturer of cutting tools with eighteen divisions in eight states. The company name was changed to the Henry G. Thompson Company, and in 1974 it moved to a new 97,000-square-foot plant in Branford, Connecticut. In 1983, the Henry G. Thompson Company affiliated with Amstar Corporation and changed its name to Milford Products Corporation. In 1999, the company became Sandvik Milford Corporation, part of the Sandvik U.S. Group, a subsidiary of the Swedish-based Sandvik AB. The Sandvik Milford Corporation closed the Branford manufacturing plant in June 2000.

1917   The Henry G. Thompson & Son Company moved into its new four-story 55,000-square-foot plant on the corner of Chapel and Mill streets in Fair Haven. The factory is of fireproof construction with concrete frame, floors, and roof, 12-inch-thick brick curtain walls and tile partitions. It is approximately 68 ft. × 160 ft. and four bays wide by four bays deep, with a flat roof, shallow parapet, and poured-concrete cornice. A four-story ell of the same construction is attached to the rear of the building.

1940   A complete metallurgical laboratory was installed, housing the most advanced metal testing and metallurgical research equipment.

1988   SUNA Associates of New Haven acquired the factory building in 1985, converted it to the Mill River Condominiums, and commenced selling individual units in 1988.

The plant is representative of early-twentieth-century industrial plants with its characteristic use of reinforced concrete and brick masonry construction. Walls are constructed in pier and spandrel method and have large open bays filled with multipaned industrial sash in metal frames. The stair towers on each corner of the front facade have a vertical band of windows at each level and are crowned with stepped parapets. Concrete is used in the base, structural members, and some details. Brick is used as infill material, enclosing walls and spandrels. Note the functional arrangement of building parts with stair towers at the corners and workspaces in between. Also note the use of the wide glass bays creating a curtain wall effect.

FIGURE 3. *A 1917 photo of the new 55,000-square-foot Thompson plant.* (New Haven Colony Historical Society Manuscript Collection, MS 258)

REFERENCES

Connecticut Development Commission. Register of War Production Facilities in Connecticut. Hartford, Conn.: n.p. [1951].

"Fine War Work Brings Thompson Co. High Award. Thompson Co., is Praised by Gov. Baldwin." *New Haven Register*, 31 January 1943.

"The Henry G. Thompson & Son Co." Clipping from unidentified newspaper, April 1946. New Haven Public Library, New Haven File—Industries.

Leading Business Men of New Haven County. Boston: Mercantile Publishing, 1887.

Milford Products Corporation. The Henry G. Thompson Company is now Milford Products Corporation. [c. 1983].

New Haven. "Report of the Building Inspector." In the *City Yearbook of the City of New Haven for 1917*. New Haven: S. Z. Field, 1918.

New Haven Chamber of Commerce. *The Industrial Advantages of the City of New Haven, Connecticut*. New Haven: Jas. P. McKinney, 1889.

———. *New Haven Industry "On Parade."* The Henry G. Thompson & Son Co. New Haven: New Haven Chamber of Commerce, January 1957.

New Haven Directory. 1880–1883, 1898, 1916, 1917, 1966–1968, 1974, 1976, 1981–1983, 1988–1991, 1999–2000 SNET Telephone Directory.

New Haven Historic Resources Inventory. Phase II, 1197 (Fair Haven). Hartford, Conn.: New Haven Preservation Trust, 1982.

New Haven Land Records. 368:22, 793:261, 3392:186, 1988 Grantor Index.

Sanborn Map Company. Insurance maps of New Haven, Connecticut. 1924, 1924 (updated to 1931), and 1924 (updated to 1961).

"Thompson and Son Co., The Henry G." October 1937. In "New Haven: Superintendent's Committee for School Tercentenary Plans, New Haven, 1638–1938," ed. Marie Campbell Gallivan. New Haven: Senior and Junior High School Curriculum Sub-Committee of the Superintendent's Committee for School Tercentenary Plans, 1942.

Thompson, Henry G. & Son, Company. Milford Hack Saw Blades. Catalogue and price list. New Haven: Henry G. Thompson and Son Company, January 1949.

Thompson, Henry G., Company. *Milford Digest. Newsletter.* February 1981.

———. "100 Years Old and Still Growing with America." Branford, Conn.: Henry G. Thompson Company, a Subsidiary of Vermont American Corporation, 1976.

———. "A Sketch." 2 July 1948. Business biography of Henry G. Thompson, 1818–1903.

Travers, Wayne E. "Sandvik To Close Facility." *New Haven Register,* 6 April 2000.

U.S. House of Representatives. The Hon. Robert N. Giaimo remarks on the country's Bicentennial observance and the 100th anniversary of The Henry G. Thompson Company of Branford, Connecticut. Congressional Record—Extensions of Remarks (11 March 1976).

The New Haven Gas Light Company

In 1847, New Haven was the largest city in Connecticut. With a population of about 20,000, it was a center of commerce, industry, culture, and education. Lively as it was during the day, the city was left in the dark when the sun set. While the streets of large cities like Baltimore, Boston, New York, and Philadelphia already were lit by gas, few cities the size of New Haven had ventured into this new era by 1847.

Convinced that gas lighting would benefit the city, Yale professor Benjamin Silliman Jr. and a group of other prominent New Haven men organized the New Haven City Gas Light Company. It was the first public utility company in New Haven and one of the earliest in the United States. When dire predictions began to circulate that electricity would put gas out of the lighting business, the company developed new uses for its product and thrived for 119 years.

A Brief History of the Firm

The New Haven City Gas Light Company was chartered by the State of Connecticut in 1847, with William W. Boardman as president. Within the year, Connecticut's first bituminous coal gas plant was built on St. John Street. The initial four miles of mains went up St. John Street and State Street to Chapel, George, Temple, Crown, and College streets, to serve New Haven's business district.

Even before the first gas lamp was lit, protesters argued that it went against nature to turn night into day. Some also feared that it would destroy the novelty and charm of festive occasions, would increase crime in the city, and encourage people to stay out on the streets all night. Nevertheless, on 16 November 1848, gaslights

went on in Durrie & Peck's bookstore on Chapel Street. A few weeks later, on Thanksgiving Eve, Professor Silliman's home on Hillhouse Avenue was the first residence in the city to be illuminated with gas, an occasion for much celebration by his guests.

The next year, the company installed gaslit street lamps and the city's nightlife blossomed as more lamps followed. Merchants began to advertise their wares with gaslights in front of their stores; soon they installed interior gas lighting as well. Within a few years, the company provided gas for 189 street lamps and 1,252 customers. The first gas cost four dollars per thousand cubic feet (whale oil for lamps was three times as expensive, and tallow candles cost ten times as much).

To meet the increasing demand, the New Haven Gas Light Company built a new, larger coal gas plant on Chapel and East streets in 1861. Following the Civil War, the company began a period of uninterrupted growth and prosperity. In 1873, the directors held their first meeting in the company's handsome new five-story office building on Crown Street. In 1885, the company built a plant for production of carbureted water gas on the East Street site.

At the same time, the New Haven Electric Light Company began to make inroads into the city's street-lighting system. In his 1887 *History of the City of New Haven*, Edward E. Atwater wrote, "The question arises whether . . . electricity will drive out the use of gas? Perhaps for lighting streets it may; but there is nothing in the present condition of electric light in New Haven to justify the belief that it will take the place of gas in dwelling houses." He was wrong. In the 1890s, many businesses turned to electricity for lighting; soon city streets and homes were also lit by electricity. In reality, the competition with electricity propelled the gas industry to explore other uses for its product. By 1895, gas was being used for cooking and heating water. From then on, new uses for gas developed rapidly.

To meet the increased consumer demand, the New Haven Gas Light Company built a new water-gas plant in 1902 and a new coal-gas plant in 1906 at East and Chapel Streets (figure 1). The project at the junction of Chapel Street and the Mill River, was impressive both for its size and for the technology used to haul raw materials and to convert them to gas and other useful by-products. Coal and other materials came by barge to the dock at the Chapel Street yard, then were trans-

ferred by overhead tramway to the huge storage building with a capacity for twenty thousand tons of coal. A track, fitted with a car and bucket, delivered crushed coal to the retort house, where it was converted to gas. The process of converting coal to gas also produced useful by-products including coke, ammonia, pitch, and tar, which the company sold.

The process of producing gas and its by-products required the skill of experienced laborers who worked in conditions that were dangerous, hot, noisy, and at times dramatic. "Purging" excess gas was one of the most difficult tasks. "We opened four doors at the bottom, and, like working at the base of a volcano, we pulled out the clinkers with a long hoe," recalled one of the fire cleaners at the plant. After each purging, the lid on the super heater was opened, and with a loud roar, released a plume of white smoke and 15-foot-long flames. "Some fellows who came in as new help didn't stay long after they saw what was involved."

The New Haven Gas Light Company pioneered the use of gas for home heating in 1926, and the following year gas furnaces were installed in one hundred and twenty residences and places of business in the city. Other present-day uses of modern gas followed, including refrigeration, air conditioning, and various industrial applications developed over the years. To promote the use of gas for cooking, the company installed a home economics department with a model kitchen in its office building, where professional cooks taught local homemakers how to cook with gas (figure 2).

The United Gas Improvement Company formally took control of New Haven Gas Light Company stock in 1927. The following year, when the company closed its original gasworks plant on St. John Street, fires were transferred from the retort as live coals to the Connecticut Coke Company's newly completed plant on a 55-acre site at the foot of Stiles Street on New Haven Harbor. Connecticut Coke Company (Koppers Coke) then became the source for coal gas.

Expansion of the company's production facilities from 1947 to 1949 nearly doubled its capacity and extended the distribution system at a cost of more than two million dollars. The project included construction of the impressive (260 feet high, five million cubic feet) gas holding tank at the plant's site on Chapel and East streets. The company's name was officially changed to the New Haven Gas Company in 1953, and that year the first pipelines for natural gas reached the city from gas fields in Texas and Louisiana.

The New Haven Gas Company and the Bridgeport Gas Company merged in 1967 to form the Southern Connecticut Gas Company. On 1 May 1979, the Connecticut Energy Corporation was established as the parent company of the Southern Connecticut Gas Company. At that time, only two buildings remained on the

once-extensive Chapel and East streets site, and one of them was demolished in 1998 (figure 3).

FIGURE 3. *The company's "works office" (building on left), designed by architect Leoni Robinson in 1912, is the only building remaining of the once-impressive plant complex.* (Photo by Henry Lord)

REFERENCES

Atwater, Edward E., ed. *History of the City of New Haven.* New York: Munsell, 1887.

Beers, Frederick W. *Map of the City of New Haven and Fair Haven.* Beers, Hellis & Soule, 1868.

"Brief History of the Gas Company." *Annual Book, City of New Haven for 1871–72.* New Haven: Tuttle, Morehouse and Taylor, 1872.

Brown, Elizabeth Mills. *New Haven, A Guide to Architecture and Urban Design.* New Haven: Yale University Press, 1976.

Connecticut Secretary of State. "Incorporating the New Haven City Gas Light Company." *Resolves and Private Laws of the State of Connecticut, 1836–1857.* New Haven: Thomas J. Stafford, 1857.

———. "Population of Towns 1756–1930." *Register and Manual, 1933.* Hartford, Conn., 1933.

———. *Resolutions and Private Acts of the General Assembly of the State of Connecticut. May Session, 1854.* New Haven: Babcock and Wildman, 1854.

Eyes, Philmer. "New Haven Gas Light Company." United Gas Improvement Company Newsletter. *The U. G. I. Circle,* December 1927.

Kelly, Cassius W. *Atlas of New Haven, Connecticut.* Bridgeport, Conn.: Streuli & Puckhafer, 1911.

Kirby, John B., Jr. "New Haven Building Permit Records, 1882–1886." Vol. 4. New Haven, February 1984.

New Haven Directory. 1854, 1859–1861.

The New Haven Gas Company 100th Anniversary Flyer. New Haven. 1948.

New Haven Land Records. 276:48; 2320:637, 647.

"The Water Gas Men Never Let the Fire Die." *The Pilot,* August 1983. Publication of the Southern Connecticut Gas Company.

Townshend, Henry Hotchkiss. "The Formative Years of New Haven's Public Utilities." In *Inventors and Engineers of Old New Haven,* ed. Richard Shelton Kirby. New Haven Tercentenary Publications. New Haven: New Haven Colony Historical Society, 1939.

"Fire Burning Here 100 Years." *New Haven Register,* 29 August 1948.

Sanborn Map Company. *Insurance Maps of New Haven, Connecticut.* 1923 (updated to 1931); 1961.

New Haven Electric Company

"When you observe the widespread strength of the present great plant, hear the buzzing of its powerful dynamos, see all the wires and know that they stretch for 250 miles, lighting about 8,700 lamps and realize that this great power is still only in the bud of its life, you must admit that the New Haven Electric Company is a corporation of surprising, unsurpassed thrift and prosperity among the most profitable institutions of the Elm City."

—*New Haven of Today* (1892)

In 1881, a group of progressive and influential New Haven businessmen formed the New Haven Electric Light Company, and New Haven became one of the first cities in America to be lit by electricity. The early decades of company were periods of innovation and outstanding accomplishment. During those years, James English, nephew of James E. English of the New Haven Clock Company, kept the company at the forefront of industry developments.

English's dedication to the fledgling company and his unique management style were evidenced during the great blizzard of 1888. When deep snow made wagon deliveries of coal to power the company's generators impossible, every available man begged coal from neighbors, carrying it to the plant in tin pails. English borrowed coal from the Post Office and Trinity Church and trundled it throughout the day and night, down Temple Street to the plant, wheelbarrow after wheelbarrow, to keep the generators running. The incident was typical of English's hands-on managerial approach, which guided the firm from its founding until his death in 1937.

A Brief History of the Firm

The New Haven Electric Light Company incorporated in 1881 with a capital of fifty thousand dollars. Dynamos, which produced direct current for the arc lights of the time, were installed on the ground floor of the C. Cowles Company plant on Orange Street. Cowles Company boilers furnished steam to power the dynamos after business hours. Within a few months, the new electric company had its first business: four 2,000-candlepower lights "to be burned all nights and Sundays, at a cost of forty cents per lamp per night and eight cents per lamp additional for each hour burned." In December, the installation of two arc lights to allow nighttime construction of the New Haven Steam Heating Plant attracted huge crowds to witness the "spectacular demonstration of electricity's usefulness."

Arc lights, with noisy, sputtering carbons that had to be renewed every day, could not compete with gaslights. Two years after its founding, the struggling electric company went under—but not for long. Within a few months, convinced that electricity would become the power source of the future, James English and several other city entrepreneurs organized the New Haven Electric Company. They bought a new hundred-light plant, engines, and electrical apparatus for $36,000, and installed them in a leased building on Temple Street between Crown and George streets. Coal to fire the boilers was hauled to the plant by wagon from coal yards on the harbor several miles away. Within a year, the new company signed its first contract with the city for thirty-one streetlights at sixty-five cents a night for one year; increased its capital to $70,000; and bought land on George Street to build a boiler house.

In 1885, James English, W. B. Hosmer and Frederick A. Gilbert, directors of the New Haven Electric Company, acquired a controlling interest in the Bridgeport Electric Light Company. As treasurer of both companies, English became the leader of two electric companies "primed for explosive growth." Improvements in incandescent lamps made them practical for interior use and by 1889, the New Haven Electric Company supplied about four thousand incandescent lamps, in addition to five hundred arc lights, in the city of New Haven. One thousand–horsepower engines generated power delivered through one hundred miles of wires. "New Haven is deemed one of the best lighted cities in America," boasted the Chamber of Commerce. "Electricity is steadily becoming the lighting power throughout the streets and the public buildings and stores. It has surpassed gas in many of our buildings, not even excepting the houses of the people."

But there were problems. Service was unreliable and available only between 3:00 P.M. and 1:00 A.M. Steadily increasing demand for electricity required more equipment and space was limited. People living in the residential neighborhoods around the George Street plant complained (some threatened lawsuits) about the constant vibration of the engines and the steady fall of "rain" from steam condensation. In 1890, the company decided to move its arc-light business to a relatively isolated site on Grand Avenue on the Mill River, near shipping and rail lines. Direct current was supplied from the George Street site to the city center until 1937, when transformers replaced the old generators.

In 1899, the New Haven Electric Company and the Bridgeport Electric Light Company consolidated with smaller companies serving area communities, to form

FIGURE 1. *"Night View of Church Street, New Haven, Illuminated with G.E. Ornamental Luminous Arc Lamps."* (New Haven Colony Historical Society; *Official Program: New Haven Week Celebration, September 19, 20, 21, 1912.*)

the United Illuminating Company (UI). Several years later, the new company supplied current to its New Haven and Bridgeport customers twenty-four hours a day, and charged them for installation of incandescent lighting. The company was on a roll, a period of rapid expansion and change began that continued through World War I. In 1908, at the instigation of English, UI began placing its distribution wiring in underground conduits and installing new turbogenerators and a magnetic arc-lamp system for street lighting. With this new system in place, it contracted with the city to install new 1,000-candlepower streetlights on bronze-coated ornamental posts on Chapel and Church streets. The December 1911 dedication of the new lights (called the "great white way") attracted an estimated one hundred thousand people, and "illuminated the downtown section of the city in a manner the like of which was unthought of by citizens heretofore" (figure 1).

After World War I, as more and more electric appliances—radios, refrigerators, electric stoves—became "must have" household items, the demand for electric power increased dramatically. Despite the expansion of generation and distribution facilities, it became obvious that a new modern plant was needed. The UI Company decided to build the plant near its Grand Avenue station, on the small island in the Mill River it had acquired at the turn of the century. The first unit of English Station (named in honor of James English) began operations in May 1929; construction of the second started immediately after. Within a year of English Station's completion, UI supplied electricity to more than 120,000 residential, business, and industrial customers (figures 2 and 3).

When transformers replaced the direct current generators in the George Street Station in 1937, most of the city converted to alternating current. With the advent of television and many new electric appliances during the 1950s and 1960s, UI's

FIGURE 2. *View of the turbine room at English Station.* (New Haven Colony Historical Society; *UI Annual Report 1947*, Dana Scrapbook, 45:260)

FIGURE 3. *English Station.* (Photo by Henry Lord)

Somber, huge, mysterious—seen only

from a distance beyond locked gates—

this building towers over the dark river.

Futurist fantasies, reveries of medieval

strongholds, and electric minarets in a

white cloud of smoke combine to pro-

duce one of the city's most haunting

architectural images.

—Elizabeth Mills Brown, *New Haven: A Guide
to Architecture and Urban Design* (1976)

residential load skyrocketed, and the industrial load increased substantially. The number of UI employees rose from 997 to 1,248.

The end of the 1950s marked a significant turning point in the production and distribution of power. It was the beginning of the age of "big" generating units, formal exchanges of power with neighboring utilities, exploration of nuclear power and statewide capacity planning. In 1958, the UI Company and Connecticut Light and Power Company bought the eighty-seven-acre waterfront site of Connecticut Coke Company for a new power generating plant. Environmental concerns regarding proposed transmission line routes delayed construction of New Haven Harbor Station until 1973. The new power plant, now jointly owned by UI and the Fitchburg Gas and Electric Light Company of Worcester, Massachusetts, took forty-six more months to build at a cost of $134 million. It will most likely be the last new oil-fired generating plant in New England.

By 1992, operations at English Station were no longer cost-effective. In addition, New Haven Harbor Station, combined with Bridgeport Harbor Station and the Seabrook plant, generated more power than UI required. The company closed English Station that year and mothballed it for possible future use.

The United Illuminating Company sold the New Haven and Bridgeport plants to the Wisvest Corporation of Milwaukee for $272 million in April 1999 and transferred English Station to Quinnipiac Energy of Killingworth, Connecticut, the following year. Now solely in the distribution business, UI supplies electricity to more than 314,000 customers in seventeen New Haven and Bridgeport area communities.

THE PLANT (ENGLISH STATION)

1927–29   The steel and masonry building designed by Westcott and Mapes was built on land and fill south of Grand Avenue Station B on 75-foot-deep piles in two sections, each one consisting of three 12,500-kilowatt units. Six 1,511-horsepower boilers designed for high-pressure operation supported each unit. The first two units of the first section went into commercial operation in May 1929. Construction of the second section followed immediately. The total capital investment to construct six units with 75,000-kilowatt capacity was less than ten million dollars.

1931   Five sections of English Station, four to six stories high, covered an exterior footprint approximately 190 ft. × 307 ft. by 1931. A special river wharf built to accommodate 10,000-ton barges received coal to power the station. Intake tunnels took water to cool the condensers from the west branch of the Mill River and discharged it into the east branch. Each unit required more than twenty million gallons of cooling water every twenty-four hours. English Station's close proximity to the Grand Avenue Station allowed a short tie-line to deliver the new station's production to the New Haven distribution system.

1941	Two additional boilers brought the station's boiler capacity up to its generating capacity.
1946–48	UI installed a new 30,000-barrel oil storage tank and a new 30,000-kilowatt generator at English Station, at an estimated cost of five million dollars.

The design of English Station is a good example of the "form follows function" style of architecture. The simplicity of the design and massing of architectural elements suggests power.

REFERENCES

Brown, Elizabeth Mills. *New Haven: A Guide to Architecture and Urban Design.* New Haven: Yale University Press, 1976.

Cooper, William. "Historical Highlights of United Illuminating." Typescript, May 1973. New Haven Colony Historical Society.

Downs, Winfield Scott, comp. *Men of New England.* New York: American Historical Company, 1941.

Fassett, John D. *U.I.: History of an Electric Company.* New Haven: United Illuminating Company, 1990.

New Haven Chamber of Commerce. *The Industrial Advantages of the City of New Haven, Connecticut.* New Haven: Jas. P. McKinney, 1889.

New Haven Chamber of Commerce. Official Program: New Haven Week Celebration, New Haven, Connecticut, September 19th, 20th, and 21st, 1912.

New Haven Directory. 1884, 1890.

New Haven Land Records. 368:365, 368, 370; 417:521; 419:425; 631:210; 722:438; 2553:226; 5483:7.

New Haven Register. 5, 6, 9, and 22 May 2000; 28 December 2000.

Palladium Company. *New Haven of Today, its Commerce, Trade and Industries.* New Haven: Clarence H. Ryder, 1892.

"Preparing English Station for the Next Century." *UI News* 6 (Winter 1992).

"Report of the Building Inspector." *City Yearbook for the City of New Haven for* 1916. New Haven: A. J. Ely, 1917.

———. *City Yearbook for the City of New Haven for* 1920, 1921. New Haven: S. Z. Field, 1921, 1922.

———. *City Yearbook for the City of New Haven for* 1923. New Haven: Ornburn Press, 1924.

———. *City Yearbook for the City of New Haven for* 1927, 1928, 1929. New Haven: Columbia Printing, 1928, 1929, 1930.

"Report of the Fire Marshal." *City Yearbook for the City of New Haven for* 1890, 1894. New Haven: O. A. Dorman, 1891, 1895.

Sanborn Map Company. *Insurance Maps of New Haven, Connecticut.* 1886 (updated to 1897); 1924; 1924 (updated to 1931).

Townshend, Henry Hotchkiss. *The U. I. C. in Retrospect.* Reprint of address at Strathmore Hall for New Haven Tercentenary Exposition, 1 July 1938.

Index

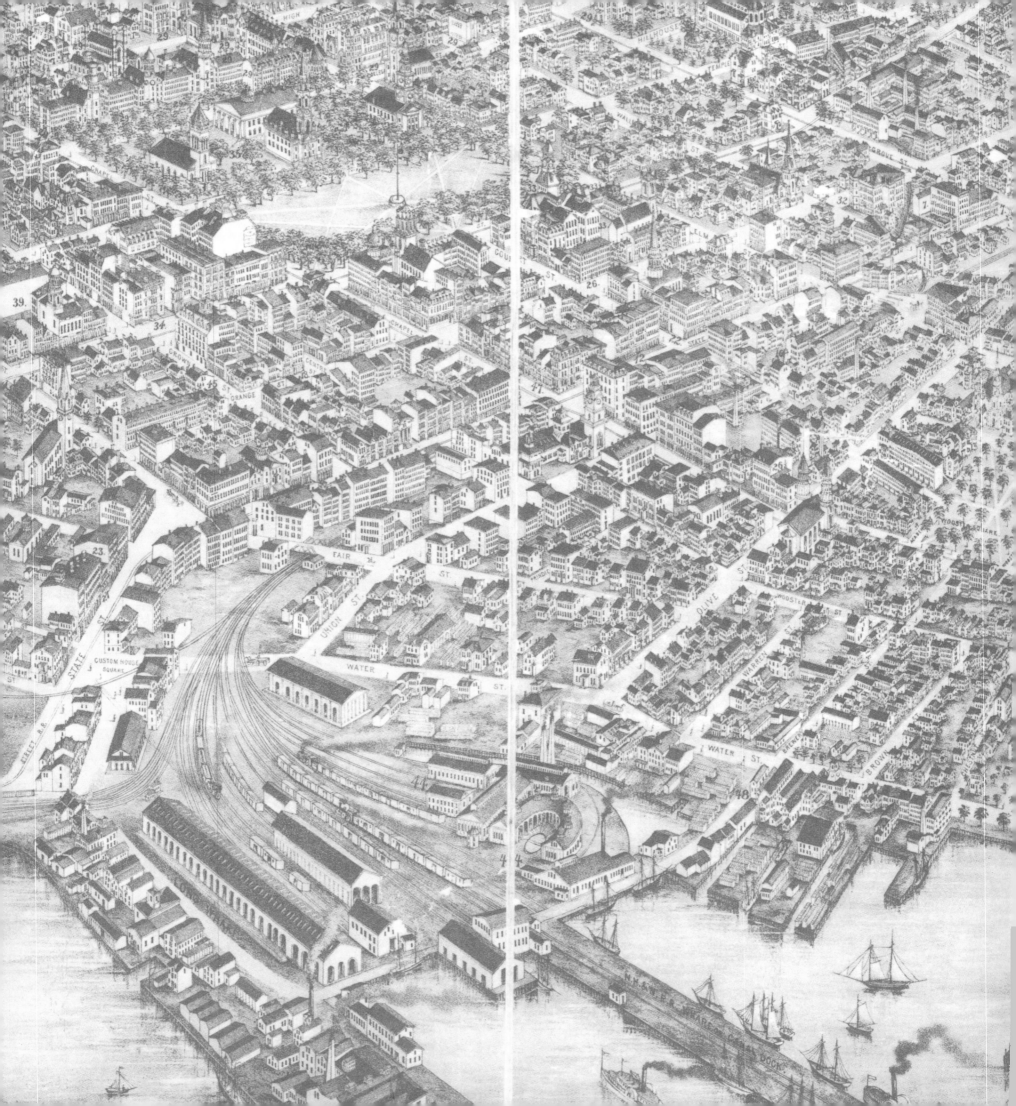